THE RUNNER'S PARADOX

the Runner's Paradox

FRAME YOUR MIND,
FIX YOUR FORM,
FIND YOUR HIGH

YING RONG MOK

THE RUNNER'S PARADOX
Frame Your Mind, Fix Your Form, Find Your High

FIRST EDITION

ISBN   978-1-5445-4339-0 *Hardcover*
        978-1-5445-4337-6 *Paperback*
        978-1-5445-4338-3 *Ebook*
        978-1-5445-4340-6 *Audiobook*

For those I've run with,

For those I've not run with,

And especially for those I'm running with.

See you tomorrow, same time, usual spot.

Text me when you're there.

CONTENTS

INTRODUCTION

THE MORNING OF THE 2017 HOMETEAMNS REAL RUN I WAS in terrible shape. I had woken up feeling feverish, but it was more than a cold or flu. Over the past year, I had struggled, both mentally and physically. I felt constantly fatigued and my workouts had been increasingly subpar. I tried different strategies to improve, but nothing worked.

Worse, I was baffled about how I had arrived here. I was ten years into my competitive running career at this point, yet I was still unable to stay healthy and strong. Each run felt so difficult and defeating, legs heavy and dragging. I would head out for an hour-long run, only to stop and walk back home after five minutes because I was so tired. I thought I had the signs of chronic fatigue, but I brushed it off as I wondered, *Why can't I just snap out of it?*

Then I inexplicably fainted at two races, and my confidence plummeted even further. I became fearful of racing, worried I would start the race and then pass out again. I didn't go to the doctor, and I didn't talk to anyone about what I was going through. I figured maybe if I didn't acknowledge my fatigue, fainting, and frustration, they would all go away.

No matter how down I felt, however, I couldn't give up running. I enjoyed my sport, even though at this point I was no longer just running. I felt the pressure to place in every single race, so I kept pushing and pushing, but in doing so, I locked myself in a self-created box of misery, pain, and exhaustion.

I thought maybe I just needed one good race to redeem myself—one easy win to pick up my confidence—so I signed up for the Real Run, a small-scale 10K at Punggol Waterway Park.

It didn't go well (that's a story for another chapter).

Afterward, I finally saw the doctor and he confirmed that my fainting, fatigue, and weakness stemmed from a variety of factors, largely stress. I decided to take a step back from racing. My friend declared that all I needed was a break in the mountains and lots of cheese. I booked a spontaneous trip to Germany, and my friend and I drove his family's campervan all over Europe.

Something almost miraculous happened during my time away. I continued running, but I did so without a watch, without target times or distances or milestones. I just ran for the fun of it across the various landscapes at each place we stopped and practised my French with the running partners I found along the way (pro-tip: if everyone is high running, nobody will focus on your bad grammar!). These fun, no-pressure runs gave me space to reassess my relationship with running. It was beautifully cold in Switzerland, and I remember snow in the parks where I ran and the bright and sharp air around me. I felt like a new runner again, in strange lands without competitors. And as a result, I reset.

In a way, that 10K race was exactly what I needed, just not in the way I thought it would be. It didn't give me a victory, but it opened the door for me to explore distance running afresh—the good and bad, the exhilarating and frustrating, the mundane and paradoxical. It gave me a chance to start at the beginning and truly learn how to run.

EMBRACE THE PARADOX

Perhaps you can relate to my story, in a way you hadn't considered until now. Maybe you've been feeling tired and burned out, with no understanding of why or how to fix it. Or maybe you've been getting injured a lot, despite your carefully constructed training plan. Perhaps you've always had that love-hate relationship with your sport—hate to train, hate to get up early, hate pounding miles in the oppressive heat, but love the high from finishing and sign up for another race the very next day—but lately the negatives are outweighing the positives. You may love this sport and feel confused as to why it is currently so unenjoyable.

How can running feel like the most natural thing in the world, yet you still struggle to do it?

As I learned, the answer to that question is at the heart of the runner's paradox: yes, we are born to run, and yet, we still need to learn how to run. And not simply on a physical level. By the time I stood at the starting line of the Real Run, I had graduated from physiotherapy school. I understood the body's mechanics, the ideal running gait, the interplay between strength and flexibility. As a result, I had fixed my problems with recurring injuries. And yet there I stood, weak, fatigued, stressed, and burned out, unable to finish an easy 10K. I clearly had more to learn about running—the mental, emotional, even philosophical aspects that can provide a healthy, enjoyable, sustainable running journey whether you are an elite or beginner.

Most of you have probably spent considerable time thinking

about the physical aspects yourselves: training plans, injury prevention, running gait. We will talk about all of these, but we're going to start with what might be the least explored facet of running, the philosophical, and then move into mental and emotional components before discussing the physical.

Why this order? To illustrate a great truth about running: there is far more to this sport than putting one foot in front of the other. As I learned in Europe, true enjoyment comes from a deeper consciousness of the whole experience: the feeling of a brisk breeze on your cheek, the sound of your shoes crunching on the gravel, the rhythmic swing of your arms, your steady, controlled breathing. Even keeping your body in top physical shape requires consciousness: paying attention to pain, how you're moving, habits you've developed both on and off the road.

Runners think they know how to run. Just lace up your shoes and go. The truth is, we all need to learn this skill, even those of us who are exceptionally gifted. Consider someone like C. Kunalan, Singapore's most decorated sprinter. Up until he was twenty years old, C. Kunalan was more interested in soccer than running. Then his speed on the pitch caught the attention of scouts for the national sprints team, and they persuaded him to switch sports. Despite his natural talent, however, C. Kunalan still had much to learn, from the way he drove his hips to the way he accelerated with his arms. With this learning, he sprinted his way to two Olympic Games and a national 100-metre record that stood for thirty-three years.

To capture the sense that we need to challenge our preconceived notions about running, I've titled the five parts with a question that may seem to have an obvious answer. As you'll learn, however, there's far more to it.

In Part I, we'll explore the question "Why Do I Run?" starting with a look at the evolution of long-distance running, the common myth that we're "born to run," and the many different motivators that push us into this sport and keep us going. Then we'll explore the paradoxical nature of running, beyond the fact that we have to learn to do this thing that is supposedly innate. In embracing these paradoxes, we can truly open our minds to all that running has to offer, far beyond exercise and weight control.

In Part II, we consider the question "How Do I Feel When I Run?" Each chapter explores a different aspect of the running experience and asks you to consider the phenomenology of running, training, racing, and the environment in which you run.

In Part III, "Do I Enjoy Running?" we dive deeper into the emotional and mental components, both positive and negative. We talk about the alienation and loneliness of the long-distance runner, as well as the potential for running to move from passion to obsession to addiction. We also explore the empowering nature of running and its ability to help us pursue excellence, not success. Lastly, we touch upon limits: understanding that though we do have physiological limits, our minds are often the more formidable barrier to reaching our full potential.

In Part IV, we at last consider the physical facet of running by asking ourselves "Do I Know How to Run?" We consider the importance of proper form and how internal and external factors influence our runner's gait and potentially lead to dysfunctional movement patterns and ultimately injuries.

Finally, in Part V, we consider the question "Am I Running Sustainably?" with chapters on injuries, rehab, prehab, and the creation of training plans that will help you achieve your running goals and stay healthy. We also look at the mental and emotional experience of going through rehab in pursuit of running sustainably, as well as difficult conversations around the "last mile" in one's running career.

To mirror the experience of a long-distance runner, this book is written in miles, with the final .2 serving as the conclusion and a chance to reflect on the randomness of the 26.2 distance, and of running in general. Like a marathon, this book may feel long, but each mile offers an easily digestible piece to consider.

At its heart, these varied chapters on running ask you not just to "act," but to stop and think. Why did you get into running? What about this practice do you love? Do you truly feel like you've tapped into its innermost potential? If you haven't, then this book is for you. It will show you how to unlock the depths that running has to offer. In the process, you'll gain deeper knowledge of *yourself*, for running acts as a mirror to our innermost being.

MY JOURNEY

In many ways, the journey you will go on in this book closely mirrors the lessons I have learned from my running career. I started running like you: with the assumption that it was a simple sport, that I was "born to do it," and that it was easy to get better and better. Across the years of my competitive career, my experiences and my attitude changed, and I went through many of the struggles you may be facing.

I write this book from a position of knowledge and empathy. I know your pain because I have lived it.

I started running in 2006, at the age of thirteen, and took part in my first 10K race six months later. Soon after, I started self-coaching myself, steadily increasing my mileage and recording my times. I bought *Runner's World* magazines, went to the library to look up training plans, and googled solutions to my questions.

In 2007, I entered the 10K event in the Singapore Standard

Chartered Marathon and competed against international female runners of all ages. I surprised myself by coming in fourth, which greatly boosted my confidence.

From 2007 to 2010, I continued self-coaching and rose quickly in the ranks of the local running scene. I participated in many races, always between 5K and 10K, and won several. In 2010, I experienced a peak of sorts. I won most of the track and field and road races I participated in, and received some wild prizes: earphones, movie vouchers, newspaper subscriptions, juices, washing machines, and of course, money—anywhere from $500 to $2,000. I also won my first cross-country title that year, and I signed a sponsorship contract with Nike.

When I entered my second year of junior college in 2011, I had high aspirations, but the training techniques that had brought me success now backfired. I lost the National Schools Cross-Country Championships because of an injury I refused to take seriously and ended up with five stress fractures. Because I had been coaching myself, I took this as a failure that reflected directly on me as a person. Coupled with the stress of college, it was a recipe for disaster. I spiralled into depression and anxiety, and almost flunked my A-level exams.

In 2012, I started physiotherapy school and gained a new understanding of the human body and the mechanics of running. With this knowledge, I created new workouts based on science, not emotion. I started paying attention to my running movements and making sense of how I felt physically, and I saw dramatic improvements in my form and performance. In 2014, I won my first half marathon, the Great Eastern Women's Run in Singapore, and in 2015, I won the 20–29 age group in my first overseas half marathon, the Taipei Standard Chartered Half Marathon. I also got the opportunity to represent Singapore at the World Cross-Country championships in China.

I graduated from physiotherapy school in 2015, but decided to put my career on hold so I could focus on running. I moved to Boulder, Colorado, with my brother, who is also a runner, so we could train full time with members of the Boulder Track Club, all of whom were trying to qualify for the Olympics. It was a gruelling experience: it was my first time training with a team, following a schedule, working with a coach, and running at such a high altitude.

I entered the 2015 Singapore Marathon with the aim of coming in the top ten in the open category, which would mean I would qualify for the Olympics. I thought I had an excellent chance after all my training. But I did terribly: the high humidity of Singapore was a far cry from the low humidity and cold in Colorado, and I wasn't able to adjust.

I was devastated. This was the first time I had dedicated myself to running so single-mindedly, and I'd failed. The spiral I fell into made me realise that while I had trained myself to become physically stronger, I was still stuck in harmful ways of thinking; I remained dependent on my outcomes for my sense of self-worth.

I took some time off racing so I could explore new sides of myself, focus on my physiotherapy career, and concentrate on running injury free. In 2016, I was invited to work with Dynasty Travel to promote the Gyeongju Cherry Blossom Half Marathon in Korea. I jumped at the opportunity: I love travel and Korean food, and I felt ready to race again, so it felt like a match made in heaven.

Not only did I win that race with a personal best, but I broke the Singapore half marathon record by two seconds. I was elated. Unfortunately, however, my post-race fatigue outlasted the euphoria. I couldn't seem to recover from the mental and physical exhaustion, so I stayed away from racing for the rest of 2016. When I started again in 2017, I kept fainting, as you learned at the beginning of this introduction, and subsequently took the trip to Europe where I reset.

In 2017, I started studying running gait more seriously. In 2018, I gave a lecture at the National Taiwan University on the power of the big toe and returned with an even deeper interest that soon developed into a running gait analysis specialty. I co-established a physiotherapy clinic to help runners improve their form. We partnered with the Singapore Athletics Association, running interest groups, and multi-sports teams such as COS Coaching, 859 Coaching Triathlon Team, and Pro Cycling SG (Singapore's first professional cycling team). As I spent time working with runners and examining their gait, my appreciation for running deepened. I saw beauty in aspects I hadn't noticed previously when I was too stuck in the game.

Though I continued racing in 2018 and 2019, and grew in my mental and emotional strength, I decided it was time to relax my stranglehold on running. I started training for duathlons and found a welcome challenge in mastering the technical skillsets required. My hard work paid off: I won several duathlons, and more importantly, I remained healthy, physically, mentally, and emotionally.

As 2019 unfolded, I realised my racing journey was complete. I had learned the lessons I needed to learn, both about the sport and myself, and it was time to move on. I decided to enter two more races and then call it quits. I ran the half marathon in the Great Eastern Women's Run in Singapore and won it—the fourth time I had done so. I also participated in the SEA Games Duathlon, which I lost quite terribly, actually, but that's a story for later in the book.

My loss at the SEA Games didn't matter. I'd reached a place where I knew my value and worth are not tied to my performance; they are found in what I make of myself and how I handle challenges and discomfort.

Now I run for the fun of it. I don't berate myself if I run less than one hundred kilometres in a week. I don't feel anxious if I run poorly. I continue to engage in runs of different distances and intensities, primarily for the mental, emotional, and physical experience and not because I'm focused on a certain goal. If I return to competitive racing, I will face the familiar challenges from a much healthier frame of mind. All because I have embraced the runner's paradox and have learned to run in every sense of the term.

FIND YOUR HIGH

Across my career, both as a runner and as a physiotherapist, I've had the opportunity to work with individuals of all backgrounds and at different levels of mobility. I've worked with nursing homes, acute hospitals, and community settings, and each time, I've treated the patient as a person, not as a condition. That means I've looked beyond their symptoms to take into account their lives, their personality, and their wants as human beings because these have an impact on their symptoms and their condition.

The same holds true for you as a runner. You cannot just examine running as an isolated aspect of your life: it works hand in hand with who you are, how you think, and what you pay attention to. This is why it's vital to run consciously: because if you're not aware of your thoughts, actions, and feelings, you can never truly tap into the potential of this sport.

This is also why I'm writing this book. Partly, it's to put down my running journey from the beginning to the end and reflect on what it taught me. But mostly it is so that everything I have learned can help you, my fellow runner. We all struggle with the same problems with running and yet we feel alone because we don't talk about it. We feel isolated and stuck because we don't know a way out.

This book is your way out.

If you're looking for a how-to manual on how to win races, then this book is not for you. Nor is this book a technical medical guide on every aspect of the body's biomechanics.

But if you're looking to change your relationship with running, this book *is* for you. Do you want to gain a new perspective and understand why running doesn't have the enjoyment it once did? Do you want to understand what good running form looks like? Or why you have all these inbuilt problems that leave you susceptible to injury? Do you want to learn strategies that can help you reflect on your own running practice and change it for the better? Then you've come to the right place. This book will teach you how to stop, reflect, and change your running practice from the ground up to be a better, faster, and more self-aware runner.

Understanding that I needed to learn how to run, even though I was born to do it, made me a better runner: it gave me the freedom to explore, redefine my boundaries, protect myself from injuries, and expand my sense of self. I believe it will do the same for you.

PART I

Why Do I Run?

HUMANS AND LONG-DISTANCE RUNNING

BECAUSE SINGAPORE IS A CITY COUNTRY WITH SCARCE resources, a high competition mentality permeates every level of society. Colloquially, we call this mindset kiasu, or "fear of losing out." In parenting, kiasu shows up as having your children load up on extracurricular activities, in addition to emphasising excellence in the classroom.

My parents were no different. They prioritised academics as well as activities that would develop my physical as well as mental strength. They figured sports would contribute to my holistic growth, so they signed me up for swimming classes when I was six years old.

My initial lessons involved simply feeling the water. The instructor wanted us to develop a relationship with it. I learned to sit with the water's weight against my body. I felt the way my arms and legs moved against its pressure. Then I learned how to breathe—how to relax my head, turn it to the side, put it back in the water. Finally, I learned the different strokes, how to propel my body forward, how to glide through the water and use its energy rather than fight it. I only started swimming and then competing after I had learned these basics.

To improve my skills, I endured many drills and dry-land strengthening sessions in which coaches broke down each stroke into different parts that we worked on one at a time. The coaches also filmed us underwater and ran through our videos with each of us individually, pointing out where our swimming strokes were improper and then helping us correct them with a combination of various stroke-specific strength work and general swimming conditioning.

After five years of competitive swimming with only moderate success, I felt fatigued and decided to stop. My parents insisted that I find another sport to stay active, so I chose running.

Unlike swimming, I just jumped into running. I didn't take lessons to develop a relationship with the ground, or understand the way it feels beneath my feet, or practice posture and form. I didn't see the need to learn the sport the way I learned swimming, and neither did anyone else.

At first, I ran after school as a way to de-stress. Then I started increasing my distance and within a few years, I was winning local races. By the time I was eighteen, I had become successful enough to secure a sponsorship from Nike.

Unfortunately, that same year, I experienced my first lengthy layoff because of an injury. I developed a stress fracture over my pubic ramus, an area deep in the butt close to the sit bone. My doctor consoled me that such an injury often happens to the more experienced distance runners due to a high volume of running. Shortly after I recovered, I was sidelined with a foot injury. This pattern of repeated injuries went on for many seasons. I couldn't figure out what was happening, nor could the professionals I was seeing.

At that point, I had known for years that I ran ugly. My running style wasn't symmetrical at all, and every running photo I was tagged in on social media made me cringe. I didn't recognize myself: it was like looking in the mirror and seeing a different reflection, one that was desperately embarrassing. It was mortifying as a teenager, but I ignored it because I was winning. I figured my style would naturally correct itself if it was really a problem.

But when I started getting injured repeatedly without answers, I went back to those videos. I studied them. There was a lot of rotation in my upper body, and my right knee turned in. Overall, it looked like I was desperately trying to run forward, but one side of my body wanted to rotate the other way and my lower body just wanted to go up and down.

After seeing several examples of my terrible form, I had a mind-blowing thought: Maybe I don't know how to run. Maybe it is a skill I have to learn.

Yes, we humans are born to run. We've been running for as long as we've been on this planet—for survival, for travel, for fun. But that doesn't mean we know how to do it.

BORN TO RUN?

In 2009, Chris McDougall published *Born to Run: A Hidden Tribe, Super Athletes, and the Greatest Race the World Has Never Seen*. The book was a national bestseller in the United States, and it reinforced many of our prevailing notions about distance running. McDougall said, for instance, that running is natural for human beings because we have run for centuries. Our ancestors ran for travel, to socially bond, and to hunt over long distances. As a consequence, our bodies physically evolved to optimise how we run.

This is the notion of running that we carry today: that running is in our DNA and is as natural as breathing. After all, we have evolutionary traits that not only make it easier for us to run, but actually bias our bodies towards running more than walking.[1] For example, we have developed thermoregulation strategies in our core and brain. We have a ligament that connects the head to the hip that stabilises us in an upright position even as we fatigue. The tendons at our hips, feet, and ankles work in a spring-like fashion, alternating between storage and generation of forces during landing and pushing off, massively saving us energy when we run. These evolutionary traits are often described in ways that make us seem like world-class marathon runners from the moment we are born. And so we wander onto the race track, with no conscious thought about how we run.

But this narrative hides the previously stated paradox at the heart of running: while we are born to run, we still need to learn to run. Runners who don't confront this paradox become crippled by injuries and confused about how they got there. Worse, they become insecure. *Humans have been running forever*, they think, *and yet I keep injuring myself while running, so what does that say about me? Am I less than human?* They cannot shake this feeling that they are somehow inadequate. Nor does common wisdom about running help: everyone says running is natural, but then they warn you about life-altering knee pain and physical damage to our joints. How can those two coexist?

To reconcile and demystify this paradox, we must understand the history of our relationship to the sport. We must look at how long distance running today is similar and dissimilar to how our ancestors did it, and deep dive into the nuances of what running signifies beyond physical activity. Once we do, we can establish a healthier relationship with it.

In the past, running played a primary role in our lives. We used it to hunt across long distances in what is now called "persistence hunting," where we tracked prey across the land and chased it for days before finally killing it. Running was how we travelled from one place to another when we were hunter-gatherers and nomads, in search of environments with better food and water. Later, when we settled into villages, we used running as a way to communicate and create larger networks. If we wanted to convey a message to another village, for example, about upcoming rain or a forest fire, or even just to ask them to share in a feast, we would send a runner. These networks were essential to creating communities that could help us survive catastrophes because we knew our strength lay in numbers. In many ways, we ran to survive.

In response to this necessity of running, our bodies evolved. We developed physical characteristics that made it easier for us to stride, speed up, and stay alive if we were being chased by animals. Thanks to how much we walked and ran, the stride became a fundamental movement.

Over time, we stopped relying so much on running for survival. We developed tools, like the bow and the arrow, that made it easier to hunt across distances. We domesticated animals like horses and mules to help us travel, and of course, many iterations later, we developed cars. We no longer needed to run between villages: we sent carrier pigeons or, today, we make a video call. Yet running stayed in our lives as this fundamental movement that we are consistently drawn to. It graduated from a necessity to a luxury, but it survived. This is why today it feels natural to run, like our bodies know how to do it. Because for decades, they have known. It is part of our history.

This is, in broad sweeps, the "born-to-run" narrative. There are truths to this version, of course: we did use running to survive once upon a time, and we don't rely on it today in quite the same way. It is also true that running is the easiest sport to just start. In tennis, you need to learn how to hold a racket so you can serve properly. In football, you need to figure out the rules. In swimming, you must teach yourself first how to float and then how to propel yourself through the water. But in running, you just lace up and go. That's what makes it so attractive to so many beginners and why the born-to-run narrative feels so true. We just know how to do it.

Yet the reality is more complicated than this story. There is nuance embedded in our history with running that we must unpack and think about if we are to enjoy running and appreciate the humanity in us.

First, research shows that while our ancestors did engage in persistence hunting, their activity was different from how we run today. Today, we run for miles at a time, not stopping, keeping up a very consistent pace. Our ancestors, however, hunted with a mixture of running, jogging, and walking. This difference in how we run obviously influences the effect it has on our bodies. To say that our ancestors were naturals at running, that they could track and tackle prey across long distances without tiring, romanticises our history to a point where it convolutes our current relationship to running. We never ran for long distances in the past, not as we do now.[2]

Second, it's important to recognize that our ancestors didn't approach running only as physical and social activities. Those were important aspects of running, yes, but our ancestors always saw the body and the mind as linked and running as having vast cognitive benefits. They were familiar with the runner's high, for instance, although they didn't give it that name. They simply knew that running could have the same effect as psychedelic plants or weeds, and create a deeply calm, euphoric state. It was a portal into a different state of consciousness.

There is also evidence that people in the past used running as a way to connect with their environment at a deeper level. Tribes of the northwestern California region ran long distances across mountains because they believed running was a way to better understand their home. The physical act connected them to the nature around them, and they believed the many steps they took allowed them to better interact with the unseen forces of their universe.[3]

This mental and physical link is overlooked in the born-to-run narrative. By focusing on our physical, evolutionary traits and framing running as a natural physical activity, we diminish a lot of what makes running so powerful: its ability to tap into the very experience of life. Did our bodies evolve as they have because we used to run? Or did these traits come about because we walked, and walking was more of a necessity than running? Does it matter? Perhaps not as much as we think it does. In truth, there is no need to romanticise our history with running, because there is already a place for this sport in our world: a place created by necessity.

Running isn't only a physical activity. It's clear that it was used in the past to develop our cognition and connect with our emotions, and it is valuable today precisely for this reason. The body and mind cannot be approached as two separate entities; they must be understood as one coherent whole. The most accessible form of exploring this whole is running. It allows us to tap into not just our bodies, but also deeper levels of consciousness. We have always used running to serve our growth as a species, to develop creativity, to serve our community, and to understand our lives better. This is the value of running. It doesn't matter if we've physically evolved to run or not; viewing it from this romanticised lens only encourages us to injure ourselves and not learn how to run. If you see running as a valuable tool to experience ourselves and the vaster universe, however, you can tap into its depths.

Today, we are drawn to running for reasons we don't quite understand. Traditional narratives put running in a box: it is a form of exercise that can be carried out within thirty minutes or maybe an hour. We set regulations and divide the mind from the body. But in truth, the value of running today is more than its health benefits. It's cognitive clarity. It's the runner's high. It's how connected we become to our bodies and the environment around us when we run. Like the tribes in the northwestern California region, running offers us a portal to a deeper state of consciousness. We should step through.

MARATHONS AND THE HUMAN SPIRIT

In many ways, marathons are a testament to the human spirit. They take endurance and commitment. A long-distance runner must overcome numerous personal challenges, but if they do, they can touch a whole series of triumphs.

The journey of a marathon is so filled with essential human experiences, it is an excellent mirror to life, and a way to reflect upon it.

But today, marathons are being used as assets. Long-distance runners boast about how much they train or what marathons they've completed. They post to Instagram or put it on their social profiles. This meditative, challenging human experience has been leveraged as membership into an exclusive, elite club.

I believe distance running is, at its core, a humbling experience. We don't need to romanticise or boast or create exclusive clubs—it doesn't need to be pushed to these extremes. If we just focused on the marathon itself, and what the experience can offer us, it could teach us more than we already know.

A NEW APPROACH TO RUNNING

At a basic level, running allows us to spend time with ourselves. It is a meditative activity that anchors us in our bodies and our minds. I see it as a special tool of understanding, a way to know ourselves more clearly. And that understanding isn't just limited to ourselves. Running is also social. We run with friends. We join clubs and run with strangers who share our love for running. Our circle expands outwards, and then we run at a national level, and then at a global level. At each stage, running links us to a vaster, wider network. It offers us connection. Each of us runs with a link to our inner selves, our quiet mind and moving body, while united with society in this common ritual.

You can see this intrinsic nature of running in the way we shape our marathons. We may not run to pass messages between villages anymore or to hunt together and eat, but we've built these social aspects into how we run today. In relays, for example, we pass the baton, a modern form of passing on a message. We work in teams, and a victory is shared by team members, just as the spoils of a hunt were once shared by the tribe. We may run around the track in a way that seems very different from the survival-based and necessity-based running of our ancestors, but we're always reaching for the same social, mental, and cognitive benefits as our forebears. It's in us. We are drawn to it. Running is intrinsic to the human experience.

We must approach running with this fullness of perspective: as a mental and physical activity, as an inheritance and a new endeavour, as a solitary and social experience. We should see it as a way to understand life. For the activity mirrors, in many ways, the act of living—the slowness of it, even the boringness of it. Running has a lot to teach us if we approach it correctly.

Learning our history to running is the first step in shaping this approach. There is a paradox at the heart of this sport that we must embrace and make peace with. Yes, our bodies have evolved to run. But they also need to be trained to run. Yes, it's true that our ancestors used to run consistently, but it is also true that their form of running is very different from how we do it today. And yes, while we no longer run to hunt or communicate, we use running in the same way our ancestors did: to connect to ourselves, society, and the world around us. We still run for the runner's high. We still run to bond with our fellow beings. We still run to be one with the world around us. It is still essential for our holistic survival.

Now that we run for fun and not survival, what are the primary motivators that keep us moving?

PRIMARY MOTIVATORS

WHEN MOST COMPETITIVE RUNNERS ARE ASKED WHY they run, they are often stumped by the question. They began running for simple reasons: either they wanted to lose weight, or they were curious about the sport, or their friends joined the track team. But ask them why they continue to run, and they don't have an answer. They might say "Because I can" and leave it at that.

Hidden in those three words is an assumption that a non-runner can never understand the quiet and complicated joys of running. But hidden in those three words is also an acknowledgment that runners themselves don't know their motivations.

My first experience with motivation in sport came when I was a competitive swimmer. Though I attended rigorous swimming lessons five to six times a week for five years, it wasn't until my final year of primary school that I actually qualified for the final at the annual inter-school swim meet. What kept me motivated in swimming clearly wasn't winning. It was improving my time, perfecting my strokes, and building my confidence.

But after five years, improvement wasn't enough. I was done with swimming laps in an enclosed space. I needed a change. So I tried my hand at table tennis, badminton, and bowling. I took part in sports camps and tried pool and soccer. Soon after starting each activity, however, I got bored. I missed the adrenaline rush I felt during training and competition. Perhaps a bit sadistically, I missed the feeling of pure exhaustion that swimming gave me. I had always dreamed of the day I could finally stop swimming training and finally take a break. But in fact, I missed pushing myself to my limits.

So I started running. It started with laps around my neighbourhood after school. Then I started setting arbitrary goals: maybe today I will run three laps around my neighbourhood, then tomorrow, if I feel good, four laps. Soon, I began mixing up environments; sometimes I ran around the park on the other side of the neighbourhood, sometimes I ran in the park and then back on the pavements. Running was interesting because of this—it was exhausting and freeing.

One day, my dad suggested that I take part in an upcoming running race at Sentosa, a small touristy section of Singapore. "Your brother's doing the 10K run. You want to do it too?"

"Oh, OK," I said indifferently.

Race day came. My dad woke me up. I grumbled, wondering why he was waking me so early, and then it struck me: I was running a race. I regretted signing up.

Grumpy and tired, I changed and made it to the race starting point. Once there, I had no clue what to do. People were milling around me, each locked in some secret activity, purposeful, knowledgeable. I decided to get closer to the starting line; it was a race after all, and getting closer to the start gave me an advantage. But when I made my way to the front, I found a ten-metre distance between me and the flag-off point.

Those ten metres were reserved for the elites. They were decked out in professional attire, their racing bibs neatly pinned to their tops. My brother was among them. *Wow, I guess he could be pretty fast*, I thought, feeling slightly impressed with my sibling. I waved to him, but he didn't see me. I tried to make eye contact with him, but he was locked in his own preparations, taking sips of water, adjusting his watch and laces. All right, I need to focus on my own game.

I looked down at myself: baggy shorts, a race event T-shirt with my bib messily pinned on, and running shoes I had chosen for their aesthetics, not their reputation. Then I returned my gaze to the elites in front. I don't stand a chance, I thought.

I was also struck by how awfully undemocratic it was for a bunch of people to have their own space reserved near the start line—and how I wanted to be one of them. Part of me also wondered what the point of racing was: by giving these elites a special spot, the race organisers had already identified the winners, and told the rest of us we were unimportant.

Motivations are tricky feelings, often shifting and difficult to pin down. My own motivations in running started with a desire to leave swimming, then to find something as physically exhausting as swimming, then to push myself in an activity I was doing alone, for fun, as I ran around the neighbourhood. Standing there at the starting line of my first official race, my motivation shifted again: I wanted to be among the best.

It's natural for motivations to change. What motivated you yesterday may not motivate you today, and that's okay—it shows your growth as a runner and reflects your ever-fluctuating personality.

But it is important, always, to know our motivations. Because our bodies were in many ways born to run, running can be a passive sport. As we fall deeper into it, our motivations transform without any conscious choice on our part. But those motivations play a large role in how we run, so it's our duty to examine them. If we don't, we will be trapped in always reacting instead of reflecting, possibly setting us up to wander down unsustainable and dysfunctional paths. An active role is essential if we want to be healthier, better runners.

It's important to get beyond answering "Because I can" when asked why you run. Know your motivations. It's how you can love this sport more dearly.

DEFINING MOTIVATIONS

Motivation today is commonly broken down into two factors: intrinsic and extrinsic. Intrinsic motivations are fuelled from within us and represent our personal drive. They include satisfaction, a desire to feel good, curiosity, a thirst for new experiences and personal bests, and a simple enjoyment of the experience. Extrinsic motivations are externally offered, by systems and society at large. They include prizes, awards, scholarship, peer admiration, commendation—essentially, the fame and laurels that come with being one of the best at what you do. Alternately, we could be externally motivated by wanting to not be the worst at what we do: not coming last in the race, or not being the lowest among our peer group. Extrinsic motivation is both the carrot and the stick.

If we peel down another layer, however, we find another categorization below extrinsic and intrinsic. At its core, our motivation is driven by three factors: (1) autonomy, (2) competence, and (3) relatedness. Autonomy refers to a sense of self and independence we can achieve from an activity, while competence speaks to our capabilities, sense of achievement, and confidence in ourselves. Relatedness is about the world around us: our sense of belonging, acceptance, and affiliation—in other words, how well we can belong to a tribe. Everything we do is driven, at its essence, by these three desires.

The problem is that we don't always see or understand the true, underlying desire. As a result, we often chase a goal believing it will give us what we want, only to achieve it and still be dissatisfied. Imagine you enter a race to win. You want the prize money or the recognition. Better still, you know winning this race will secure you a sponsorship. You win and get everything you wanted, but you're still dissatisfied. It's because those three cores of motivation—autonomy, competence, and relatedness—haven't been touched. What you really wanted was a sense of independence and power, an acceptance in your abilities. You thought the extrinsic motivators—winning, prize money, sponsorship—would give you those, but they don't.

Motivators are also confusing because they are not all created equal. Research shows that extrinsic motivation can actually reduce intrinsic motivation. For example, say someone completed a task for themselves. They enjoyed it, and they took pride in the end result. Introducing a reward for completing that task, such as money or a prize, actually diminishes this sense of personal achievement. The person's performance drops. It's almost as if extrinsic motivators overpower intrinsic factors.

Defining and understanding what motivates us is difficult, but attempting to do so is worth the effort—first, because motivations set our goals, and goals drive our actions, and second, because motivations determine how we feel. Poor motivations can lead us to ineffective, soul-crushing negativity, and they can cause every loss—whether that's missing the time goal we had set or the literal loss of first place—to feel like a failure.

If you want to be a healthy runner, mentally and physically, you must know what motivations are effective and, more importantly, sustainable. Once we do, we can begin staring straight into the sun: we can begin to know ourselves.

KNOW YOURSELF

Knowing ourselves can be a terrifying thought. The mind is like a house with many doors, and unlocking those doors is often overwhelming. It can create anxiety, as well as evoke shame and embarrassment. It's easier, we think, to leave those doors closed, to leave those emotions buried. And yet, knowing our motivations is key to truly inhabiting and enjoying this sport.

To help you open that door and distil what drives you, let's look at a common paradox that maps onto most runners.

Most runners take up the sport for recreational reasons. Some, like me, are looking for a new activity; others just want a simple form of exercise to stay fit. Either way, they run without pressure, for their own enjoyment. At this point, they want to do their best, but they're not expected to perform at a certain level; the motivation to excel is mainly internal. They form friendships within the sport that emphasise this easy, giving perspective of the world. They are happy to support each other and extend compassion because no one is a competitor.

Too soon, however, runners shift from recreational running to competitive running. They no longer run to lose weight or casually exercise. Now, they're running for times and to beat other competitors. They're running to prove they are good, to push themselves to a new maximum that will then be compared to their peers' bests. This mindset shift occurs early in a runner's career. Research shows that most runners join their second marathon because they want to reduce their time. That's how quickly we shift from recreational running to being competitive.[4]

In competitive running, our success is not based on individual, internal factors; it is endlessly relative. That's a difficult place to be because our self-value is always dependent on the outcome of a race. It's exhausting, playing catch-up like this. No matter how well we personally do, our value is found only in relation to someone else. It corrodes our self-worth.

At the same time—and this is one strange, paradoxical beauty of this sport—as we move into competitions and extrinsic motivators, we are also pulled deeper into the intrinsic motivators of running. After all, the better we get, the easier it is to immerse ourselves in it. Our whole being becomes involved in the physical act of running. Our ego falls away. The runner's high is always within reach.

This, then, is the paradox of our motivations as runners, and how our intrinsic and extrinsic motivators intertwine. On the one hand, the more we race competitively, the better we get. It is thus easier to appreciate the act of running itself and love it for what it gives us in the way of joy and satisfaction. On the other hand, the better we get, the more competitive we are and the more races we run to receive that external reward. We end up in an endless, and potentially vicious, cycle of intrinsic and extrinsic rewards. The more we love the act of running, the better we become, and the more rewards and acknowledgments we get. The more rewards we get, the more we are motivated by this extrinsic desire to succeed—or perhaps not to fail in relation to our past selves—and so the more we train, the better we become, and the more we grow to love our sport. It's a vicious cycle that's difficult to break.

One of the first steps to knowing yourself and your motivators is acknowledging this jarring shift that happens when you move from recreational running to competitive running. We don't talk about it in the running world, so it can be difficult to recognize. But competitive running is different from amateur running; the confusion you feel as you move higher and deeper into this sport is natural. Your motivators are complex and entwined. There is no simple way of understanding this.

Second, it's important to recognize that competitive running brings with it all sorts of moral dilemmas and thorny motivations. To fully understand this, we need to look at the nature of competition.

Competitive running has none of the moralistic charm of recreational running. We no longer extend support as easily; we now see our fellow runners as enemies. Every race they win is a race we've lost. Every record they set is another we have to beat. The very nature of competition is to showcase your superiority against others: how can compassion, support, or even friendship feature?

The research proves this: psychologists' studies show that athletes have lower levels of moral development compared to their non-athletic peers.[5] In other words, our motivators in competitive running are not as kind or good as when we ran recreationally. Worse, those dysfunctional motivators are encouraged. Only in sport is it okay to say, "Kick their butts." Only in competitions do we aim to crush our peers. Coaches always tell us, "It's the journey that matters," but everything—including their coaching—is focused on winning. The goal is never the journey, but always the prize.

Most runners don't confront these moral complications. They've moved from forming strong friendship circles in recreational running to seeing everyone's success as their potential loss. It's scary, it's debilitating, and it eats into their psyche. If you've felt like this, you are not alone.

In fact, you're in good company throughout history. Our sense of competition comes from how we evolved. In the past, we competed for territory and food. If someone lost out on their share, it meant more territory or food for us. Competition—winning by someone else losing—is part of the evolutionary human psyche. In some way, we're biologically drawn to it.

But it doesn't have to shape how we approach competitive running. The pursuit of sporting excellence comes with these dysfunctional drives; it pushes us deep into the heart of competition and down the rabbit hole. But it doesn't have to: not if you confront it and put new strategies in place.

Research shows that a combination of extrinsic and intrinsic motivations provides the most positive benefits for runners—but only if the extrinsic is nurtured on a foundation of high intrinsic.[6] This, then, is my hope for you: that you can reframe competitive running to downplay those extrinsic motivators—the prizes, the awards, the recognition and praise—and emphasise your intrinsic drive. Focus on your own achievements and the joy of a runner's high. Don't lose yourself in comparisons. To do this, you must be aware of what drives you and aware of when those motivations may be doing more harm than good.

THE DYSFUNCTIONAL PATH

Your motivations have far more power than you realise. They actually affect how you run. As stated earlier, the introduction of external motivators can actually weaken the presence and effectiveness of internal ones and negatively affect performance: too many extrinsic motivators reduce your natural intrinsic motivation and move you farther away from your goal.

It is vital, therefore, to understand your motivators with all their shades of meaning. You must know the cocktail of drivers that push you out onto the racetrack, and you must be very careful about how you motivate yourself, because it has consequences.

What is driving you? What strategies do you utilise to encourage yourself to reach your goal? We've already explored how extrinsic and intrinsic motivators intermingle for runners, making it complicated to understand what drives them and what to do with those motivators. But not reflecting on it can lead to severe maladaptive behaviours.

In many cultures, intrinsic motivators are considered purer than extrinsic motivators. It is better to be fuelled by love of the sport than by a prize. It is more valuable to be motivated by the runner's high than by the desire for a sponsorship. "Passion," then, becomes paramount and praised.

These analyses are not wrong. It is better to focus on the quiet, intrinsic motivators in running than on the endless competition that pushes at you from all angles. But passion too has a dark side. You can have a harmonious passion, which fuels you to be the best version of yourself, or you can have obsessive passion, which causes you to push yourself past the point of reason because you are controlled by your need to run. You show an inflexible persistence, which leads to chronic and acute injuries.[7] Most obsessive runners simply choose to ignore their injury history: anything to keep running. Research has also shown that obsessive passion makes runners push their performance markers: they keep shifting the goal post so they can keep going.[8] (For more about addictive behaviour in running, see Mile 9.)

Extrinsic motivators are as bad, if not worse. Research shows that relying on extrinsic motivators can crush creativity, and of course, as we've seen, even crush what intrinsic motivations you do possess. Extrinsic motivators lead to burnout, chronic fatigue syndrome, and reduced persistence in training. They can even lead to cheating.[9]

Rob Young is a famous example of this. He is the author of *Marathon Man* and was deeply celebrated in the running world. During his attempt to set the Trans America record, a fan of his thought he might be lonely running on the quiet roads of America at night. So this fan set out to meet him and run alongside him for company.

Young had a van following along to provide supplies, a place to rest, and if necessary, a ride to the hospital. As the fan got closer to where Young should have been jogging, this fan could see the van but not Young. Believing it to be some kind of mistake, he ran closer to the van as it drove along the road, trying to find his hero. He found him sitting in the van. Young wasn't running at all; he was taking the van at night to claim miles he didn't actually complete.

The Young case is so famous because there is video evidence of it, and because he was cheating in pursuit of a record. Young was so motivated by winning, he believed cutting corners was an acceptable way to do so. The cheating was proven without doubt: his sponsor, Skins, commissioned two independent experts from the University of Colorado, Boulder, and the University of Free State to track his telemetry data, which confirmed it. In an interview where he was confronted with the evidence, Young denied wrongdoing. It is almost as if he cannot confront the shame and embarrassment of owning up to his mistakes.

Not reflecting on your motivators can lead you down paths you never meant to traverse. You could become like Young, so scared of your inner self that you cheat and then cannot face up to it. You could push yourself to exhaustion, to injury, to mental and physical stress. A quote from a West Asian fable beautifully illustrates this: "The forest was shrinking but the trees kept voting for the axe. For the axe convinced the trees that because his handle was wood, he was one of them." This is what certain motivations are like: they seem good because they come from you, but they are actually causing great harm.

The ideas and strategies you use to reach your goals matter. Maladaptive motivators can come from anywhere: from you, your peers, your surroundings. Learning your motivations, confronting them, and correcting them are necessary to ensure your drivers are sustainable.

STRATEGIES FOR SUSTAINABLE MOTIVATORS

Sustainable motivators are positive motivators that can sustain you without leading you down a dysfunctional path. It's not easy to divide motivators into "sustainable" and "unsustainable." Passion, as we've seen, can be both sustainable when it's harmonious and unsustainable when it's obsessive. Nor is it easy to group intrinsic motivators into "sustainable" and extrinsic motivators into "unsustainable": each has its positives and negatives, which feed off each other in the world of running.

The best path as runners, then, is one of reconciliation. How do we reconcile our intrinsic motivations with our natural drive towards competition? How do we balance the desire to be the best and secure sponsorships with our deep love for the sport?

I recommend two strategies for exploring and balancing your motivations. The first is to recognize the power of perspective and adjust your frame of reference accordingly. It's important to begin your running journey with healthy ways of thinking. Yes, physicality matters, but so does your mental health. You may be able to run ten kilometres every day, but is your mindset healthy? This is critical to choosing the right motivators and setting them as your true north.

The second strategy is what we talked about at the beginning of this chapter: to reflect and respond, instead of merely reacting. So many of your motivations will change naturally during your careers. You will face incidents that break you, reshape you, pull you to new heights, or push you to new lows. Each event has in it the possibility of change. Instead of reacting to these events, you can pause, reflect, and then choose your response.

For here is the truth: we think of running as a physical sport, but it relies equally on our emotions. This is why reframing your perspectives and reflecting on your motivators matter: it's because the emotions in this sport aren't just "good, good, good" but very intense and private feelings that deeply affect our love for running.

Examining those emotions in depth is not only healthy, it is vital. To know yourself, you must know how you feel and why. In Part II we will look at this emotional component more deeply.

THE GREATEST SUCKY THING

AS STATED, I BELIEVE PARADOXES LIE AT THE HEART OF long-distance running, beyond the essential paradox that we need to learn how to do this thing we were supposedly born to do.

Think about it. Why do we complain about running long distances and then, come morning, lace up our running shoes and head out for another run? Why do we push ourselves to the point of collapsing at the end of a marathon and then sign up for another one the next day? Why do we drag ourselves out of bed for a 5 a.m. run every morning when we'd rather be snuggled under the covers?

The answer is simple, really: we put ourselves through this misery because we love our sport. Because running is the greatest sucky thing around.

In 523 AD, Roman philosopher Boethius wrote "On the Consolation of Philosophy," a dialogue between a prisoner and his nurse "Philosophy," who consoles him on the many aspects of life during his imprisonment. In 2001, Alain de Botton ran with that idea to write *Consolation of Philosophy*, a consider-ation of how philosophy can offer us comfort and meaning for how we live.

Life's paradoxes—those situations where we find ourselves up against two opposites that are equally true—offer us that same consolation. If we take the time to think about these par-adoxes, to consider them from all angles, to embrace them in all their contradictory glory without trying to reconcile them, they will teach us about ourselves and allow us to enjoy our sport to the fullest.

MIRROR OF LIFE

Modern life is often a push and pull between contradictory elements that, on closer examination, make perfect sense. We're pressured to make full use of our time, to "live in the moment"—and also to earn as much money as we can and plan for the future. The world demands we monetize our passions and hobbies—or, at the bare minimum, provide results that can justify engaging in these hobbies. But in fact, there should be no differentiation between living it up and earning money, for it is all life. The balance is found within us.

If you pause for a moment, you'll realise running is in the same boat.

Running is a unique life experience that can generate intense but contradictory feelings, often simultaneously: joy and pain, anticipation and uncertainty, despair and elation. In fact, the greater the buildup of doubt and the greater the certainty that the runner will fail, the more intense the feelings of joy and satisfaction when the runner does complete the challenging workout.

Runners fear beginning their run, but they dread not starting even more. The more they fear the run beforehand, the more satisfying it is to complete it and the more unsatisfying it is not to run at all. The more satisfying the run, the more the runner yearns to complete the same workout—in fact, the more he yearns to make it even more challenging, accompanied by the same dread. This can lead to either a motivational and empowering cycle, or to burnout and breakdowns. Both are possible. Both are not guaranteed. The path is determined by the runner, and how open he is to introspection and reflection.

The choice begins by embracing the paradoxes of running: by leaning into the sport's complexity to learn more from it, and about yourself. Each of the five paradoxes explored in this chapter offers opportunities, each with positive and negative outcomes:

- The opportunity to persevere, to negotiate our failures and our difficulties. If we negotiate well, we can climb to new heights, but we can equally fall into an all-or-nothing mind-set that leads to maladaptive behaviours.
- The opportunity to progress, to earn higher ranks in our running social circle and reach better times. This challenge can be encouraging, inspiring even, or it can send us into a negative spiral if that rank or time is not attained.
- The opportunity to forge a social identity around running— to develop niche skill sets, gain knowledge, and understand our bodies better. If the opportunity is realised, we can feel empowered—by gaining a vaster and better way to understand ourselves, creating a sense of pride and value in our work. If it is not, we can feel debilitated, having lost our sense of identity, narrowed our value to how many races we win, or suffered a loss of self-worth when we lose or get injured.

Which outcome you, the runner, experience depends on how you choose to embrace each opportunity. This is why there is inherent truth to paradoxes: they hold up a mirror to your essential self, your sometimes conflicting motivations and values, and who you choose to be.

Though there are surely more than five long-distance running paradoxes, the following seem to best console us in all the joyful struggles of distance running.

THE PARADOX OF PAIN

If you are new to the sport, distance running is just running—and it sucks because it's painful and challenging. In learning to run, however, you realise that running is so much more, especially when it sucks. Running is not enjoyable in spite of its challenges, but because of them. Running still sucks when you're an experienced runner, but that's the point. It's precisely those sucky, painful aspects—the burning muscles, difficulty breathing, blisters—that make it enjoyable.

Research shows that pain is actually what produces pleasure in running. Daniel Liberman calls the runner's high an "evolutionary adaptation that makes us enjoy exercise"—and it is.[10] The high is born out of managing pain, out of managing the despair and uncertainty. The more we push ourselves to tiredness, the more refreshed we feel. Overcoming pain gives us a sense of self-actualization and pride.

In racing, this pain paradox moves to a new level, for pain is our guide to pacing and effort. The first third of the race is mental: "I don't feel so tired. This is an OK pace." The second third is physical: "My legs still have some bounce." The last third comes from the soul. That's when we dig deep, past our mental and physical reserves, for nothing could have prepared you for this moment.

In that final stretch, pain is all we feel. To outsiders, it appears we are jogging, and they might wonder, "Why isn't she picking up the pace? The finish line is right there!" Yet we know we are sprinting as fast and as hard as we can. And though still grimacing when we cross that line, we feel euphoric. In that instant, we experience a transition of pain in its various shades. We enter an enclosed pain cave of sorts, experiencing the very rawness of our determination—a private reminder of this moment.

Happiness does not originate from a place of comfort. You can't find joy by avoiding sadness. You can't find purpose by avoiding challenges. In his book *What I Talk About When I Talk About Running*, Haruki Murakami writes that it is precisely because the runner experiences pain and precisely because he wants to overcome that pain that the runner feels alive.

This is the paradox of pain in running: the more pain we feel, the more pleasure we get.

Yet there is a warning here. Many runners get so lost in this paradox. They lose all sense of perspective. There is a threshold of pain that is healthy—beyond which our bodies break down. Often, we see marathoners pushing on that last ten kilometres in a state nothing like running at all. They limp, hobble, scurry— they're using brute force to keep moving, despite blisters. They will finish the race, regardless of the amount of damage they do to their bodies.

We can do real injury to our bodies this way. Suffering is indeed a double-edged sword. The more we engage in it, often the stronger we come out of it—till we break down. The key is knowing the tipping point.

If we stay aware and conscious as runners, and if we run for long enough, we learn to distinguish between good pain and bad pain. In other words, pain teaches us about pain. What we make of this paradox is up to us: will we embrace its potential for joy, or will we push ourselves too far and cross over into injury?

THE PARADOX OF PASSION

Passion is often seen as a good thing. After all, passion is necessary to achieve mastery in any endeavour. Mastery requires dedication, and passion provides the fuel to keep that dedication going. Running is a physically draining endeavour that requires a lot of emotional drive and mental resilience; passion is what keeps us in the game.

But there is a paradox to passion in running: the more passionate we are, the greater the chance of becoming addicted. Research shows that passion produces an intensity of emotions in us that can often erase the boundary between caring and compulsion. From there, it's one small step into addiction.[11]

In fact, passion and addiction share remarkable similarities: they both engage strongly with our feelings, although not quite in the same way. Addiction is more unstable and chaotic, whereas passion can be motivating and can help shape our long-term behaviour. Yet the underlying driving force is the same—intensity of emotion—which is why it's so easy to slip from one to the other.

In *The Passion Paradox*, Brad Stulberg and Steve Magness explain how passion can either be empowering or debilitating: it all depends on the athlete's ability to introspect. Thanks to "neurochemically charged feelings" created by passion, athletes are often pushed into all-or-nothing mindsets that encourage obsessive-compulsive behaviours that are "no different from a mogul building a billion-dollar empire."

THE PARADOX OF CERTAINTY

Many of us start running with so much confidence: it seems like a simple sport, so natural and easy, like we were born to do it. Sure, we may be slow now and our form may be uncouth, but we know we will improve.

The problem is that when we do improve, when we level up our fitness and increase our speed, we can become overly confident. In our minds, we're running smoothly, but as we will discuss more in Part IV, the body often compensates for the ways we move suboptimally, so that smooth feeling can be deceptive. If we haven't worked on fundamentals, we might have the same uncouth form, which is not only embarrassing if we think of ourselves as experienced; it can also lead to injury.

If we're honest, we'll realise that running is one of those sports where the more we run and the more knowledgeable we get, the more we understand that we know nothing at all. As we level up in fitness, attaining the next milestone becomes more difficult, especially if we don't build those strong fundamentals in body and mind. The closer we get to a goal, the more we see that the goal—what we imagined was the end—is actually just the beginning of another goal. After we finish one marathon, we sign up for another, certain that this time we'll do better, only to suffer an injury in the interim and now we're no longer certain about how we'll perform.

The journey never ends.

THE PARADOX OF FAILURE

The very nature of running is paradoxical: we break down to build ourselves up. At the end of every run, whether it's an easy twenty-minute jog or an intense half marathon, our bodies experience microdamage—small breakdowns in our muscles that are a necessary precursor to recovery, regeneration, and advancing to the next level. Thus, during every run, we experience failures and then overcome them as we recover for the next run. We have to push ourselves towards failures to earn our successes.

The same process of breakdown and buildup works emotionally as well. Failure can be psychologically debilitating, but the more we encounter setbacks, the more we realise our true potential. Failure shows us our areas of growth. It's a reflection of our efforts and we can use it as a guideline to reflect and rebuild.

Don't shy away from the uncomfortable emotions that come with failure. Lean into this paradox. Recognize that discomfort comes from simply experiencing an unfamiliar side of yourself, one that is vulnerable. Above all, introspect. Don't wallow in your sadness: use it to find those areas of growth and become better.

THE PARADOX OF FITNESS

Liebermann was once quoted as saying, "From an evolutionary perspective, not exercising every day is pathological."[12] What he meant is that evolution expected us to move about—we were never designed to sit in one place.

This is why we revere fitness and people who exercise. People who start running often do so to lose weight or get in better shape, and the more they run, the healthier they feel. They think progressing from a 5K race to a 10K to a 21K means they're getting fitter.

But are they?

The American College of Sports Medicine recommends we exercise for thirty minutes three to five times a week.[13] Running forty-two kilometres per week, for example, far exceeds that recommendation: so is that increased activity level normal, or is it pathological? According to some researchers, the level of training involved in long-distance running is clearly beyond what is necessary to acquire the basic health benefits of regular exercise,[14] and it's known that athletes generally suffer more injuries than a couch potato.[15]

In addition, you may have heard of distance runners suffering from acute kidney injury or dying from sudden cardiac arrest. Does this mean they were not fit? No. Fitness is not solely related to the ability to run long distances. In fact, it's not even purely physical. If you are physically fit but your mind doesn't believe that, you could tip into compulsive exercising in an effort to achieve the fitness you think you lack. Or you might not respect the bodily stress that accumulates over a week of long runs. It's this disparity between the mind and body that often allows injuries to take us by surprise.

This is the paradox of fitness in running: often, the fitter you get, the higher the chance of tipping into injury and unhealthiness. The key is balance: the trick to avoiding this paradox is to run in a sustainable manner, as we've talked about in this book, so you can keep on running and feel good.

EXPAND YOUR EXPERIENCE

Many of us approach running in a somewhat mindless way. We get dressed, lace up our shoes, head out the door, and run, sometimes for hours at a time, without mindfully engaging with our sport. In this chapter, my goal was to nudge you into a more conscious relationship with running by considering five paradoxes that you've perhaps always sensed but never really looked at.

This is only the beginning, the first step in deliberately and mindfully thinking about your running experience.

Now let's consider how you feel when you run. What is your experience when you train versus when you race? How do you feel when you run on different terrains or at different times of day? If you've never considered these questions, now is your chance. In doing so, you open yourself to a much deeper appreciation of this greatest sucky thing.

PART II

How Do I Feel When I Run?

THE ACT OF RUNNING

RUNNING IS A MAGICAL SPORT, THOUGH IT MAY NOT SEEM so to someone watching a runner. To the onlooker, in fact, the runner appears slightly mad. She runs in passionate circles, sweat dripping down her back, her breath laboured, her cheeks red. The runner's movements are awkward, her body unbalanced—she looks almost clumsy sometimes. Once in a while, she winces, and it is clear the consistent impact of foot to ground is painful, that there is endurance here past the limits of sanity. An onlooker thinks, *How boring* and then *how painful,* and vows never to run himself.

The runner, however—she is transported. The combination of steps and thoughts create a moment in time that can never be recreated. No two runs of the same routes, of time and place, can ever create the same experience. The runner is in her zone, her body moving in a smooth, rhythmic stride. Yes, her legs are heavy and her chest aches, but she doesn't notice it. The runner only feels empowered, aware of each inch of her body in a joyous feeling. She thinks, *I got this. Only a few kilometres more. This will be the best run of the week. It's just me and the world.* And it is. Nothing can infringe on the runner; she is in her run.

Very few runners are consciously aware of the transportive power of their run. They feel it, but they are very rarely aware of their feelings, nor can they articulate them. This detailed examination of running—this awareness of body, mind, and emotion in a relational nexus—is almost never looked at. I was the same. The first time I noticed the transportive depth of running, of how I felt when I ran, was in the Netherlands in 2017.

I was in the country to visit a friend. One morning, I set my alarm to 5:30 a.m., thinking I could run for three hours and then meet my friend to hang out after she woke up.

The run did not begin well. I was annoyed to be awake so early, out in the cold of a December morning. It was dark still, almost gloomy—I could see only a sliver of sunlight on the horizon.

I chose "Sunset Lover" by Petit Biscuit as my running track because the song has a beautiful rhythm. As I ran, however, I realised that it also perfectly matched my pace, like I'd found the music that symbolised the morning.

I settled into the run, almost cosying into the movement. The music and my rhythm synced, intersected, then flowed into each other to become almost indistinguishable. As I ran, the wind shifted. It lightened slightly, as did the sky. The horizon turned rosy, then pink, then bright and blue—a clear sky stretching across the horizon, uncut by buildings. I'd never seen anything like it in Singapore. The change was epic, a mirror to my feelings as I ran. I played "Sunset Lover" over and over for the whole three hours, captured, transported, transformed.

That Netherlands run is probably still the best run of my life. I lived the runner's high for those three hours. It's not that I hadn't felt the high before, but I had never been aware of it to that degree. Before that run, my mind always locked onto mundane things. I thought about my studies along the miles or wondered what I had to do after the run. If I managed to cull my distraction and focus on the run itself, it was always in performance-related terms. What route was I going to take? How many miles would I cover? What time would I set, and what would those results mean for my running career? Everything had a point, and the point was always expressed in numbers and measures.

I began the Netherlands run in the same way. That morning I had charted a thirty-five-kilometre route on Google Maps and strapped on my Garmin watch, but once I began the run, I was awestruck. I forgot my plan and my watch. I simply put one foot in front of the other, almost carried by the music. The weather around me changed from cold to warm, mirroring the change in my own body as I built body heat. I felt, suddenly, that what I looked at—what I focused on—would transform the run for me. I was in my own universe, with my pace and my music, but I could also explore many separate universes. I could focus on the breeze numbing my cheeks and my hands. I could focus on my surroundings, the scenery, the people, the cyclists. I was a space traveller, able to shift between worlds depending on where I wanted to go, simply with the power of my mind.

This is the magic of running. This is the pull and the power of being aware of our run and the experiences it creates, within and without. As with each of the aspects considered in Part II, this awareness is not necessarily innate. It must be learned.

SEARCHING FOR THE MAGIC: THE RUNNER'S HIGH

Every runner knows the feeling: the moment when you suddenly, inexplicably, fall out of love with running. The moment is agony, as are the months that follow. You cannot understand how something that came so effortlessly to you, that brought you so much joy, is suddenly a source of anxiety and pain. You don't know how to bring that love back.

The reason runners lose enjoyment for running is because three essential factors are out of alignment: mind, body, and environment. Matching your body and your mind allows you to convert intention into commitment and thus results. In other words, you're better able to fulfil the goals you set for yourself because your mind and your body are working in tandem with each other.

But only those two factors are not enough. Linking your body and your mind with your environment takes this experience to a whole new level. The environment may be a factor that's external to you, a thing outside of yourself, but, as Mile 6 will show, it can move with you. You can flow with it, experience it in this particular light that aligns with where your mind is and what your body is experiencing.

When all three factors meet, intersect, and flow into each other—this is where the magic happens.

Runners often call this magic "the runner's high," a state of euphoria that certain people experience when they run. Science has found three core components that characterise the runner's high: this euphoria; reduced anxiety; and sedation, a state of relaxed calm.

The physiology behind the runner's high, however, remains a mystery. So much is happening in our brains when we exercise that it is difficult to pinpoint the neural pathways fired during a runner's high. We are thus left with many questions on the actual physical process behind the phenomenon and how to recreate it.

A 2022 review demonstrated that both endorphins and endocannabinoids are produced after either (1) periods of intense exercise or (2) periods of prolonged exercise. Endorphins often find it hard to pass through the blood-brain barrier, but endocannabinoids slip through and are responsible for the state we call the runner's high. Interestingly, the threshold for achieving the runner's high changes with your fitness level. As you grow more used to exercise, you need either more exercise or more intense exercise to produce the same level of endocannabinoids.

Yet the science is not exact. No one knows, for instance, the exact exercise threshold at which the runner's high kicks in. Nor can scientists explain why some runners experience the high while other runners—who complete the same number of kilometres at the same intensity—don't.

But we can guess. There is evidence that the runner's high is not just about objective brain chemicals; there is a subjective factor as well. A large part of why research has struggled to understand the runner's high is because it is difficult to capture the phenomenon in a lab. Long-distance runners who claimed to achieve the high in the past fail to experience it when running on a treadmill in a sterile lab, no matter how intense or prolonged the exercise is. In short, their mind and body are the same—but the environment is not.

This has startling implications for us runners. It means that phenomenology—this act of choosing what we focus on, whether we're training or racing or simply running—is more vital than we think it is, both on a subjective level and a physical level. Focusing on the right sensory experiences can open you up to the runner's high and change the run for you. Not only that, but we require environments that expand our range of sensory experiences; running in a lab is not the same, for example, as running in a park.

It comes back to the paradigm we opened with: mind-body-environment. Each works in tandem. Your body may be producing the chemicals and you may need to push your body to a certain physical threshold to create those chemicals, but it becomes more difficult without the right environment to manifest a range of sensory experiences. Even if you do manifest that range of sensory experiences, your mind must focus on the right elements to access the euphoria of running. You may never know the runner's high if you remain consistently anxious or negative during your runs. You must get all three to work together.

The next time you feel alienated from running, remember this. We may not be able to control our brain chemicals, but we can control how we think and what we notice. Tap into the paradigm of the mind-body-environment, make sure they are aligned, and the magic will come.

KNOWING THE COHERENT WHOLE

Since long-distance running requires an incredible amount of endurance, we usually focus on the physicality of the run. Science especially overemphasises the theoretical aspects of running, curious to see how far we can push ourselves in the name of long-distance running. We explore biomechanics; we carefully chart out physiology. If you search online, you can find in-depth research on VO2 max, which is the volume of oxygen your body uses when it is exercised to the limit. We track and quantify the cardiovascular systems in running. We even track the psychology of running with datasets like the Motivational Marathon Scale.[16]

But we rarely consider the self as a whole in running. We explore the body separately and poke at the mind, but we don't look at the points of intersection between the two or the experiences it creates. The truth is, mind and body are one.

In 1993, Csordas found that running doesn't only exercise the body; it also exercises and transforms the mind. Just as runners build both endurance and muscle as they run, Csordas found that they develop new modes of thinking he called "somatic modes of attention." By "somatic," Csordas refers to the gamut of sensation the body experiences: not just physical pain or shortness of breath, but emotions, thoughts, and states of being. These aspects are often ignored in the literature around running, and in our conversations about it.[17]

But we must shift that focus. An awareness of ourselves as a coherent whole—body, mind, and emotions—allows us to link into the deeper state of being we access when we run.

Let's take a simple example. Say you have a training session that you are dreading because you know it will be taxing. You go through the session, registering how much pain your body has endured. At the end of the session, you feel great fatigue, but you recognize that your body has become physically stronger because of it. You have successfully clocked the run in your goal mileage, speed, and time, the numbers on your Garmin being the only thing you see.

Your focus in this session was purely physical. You dreaded the pain, endured the pain, and then measured what the run meant for your muscle strength and growth. But other aspects of you were also developed during this training session. For instance, you were constantly thinking about the pain as you trained. You were cataloguing it. You experienced it. In many ways, you formed judgments about it: This is good pain; this is bad pain. I never want to do a workout like this again. Oh, this isn't so bad. You were constantly, unendingly, thinking about your training as you did it. In other words, you felt it deeply, continuously. The somatic experience was shaped by you as you went through it.

Yet at the end of the session, you only noticed the physical growth. You didn't even see that these other aspects of you had been developed through this training session. These thoughts and emotions were neglected—but that doesn't mean growth didn't happen. This is what Csordas says: runners build somatic endurance alongside their physical endurance. This somatic endurance, in turn, is reflected in our physiology.

Never underestimate the power of our emotions on our physical capabilities. What we think about and feel changes how we run. It's like watching a comedy and thinking tragic thoughts: there is no way you're going to laugh.

The body and the mind are one. To tap into the wealth of experience running offers, we must recognize this. We must be aware of the self as a whole—and the nuanced, complex, out-of-body experiences that awareness evokes as we run.

WHY AWARENESS MATTERS

In the chapters that follow, we will deep dive into the experience of running through three different prisms: training, environment, and racing. In each of these areas, we will explore the phenomenology of the run—its physical sensations, emotions, thoughts, larger-than-body experiences, as well as the complex philosophy and interrelatedness it tips us towards.

As runners, we rarely explore these aspects of our sport. We're like practical, good students: less concerned about the experience of learning and more focused on our grades. Yet awareness is vital, not just for our overall understanding of running but as we run. My run in the Netherlands would not have been as powerful if I wasn't aware of my emotions, my movements, the depth of my inner self, and the interrelatedness with my environment, music, and body during the run. To truly get the most out of running, we must focus on what we're feeling while our bodies are in motion.

Dr. Lisa Barrett explained the benefits of this in-motion experience by looking at the relationship between our brain and our emotions. Our brains work on past data. For example, if you've fallen in the snow while running and badly injured yourself, and you ruminate on the negative experience, your brain will remember that. The next time you go out running in the snow, your brain will call upon the past experience and interpret your present moment. In other words, your brain will tell you how to feel. It will say, *The last time you were out in the snow, you twisted your ankle. Running in the snow is dangerous.* So it tells your heart to start racing. Your palms sweat. You're suddenly anxious, maybe even scared. Your brain is guessing you're going to twist your ankle, and it is making you petrified.

Emotions are essentially guesswork by the brain based on past experiences. In the preceding case, if you don't address this cycle, you're always going to be scared of running in the snow; you will never move past this barrier.

The only way to break the cycle is to collect myriad experiences that your brain can use bits and pieces of to stitch a new narrative. The way to collect those experiences is not just to do them, but to be aware as you do them. It is to choose how you think about it. It is that awareness and choosing that gives you power. You can change your thinking to embrace the challenges, rather than passively dwelling in the negativity. Being aware as you run is to notice not just your body, but your environment, your emotions, your thoughts. Instead of remembering how you injured your ankle in the snow, you can choose to remember how quiet and peaceful the world was in winter, and how serene your run was. You can choose to focus on the cold air on your face, or the shades of the landscape. Over time, as you collect more winter runs, your brain will form a new narrative, one where injury does not feature so prominently.

This is the power of awareness and why it matters. Lean into your passion as a runner. Feel it consciously, understand

it as you experience it. It will open up new worlds, in ourselves
and beyond us.

NEW WORLDS

If there is a loss embedded in our lack of awareness, it is that
we never fully see running in its full, immense potential: as a
tool of exploration.

Running is a bridge to our inner selves. When we run, mind,
body, and emotion interlock into a cohesive, powerful whole
that can transport us. The emotions we feel are raw and intense;
one study found that the stronger our mental and physical sensations, such as those we might experience through the continual
contact of foot to ground and of paying attention to our route,
the stronger the feelings we experience—and vice versa.[18] These
intense emotions would be inaccessible if we were not running.

This is why no two runs are the same, even when we're
running on the same track or route over and over again. An
onlooker may think our choices seem boring, that simply
retracing a loop day after day is repetitive and dull, but for us,
numerous factors intersect to distinguish a run. A long run,
sprint training, whether or not we did a weight session before
the run, the environment, the weather—all of these intersect
to create different body experiences in each run.

In fact, it is this repetitive nature that most reflects life. Life
is mundane, boring even, bordering on the edge of the same
thing over and over: you wake up, fall into a routine, go to sleep.
Yet, each day is different in subtle, intense ways. No hour is the
same, no moment. When we run, we tap into that essential,
intense life experience. We are brought closer to ourselves. It is
like talking to a good friend or going on your fiftieth date with
your soulmate. It's old and familiar, and yet bright and fresh.

Each run lets us peel back a layer of ourselves, lets us delve deeper into what we can experience and what it means to be us.

Yet running doesn't only shine a light on our interior world—it links us to the outside world as well. In each run, there are multiple worlds we can choose to focus on. We can focus on the pain in our feet. We can look at the leaves around us as they change from bright orange to yellow. We can focus on the flow of our breath or on how the ground feels beneath us. We can disappear into our music. Each choice holds a new way of relating to the universe around us; each shift of perspective conjures a new world.

These effects spill over from the duration of the run into our everyday ways of thinking and living. The longer we run with awareness, the better we get at understanding ourselves and the more fluid we become at choosing what we focus on. Five years ago, when I did a difficult workout, I was reluctant. I thought about the pain and wanted to avoid it. During the workout, I was hesitant to push through the pain because I feared it and didn't know how I would respond to it. Today, that workout can be as intense, but my emotions are different. I explore the pain without fearing it. I focus on the fact that the pain is temporary, but it builds an endurance that lasts. I understand what the workout does for me: mentally, physically, emotionally.

And I bring those same learnings to my life. Everything that running teaches me—strength, endurance, perseverance—can be applied to the marathon of life. By knowing my emotions and strengths, by tracking my holistic growth as a runner, I can carry those skills to living.

But for us to glean these benefits, we must begin with awareness. Awareness will make us more conscious, smarter athletes, those who can tell what kind of pain we are in, what we are experiencing and why.

Perhaps once we apply this awareness over time, we can move towards articulation. Right now, an onlooker can never know what a runner experiences when they run. Nor can we tell them, for the feeling is so raw and hidden even to ourselves. In this way, running is an individual, private phenomenon. But the urge to express ourselves has never left us. We want people to know. I remember when I began training, I complained to my family about waking early or how difficult a workout would be. My mother would roll her eyes and say, "Oh god, just quit running then." I couldn't explain the love-hate relationship I had with the sport. I couldn't articulate the layers of intensity and transformation even the pain brought me. I didn't know how to tell her the sheer joy it evokes, across this moving constellation of interacting parts.

Someday I hope I can. This is my hope for you too: that when someone asks you about running, you will have the words to lead them into the secret, rich, vibrant universe of a runner.

TRAINING

THERE ARE TWO BIG RACES EVERY YEAR IN SINGAPORE: the Great Eastern Half Marathon and the Singapore Marathon. I had won the women's Great Eastern Half Marathon twice but had failed to win the Singapore Marathon. In late 2017, I planned to change that.

About four weeks ahead of the marathon, I met my long-time training partner, Sia, at 6:30 p.m. on the National University of Singapore running track. These training sessions before the race are critical because they are confidence boosters and frame your mindset for the marathon itself.

I was feeling a bit nervous about the session, partly because it had been a rough year for me. As mentioned earlier, I had failed to finish an easy 10K and my fainting spells in general had shaken my confidence. I'd always been in tune with my body and enjoyed pushing my limits, but now I felt unknowable to myself. I questioned what I knew, what I could do, and how my body would react. I had almost lost my motivation to run and focused mainly on staying positive.

Thankfully, Sia was relaxed that evening, lightening the mood and putting me at ease. We agreed to run at our marathon race pace for two-by-four-kilometre interval sets: two sets of four kilometres at 4:15 minutes per kilometre, and a relaxed jog in the middle to break up the sets.

The training session was beautiful and comforting. Sia and I were matched in skill, which meant we could keep pace with each other and exert the same amount of effort. It was like he was my benchmark and mirror for my pace and emotions. This symbiotic relationship was especially helpful during the last leg of my marathon preparation. I was feeling pretty edgy during this period, partly because I feared I wouldn't be able to handle the discomfort that was coming. Sia helped me ease my anxiety and become comfortable with discomfort, which is what the marathon is all about—26.2 miles of discomfort.

By the second set, we were both exhausted and pushing ourselves. On one level, we were rivals; we'd sneak looks at each other and think, *Ha! You're dying. I'm going to beat you today.* On another level, we were comrades, encouraging each other, saying, "Come on, last lap. We can do it." In the final two kilometres, I dug deep, smashing the pace below the four-minute mark and held it till the end.

I completed that training session comfortably at my intended pace; I even managed to finish in a negative split. But it wasn't about the numbers. For the first time in months, I found my flow when training. I wasn't dragging my feet. I had that fluidity, smoothness, enjoyment, and reassurance I so craved. Having a partner there helped me explore my feelings: to really feel the pain of a workout and then accept it, embrace it, sustain it without overdoing it, and finally push through it.

WHAT IS TRAINING?

Training is different from simply running or even racing. When we train, we intend to deal with fatigue, discomfort, and pain.

The inflection point from recreational running to training isn't always noticeable. As discussed in Mile 2, we might begin running with an extrinsic goal in mind: to stay fit or lose weight. But over time, running takes over. Not only do we begin to love the act of running for itself, but we begin to make small changes to our lives. We make different food choices to improve our physique. We calculate our sleep schedules based on our planned runs. We notice factors that improve our ability to recover and improve from extended runs.

In other words, running becomes intrinsic to our life. At this point, we recognize that further improvements will only come from regular, rigorous exercise. In ancient Greece, a lifestyle of regular, rigorous exercise was called an aesthetic life, because it was the path to true knowledge of the self. We reach a similar realisation: if we want to explore our potential as runners, disciplined exercise is the only way to unlock it. This is when we start training.

Training goes against the natural inclinations to retreat into comfort: it is an active pushing into discomfort that distinguishes a runner from a jogger. There are levels of discomfort as well: someone training for themselves will be less willing to endure discomfort than someone training for a podium. Training is a spectrum, depending on what level of pain someone wants to move into, which in turn brings different levels of joy.

Regardless of where you are on the spectrum, training can be more fully experienced by being aware of your thoughts, emotions, and sensations as you train. In 2017, I had become so discouraged that I mentally and emotionally checked out of running. The interactions I had while training with my running groups and sometimes on a one-on-one basis with running friends helped to reanchor me in the feelings and sensations of the run, so I could move into flow. Paying attention to your run will help immerse you in the same somatic experience, which can elevate your understanding of your body and help you create somatic memory so you can develop strategies to deal with pain and fatigue. Over time, this awareness will help you develop somatic endurance, and push you towards greater satisfaction and longevity in your sport.

MEANING-MAKING

There is a point at which running extends out from a runner's body, and into their environment and possessions. They have good-luck running shoes, favourite running attire, and preferred running nutrition and equipment.

It's almost beautiful to realise how much running has manifested in your life. Those good-luck running shoes may seem silly to a non-runner, but to you, they symbolise the moment you clocked your personal best. That outfit may look like regular running gear to an onlooker, but it's the outfit you wore when you ran your first marathon. Your running paraphernalia gets ascribed different depths of meaning now, compared to when you started running, and these objects symbolise your growth and collect memories that only you can access. Your self has expanded.

BREATH

There are two types of training: aerobic and anaerobic training. In aerobic workouts, we run at a steady pace. The pace is slow and often at an effort level that can be carried out for a long period of time. During these workouts, we can feel the discomfort creeping in and building up. Anaerobic workouts, however, are designed to increase our comfort with speed and involve intense repetitions that cause an almost immediate burn.

Each training type affects us differently, offering diverging sensations, emotions, and thoughts. Awareness of these experiences creates different learnings about your body. For example, if you focus on your breath as you switch between these two workouts, you'll discover different respiratory patterns for both. Better still, you will be able to identify when those respiratory patterns falter. Researchers have explored the importance of breath to runners. They found that runners listen to their breathing as an indicator of their performance. This assessment wasn't necessarily conscious; the participants simply used breathing as a benchmark of how well they were doing naturally, without realising it.[19]

Realising it, of course, makes you a conscious runner and a better one. If you can identify your breathing patterns for your different workouts, and then deliberately use that breathing as a benchmark of how the workout is going, you will be in control of your training. You can enjoy it more and endure it for longer, for as we've discussed, your body and mind are linked. If your breath is laboured early in the run, then your body sends a signal to your brain. Irrespective of whether you're aware of that signal or not, it becomes a thought in your mind: *Maybe I am not doing so well on this workout. Maybe I am tired, and I should stop.* Awareness means you can respond intelligently to that thought. Maybe your body really is pushed beyond its limits today and you should pause. Or perhaps this irregularity in your breathing is normal, a sign that you've increased the intensity of your goals, and you should keep going. In either case, you'll only be able to respond effectively if you're aware of what's really happening.

PAIN

Training involves pain. Pain guides training. Paying attention to your pain teaches you what pain is okay to endure and what pain requires you to stop. Knowing your pain threshold and its relationship with your body is especially valuable if you're a more competitive runner who tends to overlook the importance of rest days.

Different workouts have different effects on your body and produce varying strain points. Pay attention to your body's aches: how much pain are you experiencing and in what form? Constant awareness as you train will help you create somatic memory about your body's tolerance levels. You will learn the difference between a strained muscle and a pulled one, what level of spasm you can tolerate, and what cramp you can run through. Not all pain will feel cataclysmic. For example, soreness in the shin muscles is very common for beginners as the leg muscles start learning to adapt to a new way of motion. Often, this is easily managed by reducing the running training load and intensity.

However, this soreness can easily develop into a more serious injury like a shin splint or a stress fracture, which are often caused by repetitive trauma, overuse, and biomechanical problems (more on this in Part IV). This is why you should pay attention to what you feel as you run: Are your knees hitting each other? Does your left heel hurt when you fatigue? Do you land more heavily on your right foot? Over time, through exploration and an inner dialogue with your body, you will develop your own categorization for your pain. As you notice what hurts and how the ache develops, you'll learn what's "healthy" pain— that is, pain that results from a new movement, load intensity, or load type—and what is not. If a pain is about a three on a scale of ten, but rapidly climbs up to an eight, you know you have to stop before it leads to injury. If you have to alter your gait to get rid of the pain, then it's likely time to stop that run. It's a constant process of exploration, of finding your limits and how much you can push them.

Awareness of your emotions and pain as you train transforms your body into a map. You can pinpoint your injury history on this map, and you know what dangers to avoid and what issues look worrying but aren't that serious. It can be difficult to stay cognizant of your body when you're halfway through a workout and exhausted, but this is when it matters. It will help you prevent injury, enjoy your sport, and keep running for longer.

The key is to see your body as your friend and establish a conversation with it. You learn what it likes and hates and change your strategies accordingly. Numbers make you a faster runner, but having your body as a friend keeps you running for longer.

LOGBOOK OF YOURSELF

Paying attention to your breath and pain, understanding your body, and establishing a dialogue with it feeds into your somatic memory, creating a logbook of yourself as you train.

This logbook offers you insights that feed your endurance and enjoyment of the sport. I know, for example, that if I've been sitting all day, I need to do a longer warm-up to get my body revved for the training session. This is because my calves are tight, and I cannot run through that pain; I have to alleviate it with stretches. If I encounter that type of pain during training, I won't panic or stop the session; I simply implement my stretching strategy and keep going.

These insights reinforce your somatic endurance. Because

you have recorded and reviewed the logbook of experiences, you are more familiar with how your body responds to certain workouts and terrains, so you're less worried about pain or tiredness. You trust yourself because you know what you can handle. This allows you to push your limits. Your mental narrative is of strength and tolerance: *I can do this. I've got this.* And because you believe you can, you will.

Insights also feed into the sustainability of the sport. You now know your strengths and weaknesses, which lets you try different combinations of factors with an eye towards improvement. You're not just relying on numbers for growth; you have a deeper understanding of which body parts aren't pulling their weight and you can make adjustments to your workouts accordingly.

Never underestimate the value of your logbook. In my training, I used to be scared of interval repeats. My fear made no sense to me: I had endured pain before, so why was I scared of aches now? Over time, as I kept pushing myself and stayed aware of my emotions and thoughts during training, I learned I wasn't fearful of interval repeats per se. I was scared of failing. What if I didn't hit those times? Did that make me a lousy runner? I didn't want to feel like a failure and there was a good chance I would feel like one because I wasn't great at interval repeats. I was petrified of what I was lacking.

That insight changed everything. I recognized it wasn't the action I feared, but the story around the action. I focused my efforts on working through my mental narrative. As I did more interval repeats, worked on my weakness, and fixed my timings, my story changed. The fear disappeared—I increased my ability to handle the stress and discomfort.

TRAINING WITH OTHERS

As my training session with Sia proves, training with others can be a huge emotional boost. Throughout my running career, I also had a group of friends who lived within five kilometres of my place, and we would often converge at Bedok Reservoir for an early morning workout before starting our day. We grew together through these hard runs, and they became as significant as a regular coffee meetup, if not more.

Choose your training partners carefully because their motivations and skills affect your workout. Training partners usually take turns setting the pace and encouraging each other, so someone who can't keep up will drag you down. Worse, if they're unmotivated and aren't pushing themselves, it can feel like a betrayal—like they came unprepared for a workout they promised to do. This will affect how far you are willing to push yourself.

At the same time, training with people far beyond your skill level can also negatively impact your workout. I once trained with my brother and towards the end of the session, he started whistling. I was physically dying, and he had enough leftover energy to whistle. It was discouraging, to say the least.

The best scenario is to train with people of similar skill, as I did with Sia, so that you push each other and take turns setting the pace. In a bigger group, you might have five people who are tired that day and five who are feeling great, so the group spreads out a little. Those who want to run fast take the lead, and those who want to move slower go to the back. Everyone adjusts their pace so the group can stay together.

When training with others, listen to their breathing. Breathing is a clear indication of how your partner (or partners) are faring. If you find that the pacesetter of the group is breathing harshly, then they're probably tired from leading the pack and facing the wind. Offer to take over.

The best part about training with others is that they become mirrors to your running. They know you and can recognize changes in your running style. They can point out if you're dragging your feet today, or if your foot is turning inward more than usual, or if you have a slight limp. Those insights are invaluable and anchor you even deeper in the somatic experience of the run. Training partners can even draw your attention to overall approaches you may not have noticed. There are times I am distracted by life events or close to burnout, and my training friends have noticed simply by observing my run. Their insights revealed parts of myself I didn't see.

Similarly, observing your training partners can tell you more about how you're running. If you notice a partner's posture is bent, then you automatically think about your own posture. Feedback is therefore a two-way system, whether you're the one receiving or giving it, verbally or nonverbally.

Feedback isn't always overt, nor is it only about breathing or posture; it also includes observations of demeanour. How the group endures pain affects your endurance. If your teammates are always frustrated and give up easily, you will be encouraged to do the same. Your consciousness about endurance changes: you see the "best" as being at that lower level. But if you're training with partners who consistently strive to be better, your concept of "better" also rises.

I realised this when I was training in Boulder, Colorado. My friends there gave 100 percent at every training session because they were aiming for the Olympic trials. I had never before witnessed a group strive to such excellence. In Singapore, running is never considered a viable career; it is always a serious hobby at best, so I didn't have many partners that were as dedicated.

In many ways, training with others creates a powerful intimacy. Since running is such an essential human experience, you know these friends in depth, sometimes better than they know themselves. You've seen them at their most vulnerable, in the midst of pain and misery, and you open up to them.

Running is such a beautiful and rich practice. It is a private space and yet, when you run with others, that space expands to let them into this personal community. Each runner is locked in his or her own world, but when we run together, we unlock possibilities.

WHY WE TRAIN

As explored in Mile 2, motivations around running differ from person to person, and the same is true of training specifically. Some runners do it to get on the podium, but around 80 percent aren't looking to win races. So why do they train?

Some runners train as a way to keep faith with themselves. Training is rigorous exercise on a regular basis, which means creating schedules and sticking to them. This aspect is attractive to people who want to prove that they can fulfil their commitments to themselves. They like the practice of discipline, which creates a sense of stability and self.

Others train to explore their potential in running. How far can they push themselves and how good can they become? They don't want a podium at the end of it; they just want to explore the limits of their own ability. These runners draw meaning from their sense of growth and potential. They are looking for the intensity that comes with training, and the deeper joys they can access as they evolve. They know that value exists outside their comfort zone, in moving from jogging into deeper levels of discomfort and pain, because those levels offer a deeper, and thus more rewarding, immersion into running.

Still others train for a sense of empowerment. They understand that the process of running keeps them mentally fit, giving them power over themselves. Training teaches them they can overcome challenges, run through pain, and create new thresholds for what they can achieve. Their somatic endurance leaks into other aspects of their lives and increases their faith in what they can conquer.

For anyone who trains, the focus is the journey. The race is simply an excuse to train, rather than the other way around. They revel in how aware running makes them, this bridge to an authentic inner experience. And even though they don't aim to win races, their commitment to the sport is as deep. Missing a training session can create a sense of loss, either because they broke a promise to themselves, or failed to explore their potential, or because it destabilises their concept of being fit. They even experience intense withdrawal symptoms if they miss too many sessions and may tip into depression.

Any athlete who trains must be careful of becoming obsessive. Yes, training offers rich, myriad experiences that put us in touch with the transportive power of running, especially if we stay aware as we train. But obsession can sever this natural link. If we become too attached to our schedule and routine, training will be less about the intrinsic experience and more about checking a box.

Awareness can help you evaluate your reasons for training and make sure your approach stays healthy. Stay mindful and open. Avoid rigid boundaries. Enjoy the journey. (We'll look at what it means to cross unhealthy boundaries in Mile 9.)

AWARENESS BUILDS ENDURANCE

Ultimately, training will exhaust you, drive you to the limits of your body, and cause you pain. It has to—if it didn't, it would be recreational running and not training.

Regardless of why you train or where you fall on the training spectrum, focusing on the somatic sensations of your training session will build your ability to endure your workouts. I'm not only talking about the logbook of yourself or how your observations about yourself create insights over time. I'm also talking about what you do with those insights.

How do you choose to respond to pain? How do you choose to endure fatigue? We all have a choice to not simply react to bodily discomfort, but instead pause and carefully respond. Taking the time to exercise mind over matter is how we push ourselves to be better in this sport. Training provides us with the opportunity to endure, but the choice to do so is always ours.

Being aware of your training experiences will make it easier to make a conscious choice instead of reacting. As you become more aware and your logbook grows, your decision-making power also expands. You will grow your ability to endure, not only on track but also off it.

ENVIRONMENT

IT WAS 5:30 A.M., AND MY ALARM WOKE ME FOR ANOTHER morning run. This time I was in Singapore, not the Netherlands, but I was equally annoyed. Though I knew at the end of my run I would find satisfaction, as I always did, I dreaded the repetitive kilometres that lay between me and that joy.

I dragged myself out of bed and put on my running gear, forcing myself to disconnect from my frustrated self so that I could prepare to run and, in that act, reconnect with myself. The irony was not lost on me.

When I arrived at Macritchie Reservoir, I secured my belongings in a locker, finished up my pre-workout shake, and used the bathroom, still filled with irrational anger at my own choice of how to spend this Sunday morning.

A boardwalk surrounds the perimeter of the reservoir and has several entrance points to the trail. My goal that day was two loops of the reservoir, for a total of twenty-one kilometres.

I always feel a little stiff at the beginning of a trail run. It usually takes me thirty minutes or so to warm up mentally, psychologically, and physically, and the uneven surface around the reservoir wasn't making it any easier. I felt clumsy and awkward. The world doesn't show up for you, Ying, I said to myself, and in the next breath, cursed the rock I almost tripped over.

It was particularly hot and humid that morning, not the most helpful conditions when you're trying to keep your cool. I felt like I was playing a game of Don't Sprain Your Ankle, quickly selecting the best places for each foot as I avoided the rocks and roots.

The undulating, leaf-covered trail wound its way through a mini rainforest, complete with the occasional monkey. Tall, lush trees rose up on either side, forming a canopy so thick at some points that the sky disappeared. At other spots, the trail moved through wide-open space and past a random golf course.

Leaves rustled in protest as I trampled them on my way through the manmade jungle. Kilometres passed. I tried to hold my gaze up, despite the fatigue building in my mind and body. Beads of sweat stung my eyes and blocked my vision, making it harder to run—yet I pressed on, feeling motivated to conquer the trail and the rocks impeding my progress.

I finished my second lap after about one hundred minutes. I collected my belongings and took a shower. As with every other time I had come to this trail, the journey hadn't been easy. This morning in particular had been difficult in the beginning, yet I had done it and I felt proud of myself. I had moved beyond the frustration. I had actually enjoyed the challenge provided by the rocks.

There comes a point in every runner's life when he sees a new place and immediately thinks about running. It doesn't matter what that place is—a park, an expressway, hills. He wonders what it would be like to run on it, to feel the breeze off the ocean or navigate the narrow path or feel challenged by the switchbacks.

At the same time, we can feel completely content to visit the same park and run the same circuit. Because we know that every run is unique—and how we relate to that park on any given day changes everything.

ELEMENTS OF A RUN: PLAY AND CHALLENGE

The run modifies the running environment. It doesn't matter if you choose to train in the same park each day: how you experience that park changes day to day depending on your state of mind, your activity, the temperature, and more.

For example, the time of day creates various running experiences. Running in the early morning, before the sun is up and when everything is foggy, creates a dreamlike environment that feels almost spiritual. If you run that same path after 8:00 a.m., however, when the sun is higher in the sky, the brightness will transform the route into something more ordinary.

Likewise, our experience is shaped by the type of run—jogging, sprinting, warming up, cooling down—because it impacts what we pay attention to. During cooldown, for example, I tend to appreciate the coolness of the morning, the breeze, the soft chirping of birds, because I'm in a more relaxed state of mind. In the midst of an intense interval workout, however, I might float between states of consciousness—from attempting to dissociate from my pain to enjoying my environment to concentrating on my strides—almost as if alternating between states of nightmare and reality. In other words, we establish our own meaning around and connection with our environment, depending on our intentions and our actual movement.

Because our experience of the environment is so personal, it also differs between runners. My brother and I are both runners, but we don't gain the same enjoyment from the same environments. For one of my training sessions, I was going to run in a certain park, but instead I chose to run up and down the connector to the park. I was tired from studying and just wanted something familiar; the park's varied environment was too sensory-laden for my fatigued mind. I found the terrain comforting and exactly what I needed. When I told my brother about the session, he was baffled. He had no clue how I could enjoy a two-hour run in such a boring place.

As runners, we can choose to passively experience this newness of the environment with each run, or we can choose to lean into it. I use the various environmental factors to challenge myself and change the spectrum of challenge and play. Say I'm running on a forest trail I've run a thousand times before. I can switch up the intensity of the run: I can run hard up the slopes and slow on the way down—or vice versa. Or I can pick a landmark in the park—a bench or tree or light post—and do sprint repeats: sprint to the landmark, jog back, sprint, jog. Those simple decisions will change how that run feels for me—it will distinguish the run from all the others on the same trail.

Even more crucially, though, my choice gives me a chance to strengthen myself both mentally and physically. Running hard up a slope, for example, gives me the opportunity to develop my muscles. Running slowly down the slopes allows me to flow with the descending slope and practise high turnover on my running cadence. (Side note: If you overstride as a runner, this exercise will help you correct it, as it is hard to overstride down a slope.)

Ultimately, we train ourselves to see the variety of environmental factors in a certain way and to focus on what is positive and exciting about each one. We can see the hills as boring, or we can think, *Sprinting up this section will help me develop speed skills.*

With enough conscious practice, you will be able to see the value in each terrain and each run. Soft grassy terrains and gravelly grounds are good for developing the balance mechanisms in our feet and ankles, which strengthens you as a runner. You can see slopes as an opportunity to lean in while running downhill, letting gravity work for you. You can see running with a headwind as frustrating, or you can see it as a challenge to develop another part of your body.

There are endless possibilities of play when it comes to the environment—it is up to you to stay flexible and open-minded so you can make the most of them.

FAMILIARITY AND ENDURANCE

Familiarity with your environment, far from being a negative, can be a huge positive when you're training. Because you know the terrain, you're able to anticipate the challenges that are ahead of you. You might know, for instance, that in one kilometre you're going to run on a grassy patch, so you need to be prepared for uneven ground. Familiarity keeps you from being caught off guard by the fact that halfway into your run, you're tired—you know it's because you ran up and down that hill, and it had the same effect on you last time.

On one level, there is still an element of consciousness and choice in familiar terrains. You could, for example, see the familiarity as boring and unchallenging. Or you could choose to emphasise what that familiarity gives you: a sense of courage, more mental space to focus on your body and what you're experiencing, more time to notice how your body prepares for the challenges.

Above all, training in a familiar environment offers you a sense of temporality. Because you've run the track before, you know what is coming and when—more importantly, you know what will end and when. It feeds into your ability to build endurance. Not knowing might push you to give up sooner—because you can't tell when the pain will end, you're less likely to keep soldiering on. But familiarity with the route will offer you this knowledge. You have this sense of: *I know this. I've done this before. This patch of mud or hill or slope will end soon, and then it will be easier from then on.* Such knowledge gives us mental endurance, which allows us to build physical endurance.

EXPLORE YOUR PLACE

Running in the more challenging elements of nature reminds us of our vulnerability as human beings. In daily life, it's easy to interact more passively with phenomena such as snow or rain. You can watch these elements from inside your house, or simply ignore them and go back to watching television. However, when you're outside running in these conditions, you are forced to interact with them head-on. At that point, you have an opportunity to embrace the environment with a positive attitude and learn from the challenge it presents, or you can fight against it.

Running in the snow reminds me of how vulnerable I am, how easily I could be overwhelmed by this element if I were not properly prepared. Running along the vast sea can also make me feel vulnerable and small, but at the same time, as I watch the crashing waves, I sometimes feel empowered.

Our running environment can broaden our experience of running itself and of life—if we are conscious of what is going on around us as we run. When we focus on our time or whether the run was good or bad, it's easy to run by a lake or through the rain or up a rocky hill and to have no deep connection with that element beyond knowing that the thing is there. However, if we become aware of our reaction to these natural phenomena, pause to consider how they make us feel, we can take away more than a fast time; we can enjoy a better quality run no matter what the watch says.

In running, we have a unique opportunity to explore the world around us, as well as our place in that world, and to decide how we're going to respond. Take the time to look around you, to pay attention to what you're feeling, and get the most out of every run.

RACING

I BEGAN MY WARM-UP, TRYING TO BREATHE STEADILY AND calm my nerves. I was at the start of the World Cross-Country Championships in Guiyang, China, representing Singapore among eighty-two elite female runners from around the world. My idols were here, people I read about in racing magazines long before I started running myself. I glimpsed Sarah Hall ahead of me, stretching with calm focus. It was surreal to be so close to her, to watch how she stayed in the zone, to race with her.

I was at the peak of my running career so far: I'd achieved podiums in local and international half marathons, and I'd won a half marathon in Taiwan in which I represented Singapore. I was one of two representatives the country had sent to China, and the other one was male. I was incredibly proud of what I had accomplished and excited to be here. I was also nervous. Who wouldn't be, racing alongside their heroes?

When the buzzer went off, I was in my zone. I was a competitor, a winner, and I was at the top of my game. I would give this race everything.

However, it very quickly became apparent that this race was unlike anything I'd experienced. Singapore's cross-country races were often held at Bedok Reservoir, where the terrain was mostly gravel. On the course in China, I was running through mud patches and puddles of water, in addition to grass pastures, gravel stretches, and then, out of nowhere, rolling hills. Interspersed among these obstacles were sandy spots. To make matters worse, we were at a high altitude, and at that point I had not trained in Colorado, so I had no experience of running in thinner air. I was running badly. I knew I was running badly. But I had no idea how bad until the crowd booed me.

Time slowed. Until that exact moment, I always heard applause as I ran by. Until that moment, I had been the front runner of every race I'd run as an elite. I'd gotten used to seeing no one in front of me except the lead bike. How was this happening?

As the crowd's booing engulfed me like an enormous, loud wave, I felt immediate shame. The race was three laps, and I realised I was being lapped. I knew in that moment I would be lucky to not finish last.

In this slowed-down moment, I had a choice: continue running this race with my terrible form and slow timing, with the crowd booing and my idols running past me, or quit…

IF NOT A MEDAL, THEN WHAT?

When you race, it's easy to equate racing with winning. That's what I did before the cross-country race in China. I had become so accustomed to winning that because I wasn't out in front, it was automatically a bad race. It didn't matter what time I achieved, if it was my personal best, if this was the hardest course I had run, if the people ahead of me were world champions. I didn't care. If I wasn't a contender for a podium or the top ten at the very least, I had lost.

In a way, consistently winning reinforced this mindset. I had settled into a groove, perhaps even a sense of superiority. I expected to be cheered. I expected to beat my opponents. I expected to be a worthy contender. And this expectation wasn't simply in my head. I was winning. I was making good pocket money from my talent. I had a sponsorship from Nike. How I saw myself and how the world saw me aligned.

But this alignment cemented a certain way of experiencing a race: leading the way with a top medal waiting for me at the end. The cross-country race in China changed this. There, I was forced to deal with a wide array of racing emotions, far beyond the expectation of winning and watching that expectation play out. I also felt proud to be there, aware I was at my physical best, excited to be racing among the world's best, nervous about the stakes, horrified at how badly I was performing, shamed by the crowd, and convinced I was an imposter. The conflicting joy and negativity pressed in on me. And in the middle of the race, with those boos loud around me, I had to decide what to do with it.

I kept running.

As I ran, I tried to stay positive, but being my sole cheerleader, apart from the team manager, wasn't easy. After the race was over—I placed second to last—I wanted to change out of my Singapore singlet and hide forever. I had to keep choosing to focus on the positive, to remind myself of the growth this race offered me. I had to fight off the despair. It would have been easy to let the boos of that crowd seep into me. I had to choose not to let that happen.

In a way, this is what we've been discussing throughout Part II: the need to respond instead of react. If I had simply reacted,

I would have quit. But by choosing to respond, I focused on what I learned.

I'm very glad I did. Responding instead of reacting showed me that there is more to racing than winning. The outcome didn't make this race for me: it was the gamut of emotions I experienced, the fullness and challenge of another way of racing. For once, I didn't focus on the outcome of the race but the process itself. And I was forced to ask myself: what else does racing offer me other than a medal?

Racing is a unique, challenging, high-pressure exercise, different from both recreational running and training. To experience it fully, to be aware of its unique components and emotions, you must first understand what makes this activity so singular and then learn the various riches it can offer you.

RACING VERSUS TRAINING

Training and racing are, in a way, quite similar: they require pushing out of our comfort zones and into the beyond. Runners often find themselves baffled by this pushing—after all, if we're not running from an immediate threat, from a bear or a fire, why is there a need to run at all?

But there is, in fact, an inbuilt uncertainty that draws us into training and racing. It's the shift from "I can't" to "I can." You've felt it. You're at the starting line, whether of a race or a training session, and you're staring at a route that's going to challenge you beyond your limits. You begin from a position of "I can't"—you haven't done this before, this isn't possible for you, and so on. But then you go through that training session or finish the race, and suddenly you've done it. You've moved into the "I can."

When you're standing at that starting point, though, you

don't know if you can. It's uncertain. But there is delicious hope in your uncertainty: if you can, you will be so much larger than who you are right now. The possibility is alluring.

Racing puts this uncertainty and hope at a different, deeper level. When you're training, you can always stop. But at the starting line of a race, you're pledged to a certain goal and surrounded by witnesses to your journey. There's pressure and commitment shared by your fellow participants, all standing at the starting line with you. It's like a marriage, compared to a casual relationship—there's a different set of expectations.

Still, we might intend to finish the race, but our commitment to doing so can only be tested when we're in the activity itself, in the thick of the struggle. Will we follow through on what we hope to achieve? Or will we quit at the first sign of difficulty?

The key to syncing our intentions and our commitment is leaning into the mind-body connection. Often, the gap between our intentions and commitment is a reflection of a gap between what our minds want and what our bodies say. This is why we quit, or why we procrastinate, or why we're so far from the goals we set. As we've said in all these phenomenology chapters: be aware of your mind and your body so that you choose how to respond. This especially matters in the highly charged, pressurising, and transformative arena of racing.

INTERSUBJECTIVITY OF RACING

Racing differs from training or recreational running due to its intersubjective nature. You can train with a group or recreationally run with one, but you don't have to. You can do it alone. In racing, however, you must run with a group. Moreover, you have an audience, no, a crowd of witnesses to the race.

Spectators are drawn to racing for precisely this role of witnessing. It's powerful to watch runners complete athletic feats not many people can achieve, an objective display of physical prowess. But the crowd also feels close to the runners because they're watching them struggle, fight, and endure to reach their dreams, and thus are part of the runners' emotional journeys. Witnessing a race gives spectators both these perspectives: the objective, physical journey and the softer, emotional one.

This act of witnessing is not only restricted to the spectators: it extends to the participants as well. Participants witness both other participants—how they stride, struggle, endure—and the spectators. They draw inspiration from the spectators, from the fact that strangers have a stake in their endeavour, take pictures, and encourage them over the finish line. As runners inspire spectators, so spectators inspire runners. It is a two-way street.

The unique nature of racing, then, is this tangled web of interconnectedness. Everyone is engaged in witnessing and being witnessed, creating a feedback loop that doesn't occur in training or recreational running, and contributes to the intense nature of racing. I find it beautiful that everyone at the race takes away a little piece of joy.

This interconnectedness also creates an intersubjective sense of self. Our identity isn't purely our own; it incorporates other people's perceptions of us. Humans are, after all, social creatures. We long to be seen and witnessed. This is what racing offers us: a clear gaze that allows us to know ourselves better and measure ourselves against others. Running a 10K on my own is different from running a 10K with someone else, and that is different from running a 10K with a group of people in the framework of a competition, with an audience watching us. The layers of feedback increase: it's like having more mirrors by which to know ourselves.

This intersubjective nature of racing—and thus of competition—has both positives and negatives. We explored some of the negatives in Mile 2, but they are worth repeating here: with competition, it's very easy to get attached to relative values. Competition, in fact, encourages relative values. If you came second in a race, you're not as good as the person who came first. Prize money in races cements this status of "not good enough": for example, in the Singapore Marathon, the person who wins gets $10,000, while the second-place runner gets half the reward. Sponsorships then drive the point home: as second-place finisher, you don't land any sponsorships while the person who came first secures a lucrative deal. Everywhere, the world reinforces this idea of you as "not good enough."

To truly enjoy racing, you have to look beyond these relative values. Whether you came first, or second, or won a medal at all doesn't matter. You must define your value for yourself. This isn't easy to do, thanks to the relative nature of competition, but you must stay true to yourself.

Moreover, like I did at the cross-country championships, you must focus on the other aspects of this intersubjectivity that are beautiful. Instead of thinking of yourself as not good enough, concentrate instead on the possibilities of this inter-connectedness. There is real value to intersubjectivity in that it allows you to know yourself better.

I think of it in three stages. First, there is the question every runner asks himself: Can I do this? Once that question is answered through training, the runner asks himself: Can I do it better? In other words, can I improve my overall time? Can I improve my splits so they're all below six minutes? Once the second question is answered, the runner moves on to the third, which specifically relates to racing: If both of us can do it, who can do it better? Here, the runner understands his competency in relation to the world—how do his skills measure up to others'. This teaches him what his strengths are and where he needs to grow.

In answering this third question, you're no longer thinking about outcomes. Both you and your competitor can finish this marathon or run this route; this is proven in the second stage. In this third stage, you're looking at the process.

Imagine you and your competitor are in the last mile of the race. You both will finish, although it's not certain who will beat the other, nor does it matter. What matters is how you both endure that last mile. Is your opponent coping better than you? Is she handling the pain with more grace? Is she positive despite her flagging speed? Observing your opponent in that last mile teaches you vital lessons: you reflect on how you're coping and can improve. Without competition, this reflection would be lost to you, and so would your growth.

Racing is intense, competitive, and challenging. It's full of shame, hope, uncertainty, disappointment, encouragement, and delight. It has the potential to drive your self-worth down—but only if you let it. If you reflect and respond carefully, if you focus on what racing offers you other than the medal, you can access a side of the world rich with possibility, exclusive to only the few willing to explore discomfort. You can grow in leaps and bounds, on a trajectory that wouldn't have been possible if you only ran by yourself.

HOW WE RACE

How we race is also influenced by intersubjectivity. Our strategies, even our involuntary actions, are heavily shaped by our competitors.

In most races, for example, you end up running with a particular group of people. You didn't choose this group and they are probably strangers to you, but you're all running the race together because you have the same pace, which means you naturally cluster. After a while, further into the race, you grow used to this group; they become your benchmark. When one person in the group begins to push the pace, speeding up, chances are you will follow—even if you didn't intend to increase your pace. It's a strange symbiosis, an intimate connection. It's a feeling of both "We're in this together" and "If you can increase your pace, so can I, because I know we're evenly matched and I can keep pace with you."

The intersubjective nature of racing feeds into not only our involuntary actions but also our predetermined strategies, depending on our goals. If your goal is to win the race, then there are a number of psychological approaches you can deploy. If, for example, I only want to win and am not concerned with beating a record or setting a personal best, then I just run behind the lead runner. As long as I can overtake her at the last moment, I will achieve what I want. Or, if I know my opponent is bad at the last mile sprint, I'll set the pace for the race and keep it purposefully slow. That way, I reserve my energy for the last sprint and secure the win.

In essence, there are so many factors at play in racing, because it's so beautifully interconnected. It is not an isolated sport—it cannot be. This is what draws us to it, and why it's so hard to articulate why each race is so different and alluring. It's not the outcome of the race or your timing. It's this quiet, unsaid process that makes it memorable.

FIND THE MELODY

The cross-country race in China was one of the hardest races of my life. But it was also the race that taught me the most. It shook me out of my complacent, settled approach to racing and showed me how much more the sport had to offer than a podium.

At the end of the day, when we're running, we cannot always choose how we feel or even what we think. When the crowd booed me, I immediately felt small and inadequate. In that moment, however, I could control how I chose to respond. The power of response is yours as well. Racing is composed of myriad elements: the track, your body, your mind, other participants, the spectators. Each of them interacts in many ways to create unique experiences, and you cannot always control those variables. But you can always decide your attitude to those elements.

Over time, as you get better at reflecting and responding, it will be easy to see racing as more than just the medal: as this buffet of emotions and experiences that elevate you as a runner. There's a huge amount of vulnerability in racing. It's a live demonstration of endurance and struggle: there is no space for pretence. All runners are sweating towards that finish line, their faces red, their features distorted in pain, their breath laboured. There is no beauty there, no polished appearance to hide behind. Everyone is a witness to everyone else's ugliness; we see each other at our worst. But our togetherness makes it okay. It inspires us: we push ourselves out of our comfort zone and are utterly shameless in our pain and discomfort; we feed off each other's courage. We may look half-dead as we cross the finish line, but the audience is cheering anyway, snapping pictures, shouting praise. We're united, all of us, in this single, connected endeavour.

The intersubjectivity of running makes it glorious. Yes, you can run alone or run recreationally but it won't be the same. It's like playing a single note, perhaps in different tones. There's no variation or interplay, no melody.

PART III

Do I Enjoy Running?

THE LONELINESS OF THE LONG-DISTANCE RUNNER

HALFWAY THROUGH THE TRAINING SESSION, I FELT LIKE crying. I glanced at Roberto, my running partner. How tired is he right now? He looked fine, calm and in the zone, his breath steady. So why was I in such bad shape? I looked ahead. *Don't think about it*, I told myself. Another twenty kilometres and this will be done.

We were in Hong Kong, training in a marathon simulation session for the year-end Singapore Marathon. Rob and I had it planned to the last detail. We would run forty kilometres at a four-minute-per-kilometre average, starting at 4:30 per kilometre and taking the pace down to 3:45 per kilometre by the end. We would meet friends along the way who would join us to maintain the pace for us. Twenty kilometres out and twenty back.

Rob had lived in Hong Kong for ten years, so he knew this route. I didn't, which meant I had to stick with him. Plus, I had no money, nothing on me but energy gels in my pocket. I made sure I had no escape strategy: there was no way I was not completing this workout.

I didn't let my exhaustion show, not in my breath or my features. I didn't allow the slightest disruption to my form or pace. I stayed positive by not thinking at all. The moment I thought, my mind turned to how heavy my legs felt or my increased heart rate, and then I would sink. You can't sink in a training session: either you keep the pace or you kindly show yourself out.

I sneaked another glance at Roberto. He was still composed and focused. It made me feel stressed, anxious, worried, and inspired. Jealous.

Lonely.

Because the truth was, I was worn out. Every step was a struggle. But Roberto was doing well, as were his friends. My suffering was my own and disconnected me from the pack. *Don't think about it*, I kept telling myself, but that was hard to do. If I failed to keep pace now, would it ruin the workout? Of course it would; someone would have to drop out too, take me home. I had no money. I didn't know where I was. If I stopped, I would not only fail myself but also fail everyone else. I would be a bad training partner, a bad runner.

None of the others were struggling. Why was I?

LONELINESS AND LOOKING

In our wider running culture, there is a rule about training together: either you keep pace, or you drop out and let the group continue without you. The pressure of that rule is relentless; you never want to be the person who disrupts everyone else's training session. No one wants to be the weak link.

That culture means we never talk about our struggles. I was

so far gone in that training session that I couldn't even be vulnerable in the quiet of my own mind, let alone telling the group about my issues. I felt a responsibility to be strong and indestructible. My job as a training partner was to stay the course.

But these thoughts created a profound loneliness in me. I felt alone in my pain and doubt, like I was out of sync with the group. Most runners have experienced forms of this isolation at one point or another, whether we're running alone or with others. The loneliness springs up and holds us hostage, all the more because we never talk about it.

Yet I could have escaped my loneliness that day if I had chosen to see differently. Yes, it was true I found it hard to complete the run. But Roberto and his friends chose to train with me. There was love, teamwork, and support among us. If I had focused on this instead of my struggles, I would have realised that I was cared for. Roberto, in fact, didn't let me set the pace for that session. Instead, he blocked me when I tried to lead so that I could stay at the back and conserve my energy. He was looking out for me. I was surrounded by so much trust and care from my community, but my thoughts prevented me from seeing it.

Articulating our loneliness—to ourselves, our training partners, and our family—is the first step to changing those isolating thoughts. It's funny: as runners, we believe we're unique in our isolation, but we're not alone even in this. To normalise loneliness in its various forms, to speak of it freely in its multifaceted manifestations, is to reveal how connected we are.

LONELINESS AND GROWTH

Distance running is a lonely sport. We run for miles and miles by ourselves, with no company and no one to witness how we endure or change. We're alone with our thoughts and feelings, trapped in our head, for hours at a time.

The rhythm of running itself exacerbates this loneliness: one foot in front of the other, again and again, in a never-ending, monotonous pattern. Your breath, in and out, in time with those steps. Silence all around you, stretching as far as the horizon, pressing in on you until it feels deafening. No one to break the monotony, to say something, to add a rhythm different to yours. Just you. Only you.

In many ways, the concept of growth is connected to loneliness. To truly grow, we have to push ourselves out of our comfort zone and into pain and discomfort. That pushing, this zone of the unknown and unpleasant, is a lonely place. On the other side of it is growth, and growth is what motivates us to continue, to keep pushing, to see how far we can excel. But to expand out of our comfort zones and into new territory, we must become comfortable with the loneliness of that expansion.

This is not unique to distance running, of course. There is growth in any sport, and each phase of growth brings its own loneliness, this feeling of being singular and un-understandable in our struggle. But distance running is the epitome of this loneliness simply because the sport itself emphasises it. It occurs across long periods of time, it covers great physical distances, and it is repetitive in motion. It feels like it goes on forever.

This is why it is so important to be mentally fit for distance running. On my run with Roberto, I felt lonely whenever I became negative—when I thought my breath was too laboured or my legs felt heavy. The moment those negative thoughts crept in, the loneliness followed: Why was no one else feeling like this? Why was I the only one struggling?

If you are a negative person, the isolation of the sport will likely become worse. Pay attention to your thoughts as you run and you'll find that distance running holds up a very clear mirror that reveals if you're an anxious person or pessimistic or fatalistic; in so doing, it opens the opportunity to break the cycle of negativity. These attitudes make distance running worse. If loneliness and growth are entwined and we cannot be better without struggle and discomfort, then we must learn to be friends with ourselves. We must be kinder in what we think.

LONELINESS OF OUR FREEDOM

The loneliness of distance running is also connected to another aspect of the sport that draws people to it—its freedom.

Distance running offers us independence from the overly connected world around us. It gives us solitude: a space that we carve out for ourselves where we can be by ourselves. In today's age, our phones hook us into virtual lives and a million ways of staying in touch; we are always reachable, our location always known. Distance running is an opportunity to step away from that. We can leave, we can run with nothing but our mind and body as company. We can be free.

This solitude is liberating. You feel in control of yourself and your life. You can go anywhere you desire: run over a bridge, around a park, by the side of a highway. You can run during the night or early morning. Sprint, jog, pace yourself. Listen to music, run in silence. Run with friends, run alone. It's entirely up to you. You're not beholden to anyone nor do you owe them anything. Unlike sports like tennis or football, you can enjoy running entirely on your terms.

This freedom is vital to runners. It's explored in "The Loneliness of the Long-Distance Runner" by Alan Sillitoe. In the story, Smith, who comes from a poor working-class home in Nottingham, has a talent for running. When he's sentenced to an institution for delinquent behaviour, the institution nurtures this talent. They want Smith to win races for them, to bring them glory. Smith loves running, but he resents how his love and talent are being used. In the final race, he stops just short of the finish line. He refuses to cross. No one was going to take away the freedom of running, no matter the consequences of his defiance.

This story provides an extreme example, but it gives insight into how crucial liberty is to running. Runners all over the globe have been pushing this liberty to the extreme, flirting with the limits of what we can do. We have ultrarunners, who run longer than the traditional marathon, and sky runners, who run long distances above a certain altitude.

But the freedom of running carries loneliness in its centre. The liberty to do anything also means there is no structure apart from you. No restriction, no complementary thought process—only you. Yes, you are free to do whatever you want, but there is loneliness in that freedom for there is no one to witness your journey. No one watches how far you ran today, how well you grew into your stride, or where you failed. You witness yourself, of course, and you can leaf through the emotional states and memories of your different runs. But there is no outside perspective to pin down those states or sharpen them, maybe even explain them to you in a larger context. Your growth remains hazy, unfocused. Every run feels like a transformation: you don't start the run and end it as the same person. Yet, without someone to record the changes, remember them and enjoy them with you, the detail is lost.

The missing witness exacerbates your loneliness because you feel erased. No one can understand your running journey, nor do many people care. Not the way you do. You can tell your friend you ran ten kilometres today and they'll applaud you, but it's a hollow victory because they won't hold you accountable. You could just as easily run five kilometres, say it was ten kilometres, and they'd clap anyway. They wouldn't care to check. We all want to be seen in this world: social media is designed to give you precisely that feeling of being noticed and cared for. In such a society, invisibility makes us lonelier.

LOSING THE RUNNER IDENTITY

There are points in a runner's life when, either due to injury, personal circumstances, or ageing, he is no longer able to run. During these phases, he experiences a temporary or permanent loss of the runner identity.

This loss can be crippling. Distance running is unique by nature: no two runners relate to it in the same way, nor do they experience it similarly. Your relationship to this activity is entirely your own: you've built this intimate bond with yourself about how you run and who you become when you run. This intimacy is lonely, yes, but it is even lonelier when it is taken away from you.

On one level, everything you've taken for granted is now gone. You don't have the freedom to engage in running anytime you want. Your agency is erased. If you had a community of runners that you trained and shared with, then you're isolated from that ecosystem as well. For many people, running is a coping mechanism and stress buster from the hustle and bustle of life; it's a space where they can just be by themselves. Now that avenue is closed.

All of this is alienating and you feel separated from an essential part of your life. But this separation is compounded by the unfamiliarity of what you're experiencing. Think about it: you've spent so long running, you've learned to relate to yourself—your emotions, thoughts, changes—in a particular way. The more you ran, the more you created certain strategies to cope and confront your transformations. In other words, running was a cornerstone of how you understood yourself.

When you lose your ability to run and thus your identity as a runner, you've lost this way of relating to yourself. You're in unfamiliar territory, grappling with new and strange emotions, and you must find different strategies to cope. That transformation is lonely and filled with disconnection.

In a way, then, our decline as runners is as isolating as our growth. Just as there is no one to witness us moving from strength to strength, there is no one to watch our abilities wane and our running identity corrode. This is especially vivid for elite runners. An elite runner's identity is associated with a very narrow window: when they are winning gold medals. No one watches their ascent, but once they reach their physical peak, they face enormous attention. Everyone acknowledges them, even gossips about them. But once they stop winning, that attention ceases, and it can be difficult for the elite runner to adjust. They feel alone, sometimes to the point of depression.

For two years after I decided to stop racing, people asked why I made the decision and if I would reconsider. Still others reminded me that I was a gold medalist and I should reconnect with the sport. To them, I was a single identity locked in this one moment of time: Ying as a runner who won gold medals. But I am so much more than that, across so many different points in time. It's isolating to realise they will never know those selves, not as well as they know Ying-the-runner.

Losing your running identity is scary. The unfamiliar always is. But change is inevitable. Even if you are never injured, your body will decline over time. You may run beautifully at twenty-five years old, but you can't sustain this at thirty-five or forty because your body is different. You must move on—move on from borrowed time and a borrowed body.

Always remember that even in the face of your decline, you have the power to choose how you respond to it. You define your attitudes. Choose to accept that your runner identity will morph and may even be lost. Find strength in it. We believe we can only connect with ourselves through running, but the truth is we can connect with ourselves in times of injury and old age as well. These challenges can teach us new ways of being. Embrace them.

YOU ARE THE PROBLEM AND THE SOLUTION

Throughout this mile, we've looked at the many forms of loneliness a long-distance runner must face: loneliness born from the nature of running, from its freedom, and from the identity the runner can now lose. But to truly understand and reconcile our loneliness, we must understand its very nature. And to do that, we need to look at the difference between loneliness and solitude.

Solitude is the space we create to be with ourselves. It's connected to freedom: the freedom of distance running is what allows us to shape that solitude however we like—we're free to make it what we want whenever we want. This space for ourselves is ours to define and mould. More importantly, we can create solitude when we're alone and when we're among people. Runners who train with others still experience solitude; they've carved out a mental and often physical space for themselves that allows them to access the beautiful, interior journey running gives you. Solitude is joyful. It's why we love running.

Loneliness, however, is not joyful. We hate it and shy away from it. We can be lonely when we're running by ourselves, and we can be lonely in a group. Its essential feature is disconnection: this feeling of being on the fringes, apart from the people and things you love, this sense of being un-understandable and inaccessible. When we feel lonely as distance runners, we feel disconnected from our running community, disconnected from our friends and family, who can't understand the unique challenges of this strange love, and often, we feel disconnected from the sport itself.

Solitude and loneliness merge into each other—what distinguishes them is perspective. There are parts of solitude that will always feel overwhelming and too much: when they do, they tip into loneliness. We will never be able to get rid of loneliness in distance running entirely; it's not possible. But we can manage it.

If you find yourself lonely when you run, ask yourself why. What are you disconnected from? Why are your thoughts leading you in this direction? Because changing your perspective can pull you back from the brink of loneliness and into that joyful state of solitude. It can reconnect you, either to your fellow runners or to your body, the environment, and what you love about running itself.

I know this can be hard to do. The repetitive motion of running and being locked with our thoughts for miles and miles can get us stuck. Poor coping and motivational strategies we used to progress in running now become grooves we cannot step out of. We settle into the familiar; we etch ourselves deeper. But loneliness comes from viewing running with a limited perspective. These limits give rise to those negative thoughts we talked about in "Loneliness and Growth." We have the power to change those thoughts and that narrative.

And you don't only have to change in perspective—you can also change in actions. If you've been lonely as a runner for months now, ask yourself: am I being complacent? Because there are always measures to pull yourself out of your isolation. Maybe the people you've chosen to surround yourself with are not the right community. Perhaps you need to find fellow runners who will hold you accountable to your goals, who can be your mirrors for your gait, posture, and gear, who can raise you up.

Distance running can be a bell curve: people at the top and the bottom are lonely because they don't have many people at their level. But no matter where you are on that curve, you can seek out companions. Even if you feel there is no one in your community who matches your abilities, find a running partner anyway. Maybe they won't be able to keep pace with you, but they will give you a new outlook. They can help you step back and reassess your approach to distance running. It is very difficult to do this without a partner because you need a sounding board. It's what we talked about in Mile 6: intersubjectivity matters.

Then maybe when you do go back to running solo, you'll be able to shake off your old thought process. You'll be able to approach running afresh and embrace the beauty of its solitude as you once did.

Inaction will cost you. Loneliness doesn't just remain; it festers. If you don't remedy it, it can develop into worse dysfunctional behaviours.

THE NEED TO RUN

IN PRIMARY SCHOOL, I WAS CONSIDERED ONE OF THE school's top students but when I advanced to secondary school, that reputation faltered. I was now in the best girls' school in Singapore, surrounded by very smart people; it was no longer easy to be the best. I felt the pressure to excel.

To deal with this pressure, I turned to running. My wins gave me the confidence boost I needed, a sense of self as I stood as a wallflower among my peers. Plus, I simply loved to run. I enjoyed challenging myself during training, hitting new records, and crossing the finish line ahead of the pack. Running became my coping mechanism against the stress of academics throughout secondary school, and at the same time I continued to improve. By the time I progressed to junior college, I had made a name for myself as a runner, to the point of landing that Nike sponsorship.

Somewhere along the way, however, my passion turned to obsession, and I didn't realise it.

At the end of junior college in 2011, I would sit for my A

levels, which would determine the course I could choose for university and thus my career. The pressure to do well academically kept building, as did the pressure to maintain the running reputation I had built. By the second year of junior college, I was willing to push myself to extremes to keep my sense of identity.

Enter the National Schools Cross-Country Championships. I had won the race in the first year of junior college and was looking for the rare achievement of winning it *again*—a back-to-back victory very few people achieve.

The problem, however, was that I had a shin splint. I took a few days off before the race to rest, and the pain lessened but it didn't go away entirely. I decided to race anyway. The truth is, I couldn't *not* race—who would I be if I wasn't running?

On the day of the race, I hid my injury from everyone. The reservoir where the race was held consisted of mostly soft ground, so I thought it would be okay. After all, the whole race was only four kilometres. I could do this. In sixteen minutes, it would all be over.

The race was a disaster. As I ran, the pain steadily worsened, until I was hobbling over the finish line nowhere near the top ten. The crowd was confused. I had been a favourite to win, and no one could understand how I had been so slow. I felt embarrassed and humiliated.

In the days and weeks after the race, people came up to me out of concern to ask what had happened. I was quick to assure them I was okay, but deep down, I felt deeply embarrassed, and I wanted to fade into the background. I couldn't understand why I was so affected. I knew I would return again when I recovered, and I knew it was just one race. Yet the humiliation seeped into every part of my life until I couldn't concentrate on my studies. I began to cry at odd moments, quietly and by myself.

Subsequently, I scored straight Cs in the A levels, hammering in the way I view myself as a failure.

How did something I enjoyed become such a source of pain? Very slowly. Even though I truly enjoyed running, I didn't see the extent to which I was relying on it for my sense of self-worth. In truth, my relationship with running had become dysfunctional. I had become addicted to the rush of hitting a new personal record, winning the race, consistently feeling a need to prove I was the best. I existed in a kinaesthetic bubble of my own making, and I couldn't see its transparent walls around me. I believed I was happy when I ran—and I was, in my own way—but my actions were always fuelled by fear. Fear of not winning, not hitting timings, not setting a new personal best. If I wasn't running—and perhaps more importantly, if I wasn't winning—who was I? Without running, my stability disappeared, my identity eroded, my self-worth plummeted. I ran out of grief and desperation, and I kept running to avoid thinking about it.

Dysfunctions in running can sneak up on the best of us. We all start our running journeys by falling in love with the sport, but if we're not careful, dedication can turn into obsession, which can lead to serious consequences—physical as well as mental and emotional.

PASSION VERSUS OBSESSION

As in my experience, the shift from passion to obsession is usually gradual. It can begin with something as innocent as trying to achieve a better time or run another kilometre. After a while, you find yourself chasing new goals to the exclusion of all else. You might start cancelling plans with friends because you haven't hit your weekly mileage goal. Or you might begin stressing about workouts hours before you do them. If you're winning races, then this tunnel vision gets worse; you become entirely results oriented. Nothing is more important than winning or achieving that new time. After a while, even the goals don't matter—they are an excuse to keep running to perpetuate this idea of yourself. Your identity is subsumed into that of a "runner."

Many people think elite runners are immune to this slide into obsession, but this is not so. I am but one case in point. Runners at all levels are at risk of moving from passion to obsession, and differentiating between the two is often difficult. We need to run more to improve, right? Plus, running feels good. We enjoy pushing ourselves. And it's good for our health!

Somewhere along the line, however, the feeling of "I *want* to run" can slowly, almost imperceptibly turn into "I *have* to run." At that point, we are, usually unknowingly, dealing with an addiction.

UNKNOWING ADDICT

When we think of addiction, we often picture an alcoholic or someone strung out on drugs, but people can become addicted to running and other forms of exercise. One article defines exercise addiction as "a condition of excessive or abusive exercising behavior in which moderate to intense physical activity becomes a compulsive behavior." People who are addicted to exercise exhibit a preoccupation with planning and completing exercise routines. They are driven to engage in longer and more rigorous workouts, often to the detriment of their personal, social, and professional life as well as their physical well-being. When they abstain from training, these individuals exhibit the same withdrawal symptoms experienced by those with other behavioural addictions.[20]

We can slip from passion to obsession to addiction without even realising it, partly because we love our sport. It makes us feel good. Compared to drugs and alcohol, it's a relatively healthy way to cope with stress, anxiety, and other everyday pressures, so we run more and more and more until we become unconsciously dependent on the therapeutic benefit and sense of self we gain.

There's also a biological reason we become addicted. Research shows that running delivers a dopamine hit that brings about pleasure, which is quickly followed by pain, or a come-down from the high, which leaves us searching for pleasure once again. This pleasure-pain balance served a primitive need, motivating our ancestors to keep searching for food, water, and shelter to ensure their survival. Today, however, it is often unknowingly or knowingly abused. The awaiting pleasure motivates us to endure the pain and repeat the high again and again.[21]

Because it takes time and miles to experience this endorphin rush, distance runners are more likely than sprinters to feel the high and thus become addicted to it. In addition, sprinting, by nature, is more intense and doesn't allow time for enjoying the environment and getting lost in the flow of movement. With distance running, we have time to settle into a deeply satisfying experience in which the sense of time and emotional problems seem to disappear. This transcendent state of flow makes distance running autotelic, that is, an exhilarating end in itself—an end that can be highly desirable and thus addictive.

Running's external validations can also lead to unknowing addiction. When we hit a new personal best in distance or time, we feel good about ourselves. The same is true when we place in a race or hit our times in a tough workout. As a result, we keep chasing, training harder, running farther. Keeping to our running schedule gives us a feeling of control.

Given these factors, you may wonder why some runners become addicted and others don't. Individual biases and predispositions seem to play a part. For example, individuals who suffer from symptoms of mental disorders (e.g., depression) are at greater risk for developing an exercise disorder.[22] Furthermore, dependency on exercise has been referred to as the "never alone addiction" because it often appears in conjunction with other disorders, most commonly obsessive-compulsive disorder, eating disorders like anorexia, and body image disorders.[23]

In addition, some people have a hard time expressing strong, uncomfortable emotions, and look for a physical outlet. They might turn to running because the predictable, repetitive nature helps them "pound out" their feelings—as opposed to dancing, for example, which requires a more conscious expression of emotion through motion.

The problem is that we can become dependent on that emotional outlet, such that we have an even harder time coping with our emotions through any mechanism other than running, which then tips the scale into addiction.

CONSEQUENCES

Just like any other addiction, a dependence on exercise can have far-reaching consequences. After I finished the cross-country race with a shin splint, I went straight to the doctor and found I had five stress fractures on my foot. I had to walk on crutches for months, a high price to pay for a lack of self-awareness or rather, a series of ineffective habits I had cultivated over the years.

Overtraining is a severe phenomenon and must be treated seriously. It's not only the obvious injuries, like shin splints, fractures, or permanent damage to our knees and ankles, but also the hidden effects on our bodies. Overtraining can place excessive stress on our heart and lungs, for example. It can affect the minerals in our bones and cause our bones to break down faster. It causes high blood pressure and puts an enormous strain on our nervous system.[24]

In addition, the nervous system can become deregulated such that the body becomes confused about what relaxes it and begins to misinterpret exercise as something soothing. If exercise is our only coping tool for stress and intense emotion, our evening jog to relax could be causing more harm than good.[25]

Addiction makes us lose perspective. Sportspeople who are addicted to the runner's high begin to chase it at the expense of all else. They withdraw from their family and friends and refuse to let anything—not a dinner or party or casual drink after work—disrupt their training schedule. They isolate themselves, which leads to a further dependence on running as the only thing in their lives that gives them joy, purpose, and control. If they don't run, they get withdrawal symptoms; they become anxious and stressed.

Ultimately, addiction affects our mental health. If running is all people have in their lives, any perceived failure in running leads to a mental health spiral. Any perceived *success* only fuels the addiction, and encourages the runner to push themselves harder, to set a new goal. It's a lose-lose situation, and runners sacrifice their sense of well-being because their values and identity are based on the sport.

EVALUATE YOUR RELATIONSHIP TO RUNNING

How healthy is your relationship to running? To avoid the consequences described here, you need to be willing to do some honest introspection and then take steps to address the issue, whether that means seeing a therapist, talking to your coach, or sharing with a friend. Here are some questions to help you with this evaluation.

1. How do you process setbacks in your running? Do you get upset for days when you fail to reach your targets?
2. Is running hurting you physically? Do you consistently find yourself getting injured and have little or no energy to last the day?
3. Has running brought you closer to your loved ones, or pushed you further away from them?
4. Is running a source of happiness or suffering?
5. How do you see yourself? Is your self-image wrapped up in racing times?
6. Is your self-talk compassionate, or consistently negative and hurtful?
7. Do you fear giving up a certain level of training because it will cost you an image that you feel pressured to maintain?

YOU DON'T NEED TO RUN

A dysfunctional relationship can be difficult to catch. In junior college, I didn't understand that I was leaning on running for my sense of stability and self, and as a result, I entered one of the worst mental health periods of my life.

Six years later, when I stood at the starting line of the HomeTeamNS Real Run, I was still struggling mentally and emotionally. Exercise addiction is not easy to fix.

But it is fixable.

My journey to a healthier relationship with running started on my trip to Europe where I ran for the fun of it, no watch and no pressure to perform. I was reminded that I did find true joy in the act of running. I also became more reflective and started journaling after each run. I was very thorough, recording exactly how I felt and what I was thinking. Finally, I started sharing my feelings with my fellow runners and found that I was not alone in my struggles. Verbalising my experiences grounded me and made me more compassionate towards myself. In the end, I found a friend in me and some of my loneliness disappeared.

Today, I am able to look back and see that my failures are all part of my journey. They make me who I am. They did not decrease my value, but rather increased it because I learned how to respond to them. I learned that I didn't need to run to boost my worth. I could run simply because I enjoy it.

Maybe I could have shortened the time I suffered if I knew how to recognize the signs. This is what I hope you can do for your own relationship with running: consistently evaluate it to make sure you're on the right path. It's okay for running to be an important activity in your life, but it's dangerous the moment it becomes the *most* important activity. If all you can think about is running, if you're willing to sacrifice your relationships so you can keep a training schedule, and if running is affecting your emotions to a disproportionate degree, you may be sliding down the spectrum into obsession.

Remember, also, that motives define a relationship. Ultramarathon runners, for example, regularly push themselves more than the average person but this doesn't mean they have a dysfunctional relationship to running. They are simply training for a really long race. But it could be dysfunctional if they are using an ultramarathon as an excuse to run excessively, to escape instead of confronting their fears.

Think about someone running a 10K who is just happy to be out on the path, running with others on a Saturday morning. Compare that to someone who is also running a 10K, but who is obsessed about his time, worried that his form or gait has slipped in the past few months, and obsessed over his dip in performance, fearing that he may lose the next race. Both runners are engaging in their passion, but the second is setting himself up for a dysfunctional relationship with it.

Running isn't disconnected from your wider life. How you act or think outside of running feeds into your moments on the road, and the experiences you open yourself up to. Similarly, running can show you sides of yourself you may want to address—perfectionist tendencies, for example, or your need to look a certain way. Managing your relationship with this sport helps you have a healthy balance in all aspects of your life.

RUNNING AS EMPOWERMENT

WHEN I WAS TEN, MY SWIMMING COACH PUT US THROUGH gruelling sprints during one practice. It was so hard that I still remember it, nineteen years later. We were supposed to dive off the board, sprint fifty metres in freestyle as our coach timed us, then get out, dive in again, sprint fifty metres, and so on. Twenty times.

On one of these rounds, I was pushing myself to the absolute limit. I thought I was going fast, even faster than the ideal time set by my coach, but when I touched the wall, I found I had missed it by one second. He began shouting at me for not taking swimming seriously, and I was so exhausted and overwhelmed, I burst into tears.

That practice was my first taste of enduring discomfort and pain and not knowing what to do with the emotions that came with it. All I could think about was escaping. After the coach yelled at me, the last thing I wanted to do was dive in and do it again.

Today, I can recognize that moment in the pool was a learning opportunity. I was given a chance to stay with my discomfort and grow from it. But I was too young and so I did what came naturally to me: I sought to avoid it.

If you love running, then you already know that it's an incredible sport that gives you joy. But running can do more than that—it can empower you. It can teach you how to grow in different ways, and make you a stronger, happier person.

But you have to let it.

Swimming was a challenging sport that could have empowered me in similar ways, but I was too immature to fully embrace the opportunity. In many ways, I was lucky my parents kept me disciplined enough to go, otherwise I would have happily avoided every training session. As adults, the responsibility for how we engage—and how *much* we engage—falls squarely on our shoulders. Take ownership of that power.

If you let running become your teacher, if you lean into the hard learning moments instead of shying away from them, you'll see just how much this sport can give you.

POWER TO ENDURE

Like swimming, long-distance running provides an opportunity to grow stronger through pain. It teaches us that tough situations may bend us, but they don't have to break us. Mile after mile, we build up our ability to encounter and navigate discomfort, physical, mental, and emotional. And the more we endure discomfort, the more we build memories of ourselves doing it, and thus create awareness that we can *continue* to do it, into the future, with each new challenge.

This, essentially, is the heart of self-efficacy. It's the ability to confront an obstacle with the knowledge that you've overcome challenges before and so can overcome this one as well. It gives you courage and confidence and increases your motivation because you believe in yourself.

Running is a vehicle to build self-efficacy, a skill that is, of course, applicable in all areas of your life. People with a high sense of their capabilities are more likely to lean into challenges and not quit when the going gets tough.

They are also more comfortable with vulnerability. Think back to when you were a child: most children react to uncertainty and discomfort with extreme emotions, just as I did in the pool that day. They cry, they scream, they throw a tantrum. They're overwhelmed and they don't know what to do with the pain because they've had no practice. Their first response is to escape. As they grow, however, they learn to become comfortable with uncomfortable situations; they grasp how to overcome, endure, and persist.

As we will discuss further in Mile 12, learning to endure physical pain also builds our mental endurance. During physical exertion, the brain releases adenosine, an inhibitory neurotransmitter. Adenosine has a fatiguing effect on the body, via increasing our effort perception. The body learns to process adenosine better over time and gets better at handling mental fatigue. This endurance is processed at the level of the brain as much as it is via the body.

Running allows us to further develop these physical, mental, and emotional skills. It helps us embrace vulnerability in all forms, and thus lean into stronger versions of ourselves, mentally and physically. As we grow, we become less fearful of the unknown and thus more willing to take risks. Through running, we can access a version of our lives that's wilder, freer, and braver.

POWER TO CHOOSE

In every part of our lives, we face both the finite and the infinite: aspects that are entirely out of our control, and circumstances we can shape. Family, ethnicity, where we're born in the world—all of these are examples of the finite factors in our lives. The infinite factors we can influence include how hard we work or how we choose to respond to the stressors.

Running is a synthesis of both the finite and the infinite. For example, there are finite factors we have no say in: how old we are, whether our knees are disintegrating, whether we were born with a weak heart. Yet, every single moment we're logging miles, we're also faced with the infinite: how far to run on any given day, which trail to follow, how hard to push ourselves.

Understanding this synthesis empowers us: we have the freedom to choose what we focus on. Focusing on finite factors will only toss us into a negative mental spiral. Focusing on the infinite, however, enables us to push ourselves and to grow.

And running, ultimately, is a prime place to exercise this freedom. I call it a "brainless" way to teach us about life—brainless, because running begins with your body. No one can run for you. If you want to run, you have to do it yourself. It's linked irrevocably to *your* body.

Localising yourself in that body and in the running experience puts you right at the centre of possibility. Every run is a chance for exploration. Every run has a million possible paths regarding how it can turn out, all hinged on the choices *you* make. You're constantly at the edge of the unknown and the immense possibility contained in it.

And so it is with life. There are many finite aspects outside of your control—natural disasters, work layoffs, illness—but there are even more infinite factors that you can influence, and you have the power to choose where you place your focus. Running can help you fine-tune this power.

Along with the freedom to choose comes responsibility for the consequences of those choices, whether in running or in life. As we saw in the last chapter, for example, if you're addicted to running, then you have to face up to the consequences of injury, exhaustion, and maladaptive behaviour. As Jean-Paul Sartre once said, "Man is condemned to be free; because once thrown into the world, he is responsible for everything he does." But consider the alternative: a life in bondage to the whims of fate.

Ultimately, where we choose to place our focus, on the finite or infinite, determines our experience. What we choose to endure defines how we experience it. Are you threatened by something, or do you see it as a challenge? How you approach it defines what you gain from it.

POWER TO CREATE MEANING AND VALUE

Running also empowers us because it's a blank slate: it allows us to create our meaning and value on every run. Inherently, running is meaningless. It's one foot in front of the other, with no discernible purpose—unlike our ancestors, who ran with the clear goal of hunting and surviving. In that way, it mirrors an existential view of life.

Existentialism holds that no lives have any inherent meaning or purpose, other than the purpose we ourselves create. Running is exactly the same: it imbibes the meaning *we* give it, the value *we* form.

On a granular level, this means we get to control how we undergo pain or pleasure, rather than allowing pain or pleasure to control us. Think back to Part II, our chapters on the experience of running, where we explored the concept of responding instead of reacting. When we feel pain, for example, we can focus on the pain, allow it to become all-encompassing and dictate our every choice. Or we can dissociate from the pain, understand that it is telling us something, but it is not the totality of our experience, and instead focus on the movement of our bodies, the synergy of the run, our environment. In other words, we control the experience—we shape what it becomes and the value it holds.

It's our consciousness that allows us to create meaning and value. Consciousness is what separates man from machine: our computers may have far more processing power than us, and may be smarter in many ways, but our consciousness is what makes us human.

I always find it fascinating, our ability to create meaning where no meaning exists. Across time, mankind has forged mythologies and stories to frame how we endure and survive. Running harnesses that storytelling ability, this skill of finding value in blank slates. It gives us a chance to experience meaning—but only if we're participating consciously.

This conscious participation is key. Eliud Kipchoge, widely regarded as the greatest marathoner of all time, once said, "Only the disciplined ones in life are free. If you are undisciplined, you are a slave to your moods and passions." The freedom of running, our ability to make meaning out of it, all depends on our willingness to focus and engage—to pause, reflect, and make a conscious choice instead of floating along in a passive state and reacting to every stimulus that comes your way.

POWER TO REGULATE OUR RESPONSE TO STRESS

Running is also an excellent tool to regulate stress in our everyday lives.

Anxiety is on the rise in society today, as is stress. With our phones and our constant connection to the world around us, we are increasingly inundated with information and consequently overwhelmed and anxious.

Most of us try to battle anxiety through self-talk. We analyse the situation, try to identify the causes, and then talk ourselves out of it. If the feeling persists or happens frequently, we may go to therapy or talk more to our loved ones about what we're experiencing.

The problem with talk alone, however, is that it doesn't deal with the physiological changes to our bodies when we become anxious. That's where running comes in.

There are two sides to our brain: one part that controls consciousness and the other that controls emotions. The moment we become stressed, the brain turns on the sympathetic nervous system and the body reacts. Our heart rate or pulse might increase. Our breath becomes faster and shorter. We may feel indigestion.

When we try to talk ourselves out of the anxiety, we ignore these physical changes and focus only on our minds. But our bodies are already triggered, no matter what we're telling ourselves. Explaining to ourselves why we shouldn't be anxious about a test or a meeting with our boss may fix our thoughts, but it doesn't regulate our heart rate or lower our pulse. As discussed earlier, emotional pain is mapped into the body as somatic memory. Focusing on logical reasoning and mental talk can be ineffective when the body remains triggered.[26]

This is why a solely mental approach to anxiety often backfires: our brains begin criticising us for still being stressed, even after all the pep talks, while failing to recognise that our bodies haven't been soothed at all.

Running offers what is called a body-first approach to stress in which you regulate your stress response through your body, rather than trying to talk yourself out of it. The basic physicality of running—that process of one foot in front of the other—grounds us; it calms the brain. Focusing on how our soles hit the pavement and how our bodies move through the environment allows us to pay attention to our bodies and create space for healing.

Note, however, that attention is crucial for the body-first approach. It doesn't happen automatically: you cannot continue to ruminate about the stressors of your life while you run and expect to lower your anxiety level. Your body will remain triggered. But if you pay attention to your body and environment and how they interact with each other through mindfulness, you can decrease stress.

Could lack of physical activity be why so many people today are so stressed?

THE BEST TEACHER

As athletes, we're often trained to think in extreme ways. What we do or how we do it doesn't matter as much as the outcome. The outcome is *everything*. The world expects athletes to bring home victories—this is their only role.

But focusing on the outcome can blind us to the journey, and often means we miss the point. Running offers growth and skills built into its *process*. Simply running teaches us about freedom, choice, and navigating our limits while making the most of our potential. It helps us cope with stress and teaches us to endure pain, whether mental, physical, or emotional. We learn to embrace discomfort and lean into our uncertainty. We learn to be brave.

If we only look at our victories, we risk losing sight of these gifts. If we only care about outcomes, we are often devastated when we miss those goals—we shy away from failure and what it can teach us; we refuse to find value in the journey itself. But it's the journey that empowers us. It's our best teacher.

THE PURSUIT OF EXCELLENCE

WHEN I DECIDED TO JOIN MY BROTHER FOR TRAINING IN Boulder, Colorado, my heart wasn't in it. I had just wrapped up my physiotherapy studies and I didn't have a clear plan for what was next. At that point, my running journey had been mixed: I'd experienced some great victories on a global stage, but I'd also been booed at the World Cross-Country Championships, and I found myself plagued with doubt. Did I have the physique to truly be a great long-distance runner? I didn't have the skinny legs and the long strides of the Kenyan athletes, for example—would that always hold me back?

With these doubts at the forefront of my mind, I didn't really have a goal for my time in Colorado. Whereas my brother wanted to improve enough to qualify for the Olympics, I wasn't sure that I would qualify even if I did put in the extra effort. I ultimately decided to go, more because I had the time than because I really thought it would help me.

My lack of clarity affected my whole trip. I wasn't focused on my training. Whereas my brother took naps after tough workouts, I went hiking and biking between sessions. While he spent his recovery days stretching and doing prehab work, I went camping every weekend.

In the end, I didn't qualify for the Olympics, nor did I deserve to. I didn't lean into the process in Boulder. I wasn't consistent in my efforts, and I didn't really give training 100 percent of my focus.

If I had put my all into workouts, trained consistently and wholeheartedly, I would have achieved excellence, even if I hadn't made the team. My shortcoming was in the way I approached the process, not in the fact that I didn't qualify.

Many of us view excellence as being synonymous with success, but they are actually quite different. If I had succeeded in qualifying for the Olympics even with the half-hearted, inconsistent effort I put in, would I have been excellent in my success? I don't think so.

Excellence is all about our mindset. It is the persistent consistency between mind and body, between our goals and the effort we put in to achieve them. It's not about achieving them.

If we pursue excellence throughout our running career, rather than success, we are much more likely to find the journey enjoyable and fulfilling for many years.

REDEFINING EXCELLENCE

What is excellence?

If you're like most people, you might immediately think of things like "Winning my age group" or "Setting a new PR." You might look at numbers as the standard for excellence: the better the numbers, the better the runner.

I suggest that these are actually indicators of success, which is not the same thing as excellence.

SUCCESS VERSUS EXCELLENCE

Let's start with success:

- *Success is relative.* It is only found in relation to a standard: achieving a certain time, winning a race, beating everyone else in your age group, qualifying for the Olympics. There are only three positions on the podium, and there can only be one winner.
- *Success is fleeting.* Winning today doesn't mean you'll win tomorrow or in three months. World-class runners on the podium in the Olympics now may not even make the top ten in twenty years. In addition, records are meant to be broken. From 1908 to 2022, the men's marathon record has been set and broken fifty-one times!
- *Success is all or nothing.* You either achieved your goal or you didn't—there's no middle ground.

Compare that list with what constitutes excellence:

- *Excellence is a mindset.* It is the way you mentally approach the work you do with your body.
- *Excellence is all about consistent, persistent effort.* There is no element of luck.
- *Excellence is defined by the person pursuing it.* It is not based on our performance in relation to others.

In short, excellence is about the journey and the process, not the outcome. We can *all* achieve excellence, even if we don't obtain the desired result—an opportunity I missed out on in Colorado because my effort was lacking. Even an amateur runner who never places can achieve excellence if she gives her best in every run.

At the same time, excellence does bring us closer to success. If we remain rooted in consistent, persistent effort, we will achieve breakthroughs and improve our times. We will reach new heights in our running journey simply because we are constantly putting ourselves in the place to achieve our goals.

Pursuing excellence is sometimes difficult because we say A and do B. Our mind and actions do not match. In this sense, excellence can be defined as consistency in action in pursuit of one's goals. Excellence in this sense requires planning and dedication: if you want to achieve A, you have to figure out steps to get A and then do them. Actions are not the result of mind or body; it's both.

WHAT WE CAN CONTROL

We've been taught to view sports as a level playing field on which the most dedicated and hardworking can compete even if they lack some of the natural talent. The truth is, we don't begin on equal footing. Many factors completely outside of our control—upbringing, genetics, personality, socio-environment, training environment—influence how far we go in sport.

Genetic makeup, for example, can influence anthropometric and physiological structure, giving someone an advantage in energy metabolism, respiratory and circulatory efficiency, muscular strength, endurance, speed, and power. Research has shown, for example, that the ACTN3 genotype gives people a 20 percent advantage in becoming an elite sprinter over those who lack it, and the COL5A1 gene is associated with ligamentous injuries.[27] Genetic architecture even influences personality, predisposing people to certain mindsets and behaviours, which in turn impacts dedication and performance.

Even some factors seemingly within our control are themselves a function of our environment and upbringing. For example, where you train determines how you think about sport and its place in one's life. In Singapore, running is viewed as a hobby, something complementary to academics and personal growth, but not a career option. That perspective played a huge role in how I viewed myself as a runner. Training in Colorado allowed me to immerse myself in a completely different attitude. We started workouts at eight o'clock every morning, the optimal time to start according to the coaches. Such a time would not have been possible in my home setting, partly because it would be too hot and partly because we had to be at our "real" jobs by then.

If we let society define excellence for us—as success, determined by numbers and medals—these aspects outside of our control can seem to keep us from excellence. If we choose to define excellence for ourselves—as something based on our effort and mindset—we can all achieve excellence, no matter how unlevel the playing field. The fact is, even the most genetically talented still need a framework of excellence to achieve success. It doesn't just happen.

It's time to redefine excellence as making the best out of what you can control. We need to play with the hand we're dealt—work with it to create the best outcome. In doing so we pursue excellence, even if we don't finish in the top places or run a certain time. We can all define excellence, which puts it well within reach for each one of us.

WORKING WITH FACTORS BEYOND OUR CONTROL

For years, ultrarunner Diane Van Deren suffered from epileptic seizures as often as two or three times a week. The number and timing of these episodes was completely out of her control, so she focused on what she could control: trying to fix them.

At age thirty-seven, Van Deren opted for brain surgery to remove part of her temporal cortex where the seizures occurred. The surgery was a success, but it also left her with poor memory and impaired her sense of direction and ability to track time. One might expect this to negatively impact her ability to race, but these side effects actually kickstarted Van Deren's success in ultramarathons because she would simply lose track of time. She could run hundreds of miles and have no idea how long she had been running.

Of course, Van Deren could not have predicted the outcome of her surgery. But that's my point: there are always factors beyond our control and even our ability to predict. Sometimes those factors are good, sometimes they're bad. Excellence involves working *with* them, consistently, to see past outcomes and focus on what we *can* control. Effort is excellence.

PAIN AND EXCELLENCE

Emil Zatopek is a legend in long-distance running. A three-time gold winner at the 1952 Summer Olympics, he was known for his difficult and often torturous workouts. When Zatopek ran, he ran with an expression of acute pain on his face—so much so that it inspired the term "Zatopek pain."

The concept of Zatopek pain points to an interesting phenomenon in running today: the fetishization of pain and the romanticization of meritocracy. Zatopek was a champion, but his champion status is often attributed *to* this pain. People believe he succeeded only because he was willing to put in the effort to the point of intense suffering.

This narrative emphasises effort as the sole determinant of success, which, as we saw in the last section, isn't true since it doesn't take into account genetics, environmental, socio-economic, and sociocultural factors. Very rarely will you find people romanticising the efforts made by, say, an athlete who finished last. Victors are victors, we believe, because they practise, they labour more than anyone else, and so come out on top. Likewise, Zatopek's outward display of pain also mattered. His suffering would not have been judged as important or noteworthy if he had not won.

But is that the way it should be? If true excellence is based on effort, then every display of consistent, persistent effort should be celebrated.

The truth is that your efforts are valuable whether or not you win the race. After all, being a slow runner does not mean you worked any less. Moreover, your pain is valid whether or not it shows on your face, and whether or not it leads to a championship. Outward displays of suffering do not mean you suffered more, and they do not guarantee success.

We must create our own yardsticks for excellence and measure ourselves by these—yardsticks that involve doing our best. Yet, herein is another expression of the runner's paradox: when we finish our workouts and races, we feel tired and equate this with doing our best. But if we feel we have failed because we didn't place or reach a new PR, then we show that we need to learn what "doing our best" really means. We need to learn how to focus on the journey and our effort. In doing so we ensure we have attained excellence, and that is good enough.

PURSUING YOUR EXCELLENCE

In the world of competitive racing, it's so easy to compare ourselves to our peers. We measure times, sponsorship amounts, number of podiums. But the comparison game is a trap.

Focusing only on the numbers urges us towards more extreme methods to attain that excellence, such as doping and steroids. We become discouraged. We may feel there are inequalities between us and our fellow runners, which makes us question if we should even bother trying. *If I'm never going to win that marathon or break that record*, you might think, *then why try at all?*

But this is the wrong question, and it comes from a faulty definition of excellence as outcome-based. Our effort doesn't guarantee us a win, but this is not the point of running. The beauty is in the process, and how we grow from managing the various nuances that make us who we are.

Outcomes do have certain merits: they help us know where we stand and how to improve. If, say, you usually complete a marathon in just over three hours, but you want to run faster, you can consider what steps to take. Maybe you need to change your racing strategy or focus on your running style. At the same time, that outcome cannot be your sole goal. Instead, focus on your growth and journey, on acquiring knowledge and developing skills, on expanding your perspective to include more than the result. By sticking to the value of excellence, you acquire the skills and experience to put you in a better position of achieving success. And even if you don't win or set a PR, you have still set yourself up for a rewarding journey with many opportunities for growth.

If these are your standards of excellence, you are sure to succeed in meeting them.

HITTING THE WALL—AND BREAKING THROUGH IT

BACK TO THE 2017 HOMETEAMNS REAL RUN MENTIONED earlier, the 10K I hoped was going to give me a much-needed boost after a disappointing race season filled with fatigue and fainting.

An hour before the race, I met my friend Desmond to warm up. Then we made our way to the starting line, where we joined a few other people we had trained with now and then. As I looked around, I saw some of my usual competition and figured I could probably finish in the top three. This really could be the race to help me regain confidence.

Yet, as I waited for the race to start, I still felt anxious. I couldn't calm my breathing, and I felt embarrassed about feeling so stressed at this no-pressure fun run.

By the time the gun went off, the sun was blazing, and I struggled to settle into a comfortable pace. I managed to join a pack of four or five runners, but I could tell my breathing was much more laboured than those around me. I was dragging my legs and throwing my body forward in a desperate attempt to keep going. I didn't feel calm and comfortable as I usually did, especially at this early point in the race. I was literally forcing myself to run.

This unhappy state continued to the turning point of the out-and-back route. After we made the turn, I started lagging behind the pack. I felt so hot and exhausted. My breathing was out of sync. I watched the pack move farther and farther ahead, feeling crushed at my performance.

The next thing I knew, I was on the ground, lying on my back in a makeshift tent. I was drenched in sweat, and sand stuck to my arms and legs and my Nike-sponsored running shorts and top. I realised my dad was kneeling next to me, and I was surrounded by paramedics.

"Can you breathe?" one of the medics asked.

I tried to tell him no, but I couldn't even speak. I frantically gasped for breath, desperately trying to fill my lungs with air. I felt like I was suffocating.

Then it hit me: I had fainted again.

Despair and disappointment overwhelmed me. I had won marathons and half marathons, and now I couldn't even finish a 10K without fainting.

I closed my eyes. I felt like if I stopped fighting it, I would stop breathing and quietly pass on. Part of me was okay with having this be the end, and part of me was so ashamed that I could give up so easily. I was a mess, emotions warring inside for attention.

All the self-help books and meditation guides tell you to be in touch with yourself. But it's not that easy, is it? Throughout my whole competitive running career—despite the wins, despite the sponsorships, despite the record I'd broken—I wasn't really in touch with myself. I hadn't paused once to reflect on and understand my emotions or my mental state when it came to running. And so I found myself here, on the ground in a medical tent, struggling to breathe, one part of me wanting to let everything go, even living, and another part of me fighting to survive and then get up and win. I didn't know which part of me was dominant, or which part of me was really me.

This is what hitting the wall looks like in the extreme: I had reached the limits of my physical, mental, and emotional endurance and literally couldn't take one step further. My experience points to the larger truth that we humans are not machines. We will reach the limit of what we can handle, and if we're physically and mentally unhealthy, we'll hit that wall sooner rather than later. We may collapse or suffer a heart attack or even die in worst-case scenarios. It's easy to push ourselves to the point of breaking.

That said, it's also easy to underperform, to stop short of what we are truly capable of achieving. We are not robots, but we can endure more than we think we can—*if* we properly train our bodies and, more importantly, our minds.

PHYSIOLOGICAL LIMITS

When we talk about "limits" in sport, people naturally think of physical limits. And it's true: physiologically speaking, there are limits to human endurance. Because of several factors beyond our control, we can only go so far, so fast, and then we hit the wall:

- *VO2 max.* This is an index of aerobic capacity: how efficiently your body processes oxygen and distributes it to the muscles. Some people have a naturally higher VO2 max because their genetic makeup allows them to adapt to training stimuli more efficiently at the heart and lung level. However, even these individuals have an upper limit on aerobic capacity.

- *Lactate threshold.* To function optimally, muscles require a certain uptake of oxygen during physical exercise. When the body's uptake of oxygen dips below that threshold—known as the lactate threshold—lactic acid starts to accumulate in the blood, causing runners to experience a certain heaviness in their legs. There's a genetic influence upon the threshold.
- *Physiological makeup.* We are all born with different limb lengths, muscle fibre strengths, and other genetic factors that impact endurance. You can work on strength and flexibility, but you'll never be able to change the length of your legs, for example.

Because we are not machines, it is difficult to identify where our true physiological limits lie. Running consistently enlarges our heart muscle, which is a good thing—until it isn't. If we train too hard without sufficient rest, our hearts can become inflamed to the point of weakening the muscle. Otherwise fit long-distance runners have died because they pushed their hearts to the breaking point. Ryan Shay, a twenty-eight-year-old marathoner who died in the Olympic Trials in 2007, is but one example.

Certainly, we can take certain measures to maximise these physiological limits. We can implement a training plan as discussed in Mile 25. We can work with a physiotherapist to correct poor form. We can pay attention to nutrition and hydration and figure out the exact blend of calories that gives us the most sustained energy.

But even still, our efforts to reach our potential will fall short unless we engage our most important asset: the mind. For it's not only our physical limits that determine our endurance level in long-distance running. It's our mental ones.

Let's say a runner from a cold, dry climate visits another country with hot, humid weather. She goes for a run and soon begins to struggle. Why? It's natural to assume that the heat has had an adverse physical effect on the body: maybe she's sweating profusely and thus losing more water than usual; maybe her muscles are cramping painfully from dehydration. But science shows that the most significant impacts from a change in climate happen at the cerebral level. The runner slows down, not because her body is affected, but because her brain judges the unfamiliarity of the situation, perceives fatigue, and reacts in protection of the body before failure happens. As a consequence, performance is disrupted.

In the book *Endure: Mind, Body, and the Curiously Elastic Limits of Human Performance*, Alex Hutchinson speaks of an incident in which he was misled into thinking he was running faster than he really was. For each lap of the mile, the lap counter called his times out as three seconds faster than they actually were. Perhaps the lap counter had started his watch three seconds late, or perhaps his effort to translate French to English caused a delay. Either way, Hutchinson believed he was running faster than he actually was, while feeling quite good. As a result, Hutchinson "unshackled himself from [his] pre-race expectations and ran a race nobody could have predicted." Indeed, he set a personal best by a full nine seconds.[28]

In short, all our physiological limits are consistently filtered and processed through our mind. Our mind then interprets these limits and acts on those interpretations, affecting our performance. It's a cycle: physical limits impact how we feel, how we feel informs our perception, and then our perception, in turn, interprets the situation to improve or disrupt performance.

The beauty of recognizing this is that you can disrupt this cycle. Through training, you can work to overcome your mental limits and improve your performance. It's mind over matter.

MIND OVER MATTER

Where do we start? After all, reworking one's mental limits seems like a large undertaking. One factor in particular influences how we define and respond to our boundaries: our ability to endure and adapt to pain.

USING PAIN

We don't need to block out pain—on the contrary, in fact. We need to accept that it's necessary. Studies show that runners who use nerve blockers—in order to limit the pain when they run—have actually faced worse outcomes than simply enduring the pain. A lack of peripheral feedback inhibits central motor output. Pain guides pacing. It shows us how much we can push at each point of the run based on how we feel at that point.

Teaching ourselves this endurance is integral to a successful running career. It's easy for a runner to simply quit when he encounters pain. But that attitude leaks into his running approach: it becomes easier and easier for him to not show up for the difficult workouts, the challenging sets, the training that will help him grow to the next level. That approach can expand to include fatigue ("Oh, I'm tired today, I'm not up for it") or any form of discomfort ("This is harder than I imagined; maybe I'll just quit"). Pain, discomfort, and fatigue are part of the running journey, and not just while we're out on the track. They are present *between* training sessions, during recovery, before a race, after a race. We cannot avoid them.

Working to improve your acceptance of pain will change how your mind responds to your physical limits. You will be able to acknowledge your mental barriers and take ownership of them. In doing so, you'll be able to break them.

INTENTION, ATTITUDE, ATTENTION

The key to taking control of your mental limitations is through a three-pronged approach: intention, attitude, and attention.

Intention is all about your personal vision. What do you want to achieve? Intention isn't as granular or specific as goals, but more focused on the overall direction. Think of it as a compass: it's about knowing where you're going and why. Intention sets the stage for what's possible and anchors you in your journey.

Intention works in tandem with attention and attitude. Becoming clear about your compass, so to speak, helps you focus and thus triggers sustained attention in that direction, which in turn, reinforces the type of attitude you want to adopt.

Attitude is the quality of your attention—it's how you relate to what you focus on. Choosing your attitude is important because the wrong approach can take you further away from your intention. Say a runner consistently misses his running times during training. He has two options: he can be harsh and berate himself, or he can be kind and forgiving and vow to do better. The first approach leads to a negative spiral. The second leads to change.

This is why attitude is so important. Like the hypothetical runner, we always have a *choice.* What we choose determines what we experience. If we decide to consistently berate ourselves, we can fall into a habit that will permanently affect our running performance.

Attention. What you pay attention to matters. It not only

affects how you feel but how your body responds, which in turn affects how you feel. For example, focusing on the people watching you or on your competitor's preparations instead of focusing on your goals (e.g., the opportunity to give your best) will affect how your body responds.

One professor proposed that in stressful situations, individuals can either have a "challenge response" or a "threat response," and each is associated with different physiological patterns. Because these situations are processed through our minds, we have the ability to set the stage, anticipate, and utilise these responses to our advantage.[29]

Intention, attention, and attitude all work together. We can't have one without the other two; they lean on each other. The goal is to be able to take control of our emotions and mind, and if we can do so, we are in control of the process and that affects our experience, as well as the outcome.

And strangely enough, embracing pain and tackling it through this three-pronged approach changes your relationship with reality, specifically pain. Accepting pain *decreases* your suffering because your mind is now on your side. It's working with you to push past your limits. Not embracing pain, on the other hand, tips you into a negative spiral: the more you fear discomfort, the more you react to it and the more you react to it, the worse you suffer.

PERCEPTIONS

Another way to expand our mental limits is to understand the way perception influences reality, specifically our ability to physically endure.

Our Limitations

How we view our strengths and weaknesses, our abilities or lack thereof, and our bodies' limits all influence our perception of reality. We may not be able to change the limitations themselves, but we can change how we view them, which will ultimately impact how we respond to them and what we can accomplish. Research has demonstrated that if we view our limitations as something fixed and unchanging, our ability to perform will be affected. In addition, we tend to focus on the end result, which affects the sustainability, depth, and satisfaction of the journey towards the goal.

But, if we believe we can improve, we will ask ourselves, "What's the next thing I can do to move forward?" If we believe our ability can be modified, we often demonstrate adaptive responses such as increased motivation, satisfaction, and greater persistence, focusing on the journey and quality of growth rather than the outcome.[30]

Social Support

Perception of social support—that is, believing that we are part of a community—can reduce perception of difficulty and raise physical output. Humans truly don't work alone, even when they are running by themselves in a workout or race. The perception of belonging in a social group increases stress resilience of all kinds, including physical.

Group training, especially during high-intensity workouts, leads to a beneficial psychological effect, which can enhance fitness by lowering RPE (rate of perceived effort) and increasing the satisfaction of the training, while mitigating the discomfort experienced.[31]

A study on Parkrun, a type of community time trial first

established in Australia, demonstrated that social runs done in high intensity provided a perceived satisfaction, confidence, motivation, and higher "subjective energy," which was in turn "associated with faster run times without increase in perceived effort." This same study found that perceived social support impacts homeostatic regulation of stress, fatigue, and pain and that rewarding social experiences activate neurobiological systems that are involved in modulating responses to painful stimuli and in sustaining endurance exercise.[32]

Effort

In a field of equal competition based on physical ability, the one with the strongest mind wins. But what makes a strong mind? It's not motivation alone, because every one of those runners wants to win. They are all willing to exert maximum effort to that end.

The difference maker in such a case is not motivation; it is the perception of effort. What we pay attention to affects effort perception and, subsequently, performance. Research compared two settings of three-kilometre time trial running. Participants had to finish the three kilometres as fast as possible in two different settings:

1. Hitting certain RPE values at various distance markers; in other words, they focused on their feelings and how hard it felt like they were running.
2. Running at fixed paces on the treadmill.

Researchers found that runners who focused on their feelings ended up running slower, whereas the runners who focus on pace were able to relax. Why? Because when the first group hit the pain phase, they were hyper-aware of their discomfort, which impacted their perceived effort and caused them to run slower. The cognitive strategies selected are crucial in performance because they modify the perception of effort.[33]

Mental fatigue, or feeling tired, doesn't impact our physiological performance. It has no effect on heart rate, blood concentration, or lactate concentration. Instead, mental fatigue impacts our perception of effort. If I feel tired, I will perceive all effort as much more strenuous and difficult, which will impact how hard I will run, how much I can endure.

Thus, it seems important to reduce mental fatigue. Research shows that training-induced adaptations helped cyclists conserve cerebral fuel and thus tolerate a greater cognitive load (feeling tired) before they experienced detrimental effects on their endurance.[34]

Another study showed that listening to music while running can reduce mental fatigue and thus lower the perception of effort. These researchers found that "listening to music in a mentally fatigued state can restore endurance running capacity and performance to a similar level as observed when no MF [mental fatigue] is present."[35] The shared involvement of music processing and rate of perception generation allow for music to counteract the effects of mental fatigue on endurance exercise capacity and performance.

Completion

Perception of effort doesn't allow us to reach max exertion, but perception of completion does. The closer we are to the finish line, the greater the likelihood that we will finish and therefore the more willing we are to dig deep and expend every last ounce of energy.

REFRAME YOUR MIND

Adopting the process of intention, attention, and attitude is an ongoing journey that demands a paralleled growth and understanding of the self. Both require practice, so be kind to yourself. Don't fixate too much on the outcome. Just keep at it, slowly, and you'll find a balance.

John Landy was the second person in recorded history to break the four-minute mile. Just before he finally succeeded, he didn't think he could do it. Only one other person had done it before. When he came two seconds short of breaking four minutes, even then, he said he couldn't do it. He believed it was impossible right up until the point that he broke it.

Landy knew what his intention was, he knew what his attention was focused on, and he knew the attitude that would get him there. He practised all three. Whether or not he believed the outcome was likely, he practised all three. And it worked: he redefined the limits of what was possible.

In other words, your outcome should not be your focus. Concentrate on the journey. Push barriers *within* your journey: in how you think and show up. It makes all the difference.

PART IV

Do I Know How to Run?

RELEARNING TO RUN

IN NOVEMBER 2015, I WAS LIVING IN HONG KONG TO train for the upcoming Singapore marathon. On a few mornings after I finished my workout at the Hong Kong Sports Institute, I would buy a bowl of noodles from the canteen nearby and then sit on the steps near the track, watching others run.

One morning, there was a team performing interval repeats of 800 metres. As I ate my noodles, I watched the star runner leading the reps. The physiotherapist in me immediately noticed some issues with his gait: He ran with excessive upper body rotation together with excessive cross-body arm swing. His shoulders were hunched forward and his neck craned forward, like he was pulling himself forward with his chin. In addition, he kept slamming his heels into the ground with each step.

I could see several reasons for this form, as well as the ways it could cause him problems:

- Excessive upper body rotation: Restriction in his upper body could result in excessive motion here, potentially impeding diaphragmatic breathing.

- Excessive cross-body arm swing: This motion was probably creating tightness through his chest. Along with the excessive upper body rotation, this arm swing demanded greater counterbalancing work from his core muscles, which might tire out prematurely, causing his posture to deteriorate at a faster rate.
- Hunched shoulders: Along with his rounded upper back, his hunched shoulders were limiting proper core and diaphragmatic engagement. This forced him to breathe more from the upper chest, causing his neck muscles to tighten, which led him to unconsciously stick out his chin.
- Neck craned forward: He looked like he was using his head to pull himself forward, which indirectly shifted his centre of mass backwards, worsening his overstriding.
- Slamming heels: Because he was overstriding and landing beyond his centre of mass, he slammed his heels into the ground as a kind of braking force. This slamming is a surefire way to create excessive impact from the heel into the shin.

The diagnosis was clear: this top runner had poor form. And yet his coach kept praising him, shouting loudly in Cantonese, "Good job!" I did a quick scan of the other runners and found the same: excessive leg flicking, back arching, and chin jutting.

It's difficult to spot poor form if you're not looking out for it, or if you don't know what it looks like. Most runners think that if they're getting faster, they must be running correctly. The truth is that you can become a very strong runner with poor form—and that thought should petrify you. No matter how fast you're going or how many races you win, poor form leaves you open to injuries and to movement patterns that become harder to shake the longer you don't correct them.

It's intriguing that how we feel when we run doesn't reflect how we appear when we run. I'm sure the star runner at that team training session thought he was running beautifully, reinforced by his coach's "Good job!"

Likewise, I find it interesting that nobody talks about their running form, as if it's an off-limits topic like our weight or political orientation, something you don't discuss at the first meeting. The reason we don't discuss form, however, is not because it's taboo or too personal; it's because we often take it for granted. We think we either run well or don't, a birthmark we simply come to accept.

And sure, genetics do play a role. Some people are more adept at slower, aerobic running. Some are born with a higher proportion of fast-twitch fibres, enabling them to leap off the block without much training. Genetics also influences joint structure, how muscle tendons are built, and how they insert into the bone, which influences how easy it is to activate certain key muscles. All that impacts our running form.

But it's also true that our bodies are not blank slates. We are also influenced by our lifestyles and our training, all of which work upon our muscles and change them. As you'll see in Mile 15, poor movement patterns are often created by small, daily habits that add up.

Changing our running form is not easy. It takes time to identify poor patterns and even more effort to diagnose the root causes, which come in various forms: body build, past injuries, posture, and more. It then takes discipline and perseverance to work on strengthening those weak areas, first in isolation and then in combination and then in the act of running itself.

The process is tough, but it's worth it. Your long-term enjoyment of running really depends on it.

As we've said from the beginning of this book: running does come naturally, but running effectively does not. We need to learn how to harness the body's strength and flexibility into a healthy, effective form that doesn't lead to injury.

THE SELF-ORGANISING BODY

In the rest of the chapters in Part IV, we'll discuss the various ways we engage in dysfunctional movement patterns. Like the runner I watched that day in Hong Kong, we are often unaware of these suboptimal patterns because our bodies are self-organising—they naturally adapt to innate and learned running motions to enable us to move forward, sometimes very quickly and sometimes to our detriment.

We all know how to stand up, to walk, to jog, to run—our bodies instinctively reach for the movement pattern without conscious learning. What we don't realise, however, is that our bodies organise this movement pattern within the constraints of our internal systems according to a variety of external factors:

- Our environment—what terrain we're running on, what the weather is like
- Running stressors—how we train and develop our bodies through exercise
- Non-running stressors—how we sit when we watch television, our work, our posture
- Thoughts and mindset—loneliness, doubt, positive outlook, addiction
- Biology—body shape, limb lengths, foot structure, fibre type
- Injury history—prior injuries that led to scar tissue buildup

and bodily adaptations; though the pain is gone, the compensation continues
* The echo of pain—current injury that causes pain in one area leading to compensation in another

A runner's gait is a complex interplay of constraints and drivers. Behind these adaptations is the body's consistent calibration of metabolic cost. Running is a costly habit: the constant strain of running optimally, of keeping the body upright against the consistent gravitational forces pulling it to the ground, requires extra oxygen costs to keep the postural and core muscles working properly. This cost gets higher when you run across distances. Thus, your body is always optimising your gait for your metabolic cost, in an attempt to keep you going for longer.

In addition, our bodies naturally work to minimise certain costs over others, and minimising metabolic cost is one of the top priorities, compared with minimising impact forces, for example. This is because our cardiovascular system is more sensitive to demands placed on it, compared to our musculoskeletal and neural systems. In a way, we further desensitise these latter systems by wearing heavily cushioned shoes, which sets us up for injury because we are able to run farther without feeling the high-impact effects.

WHY CORRECT OUR RUNNING FORM?

Think back to our lead runner at the Hong Kong Sports Institute. He had poor form, but he was able to complete all the interval runs his coach gave him, and he was able to do so within the time required. He was, in other words, fast. If the ultimate aim of running is to be fast, and if our bodies self-organise to the point that we can be fast without correcting our form, why bother fixing it?

To understand why, we need to take a look at our areas of efficiency. Most people think running is only about biomechanical efficiency, but there are in fact three core areas: (1) neuromuscular, (2) physiological, and (3) biomechanical. Neuromuscular efficiency refers to the brain-muscle connection, and our sense of smoothness and coordination. Physiological efficiency refers to our heart, lungs, and metabolism. Biomechanical efficiency refers to the efficiency of our muscles and bones, specifically in terms of muscle activation (i.e., posture, movement patterns).

When we first start to train, we see enormous gains in neuromuscular efficiency and physiological efficiency. This is why we get faster, even though our gait and form (biomechanical efficiency) are terrible. But this progress is unsustainable—at some point, we plateau. Worse, we get injured.

I think of biomechanical efficiency as the very foundation for our running. Both neuromuscular efficiency and physiological efficiency are involuntary. We can't tell our heart to pump faster, nor can we tell ourselves to react faster. It just happens. We can improve these efficiencies, but improvement doesn't start at the conscious level. Biomechanical efficiency, on the other hand, can be consciously worked on. And we must, if we are to enjoy a long, injury-free running career.

If we ignore biomechanical efficiency—in other words, if we don't help our bodies organise in an optimal and sustainable way—we'll hit a barrier. That's why so many runners get injured at a certain mileage or level of intensity. If we do work on it, however, we can use that firm foundation to increase our neuromuscular and physiological efficiencies by creating new patterns.

It all starts with form.

MISCONCEPTIONS

There are so many misconceptions about running that it's no wonder our form doesn't get addressed. People hold incorrect fundamental beliefs on movement patterns and posturing and remain unaware of how these factors can create pain. Most people, for example, believe they can sit or stand or move in any way without any consequences. They are then shocked when they experience knee or back pain. But every action has a result—it might take a while for our poor actions to manifest as injury and pain, but it will happen. It's like a poor diet: even if you have the best metabolism in the world, a poor diet over time will create health issues.

Being aware of these misconceptions can start you on your journey to correct form. Let's take a look at the most prevalent myths.

MYTH 1: RUNNING INJURIES JUST HAPPEN

Runners believe that their injuries simply happen, and they expect to "delete" their pain just as fast as it comes. They remain unaware that the progress of pain often begins way before symptoms manifest.

Unfortunately, many medical professionals remain fixated on the relationship between pain and structural causes, discounting the consequences of our movement choices. This leads to ineffective advice that pain can only be effectively resolved through medication and surgery, which in turn leads to the belief among the masses that injuries demand only passive treatment, with no change needed on their end.

One thought leader in movement analysis advises us to take a different perspective. Shirley Sahrmann was one of the first physiotherapists to advocate the truth that pain is not an isolated temporary inflammatory event, but rather a progressive condition greatly influenced by lifestyle.[36] She believes that most running motions are built on poor movement patterns in our daily lives away from the track or road, as we'll explore in greater detail in Mile 15. These poor movement patterns continue for years without providing any symptoms, but they get aggravated with running. Ultimately, the runner gets injured—and when they do, they blame running, even though running was only a messenger for a more chronic issue that existed in the background for years.

MYTH 2: ANYONE CAN DO IT, RIGHT NOW!

We're back to the born-to-run idea. No gym membership, no equipment, no playing partner required—heck, you don't even need to learn the skill. Just wake up one day, put on your running shoes, and go. As we've seen, however, it isn't that simple.

We live a sedentary lifestyle, where we spend Monday to Friday hunched over our desks, creating a lengthening and weakening of our postural muscles, and then we expect to run a 30K with an upright posture? It's not going to happen!

Most people think running is just about moving forward. And it is—but how you move forward makes all the difference. There is an ideal way to run and several dysfunctional variations, and if your body is already affected by your sedentary lifestyle, then those dysfunctions will only get worse with running. New runners assume their bodies are naturally built for this, that they will immediately find the ideal way to run, but that rarely happens. Because, as we will see in Mile 14, your body is not optimising for the ideal gait, but for efficiency.

MYTH 3: RUNNING IS A SERIES OF HOPS

A final misconception about running is that it is a series of hops. This notion fails to take into consideration the helpful effects of gravity. This mindset is unsustainable and unhelpful because it presumes that running is an entirely active process, and this is far from the truth. In reality, running is a series of falls, assisted by gravity. We are continuously creating a falling forward motion and subsequently catching ourselves and rolling on, with as little braking force as possible.

Rather than thinking of running as a series of one-legged jumps, bounding from one foot to another, it's more useful to think of it as a cycling motion. While one leg lands, paws back into the ground, and drives the body forward, the other leg simultaneously picks up at the hip, lifting the body and effectively lowering the amount of force needed for the "down" leg to hold the body up. The simultaneous counterrotation in the upper body builds up energy into the next stride. In other words, the ideal gait consistently harnesses the power of angular momentum to drive the body forward.

LOOK AT YOURSELF

Even though the runner I watched in Hong Kong was already running fast, he could have been running with a form that takes him to speed with greater ease. He may not have been feeling any pain, but that still doesn't mean he was running correctly. His body had simply reorganised its movements in a way that allowed him to move forward quickly, at least for now.

Our bodies are amazing self-organising, self-calibrating machines. They naturally set us up for the smoothest ride possible. As we'll discuss next, however, smooth doesn't always mean efficient or sustainable.

CALIBRATING A SMOOTH RUNNING EXPERIENCE

THE FIRST TIME I SAW A PICTURE OF MYSELF RUNNING was in 2009, two years after I started racing competitively. By that point I had optimised my training for speed and efficiency, and it was paying off. No longer were my legs heavy and my breathing laboured; no longer did each race feel impossible. I had found the flow and was beginning to feel more in tune with my body. I was running faster, and I was winning races. For the first time, I believed I had potential to go far in this sport.

I came home from that 2009 race feeling on top of the world. I logged onto Facebook to see if anyone had posted pictures of the race. They had. And I was horrified.

I didn't see the streamlined, graceful woman I saw in my mind. I didn't look like a young Sarah Hall or Paula Radcliff. I looked like I was trying not to fall over. My knees were knocking into each other, and my feet turned in as they struck the ground. The way I drove my leg back looked unsightly: I twisted at the waist, like I was desperately trying to throw myself forward. I won't go into my facial expressions because they were truly awful, but even ignoring those, I looked like a woman at war with herself.

In the two years I'd been racing before that day, not one person had commented on my form. I looked at the spectators in the pictures, and all of them were clapping and cheering, not one of them confused about how I could be winning and running that badly. Had I not seen the photos, I probably wouldn't have believed someone if they had said something because my experience depicted the exact opposite: I felt so controlled, so compact, so smooth.

It's difficult to categorise what we mean by "smoothness in running," but you know it when you see it—especially when you observe an elite runner. The recognition of good form is almost intuitive: you feel the runner's body in flow, you can sense the grace. It's an art form in itself, with its own kind of beauty. It's a combination of factors that creates this smoothness: how the runner controls their posture, how their joints line up, the combination of the body's muscles from hip to toe as they absorb the shock of each step. It's beautiful.

As my story shows, personal experience can be deceptive. I felt smooth, but to the outside observer, I was anything but. How can that be? Just as the body self-organises and adapts to internal and external factors to keep us moving forward, so it works hard to create that feeling of flow. The body calibrates and compensates across multiple physical and psycho-emotional systems to create a sense of seamlessness. It's brilliant—but also detrimental if left unaddressed.

If you want to make the most of your running journey, then you must be aware of your body's default mechanisms. Let's take a closer look at how our bodies engineer this sense of smoothness, and what it means for competitive running.

CALIBRATION AND DYSFUNCTION

One researcher proposed the very first theory on how the body creates a sense of smoothness, called the minimum jerk theory. According to Hogan, the body adapts to its internal (neural and anatomical) constraints and external terrain to minimise acceleration changes and optimise smoothness. In other words, we calibrate for our surroundings when we move, creating this impression of seamless automation. Our bodies don't do this for aesthetic reasons—it's to reduce the cost of energy. The less jerky we are when we move, the more energy we save.[37]

For a smooth running experience, the body calibrates three systems: the neuromuscular system, which includes our reflexes and muscle activation; our cardiovascular system, which deals with the health of our heart and lungs, including our metabolic adaptations such as our heart rate, oxygen uptake, and blood haemoglobin levels; and the psycho-emotional system, which is our cognitive state during the run. Research shows that most of us move in fundamentally similar ways. A group of healthy people with no injuries or no constraints on their movements should show similar posture movements. We're all variations on a common model.

But we all don't move in the same manner because these three systems are affected by a number of factors. Ageing is a big one, but so is tiredness, injury, and how our bodies mature. These small factors create aberrations in our movement. Think of the body as a smart, efficient machine that's trying to reduce energy costs at every point. Say it is trying to pick up a cup. There is an optimal trajectory path of the hand that keeps energy costs to the absolute minimum, which is what the body tries to execute. If, however, the shoulder becomes stiff from working in front of a computer all day, that will impact how the body executes the optimal movement—creating aberrations. If someone else's wrist is too tight, that will impact the optimal movement in a different way, creating a slightly different movement.

The body's biomechanics are extraordinarily complex. The body is constantly calibrating and compensating to give us a smooth and seamless experience of the world. Take uneven surfaces, for example. In 2019, researchers explored how the body copes with uneven surfaces to maintain balance and offer a sense of coordination. They found that subjects exhibited greater leg stiffness when running on uneven ground as compared to a level surface, the body's natural compensation to decrease ankle work. Our bodies regulate a continuous cyclical action of the legs using feedback from the ankles, allowing us to rely less on visual feedback for balance, creating a sense of smoothness so we can zone out and enjoy our surroundings as we run.[38]

In other words, we all share similar control mechanisms for handling an uneven surface: healthy runners will automatically stiffen their ankle joints and lower legs, which creates a reduction in ankle motion and thus protects the Achilles tendon. Any aberration in this common movement comes from variations in the three systems. Runners who have had multiple ankle sprains, for example, will struggle to recreate that same level of stiffness needed for the proprioceptive feedback—the ability to sense the environment—seen in healthy runners.

It's important to examine the body's common and instinctive calibrating strategies because not all of them are good for us. Our tendency to stiffen our lower legs and ankles when running on uneven surfaces is great, of course, and prevents us from falling down. But the body can also go into a more crouched leg posture when we run on uneven surfaces or even on unfamiliar ground, a posture that helps us feel more in control, but, as Voloshina and Ferris found in 2015, is detrimental for the runner in the long haul. Alas, what feels smoother is not necessarily good for us.[39]

And our brain is constantly adjusting for smoothness. Even something as simple as adding a small weight to one hand changes how we move. One study found that doing so created changes in limb coordination: there was increased muscle activity in both arms, increased amplitude in the hand without the weight, and decreased amplitude in the hand with the weight. This allowed for the relative frequency between the arms and legs to be maintained while walking, even with the additional weights.[40] In another study, holding hand weights caused the subjects to unknowingly walk faster, presumably to compensate for the added weight.[41] Ever carried a water bottle while running? You'll notice after a while that it seems natural—like it's a part of you. It's because your body reorganises itself and adjusts your movements to account for it.

Our body is a smart tool that is always assessing, judging, and changing depending on the circumstances. But its aim is energy efficiency, and it achieves that by eliminating any jerkiness—it doesn't care about long-term damage that results from the tactics used to remain smooth. Just because it feels right doesn't mean it is right. As runners, we must examine our common coping mechanisms and see which actions genuinely help our muscles and joints in the long run.

Most of us assume our bodies have an inbuilt mechanism to correct for any major deviations from the ideal gait or any compensation strategies that will harm us in the long run. If we're leaning to the side when we run, for example, shouldn't our bodies know and tell us? Yes—and no.

Yes, because the body does have sensors for precisely this purpose: they're called proprioceptors and are located in our core muscles. Proprioceptors provide spatial awareness; they play an important role in keeping us upright as we run (no matter how tired we are) and in managing perturbations that occur from running on rocky terrains, downhill, or in strong winds. In short, our proprioceptors are responsible for our awareness of the body's positions—are we slouching, for instance, or are we leaning more to one side?—and their feedback helps us respond to the environment. So if we're running into a strong wind, then our proprioceptors will signal that we need to adjust our upper body position to make sure we're staying upright: we need to lean forward, for example, to counter the wind's force. Feedback from the proprioceptors activates the right muscle groups and helps the body instinctively react.

No, because the proprioceptors are not foolproof. If we have a weak core, then our proprioceptors might be weak and their feedback poor. They may not notice we're leaning to the side or running with a slouched back—they're simply not sensitive enough to pick up on it. Because their feedback is poor, the right muscle groups are not activated in the right circumstances, and we continue to run with a slouched posture or other poor compensation techniques. Over time, our muscles will set in this position, and it will be difficult to remember that this isn't the ideal gait because it feels so familiar.

Also remember that our compensation movements aren't just biomechanical; they rely on different systems to function properly. Say you're on a trail and you trip over a rock. That trip creates a reflex action in your arm—you put out your hand to break your fall—which is triggered by the distal tibial nerve in the arm. The reflex is dictated by neural connections between the legs and the arms, not the body's biomechanical system. Runners who practise a lot on trails will have better reflexes in this regard because they will be used to encountering unexpected obstacles.

Understanding this complex muscle and mind interaction is crucial to correcting our running styles. So often I hear coaches tell runners to reduce their cross-body motion by changing their arm swing. But it's not so simple—they can't just decide to force a straight arm swing. If their knees are moving inwards, or if they have a lot of lower body rotation, or if they don't have sufficient upper thoracic strength to pull their arms back, they aren't going to be able to correct their posture—not sustainably. Their incorrect arm posture is connected to their legs and the rest of their body with neural connectors; simply fixing their arms won't fix the problem.

In simple terms, our body is an interconnected web of relations. Think of your joints as sensors, with feedback provided to your brain, which then calibrates and coordinates it to provide as clear and cohesive an experience as possible. Some of the experiments conducted to prove this level of coordination are fascinating. Zehr et al. found, for example, that the movement of one limb affects the movement of the other: if one leg is in the air for a longer time, the second leg will stay connected to the ground to compensate.[42]

Experiments have been conducted on a split-belt treadmill to prove this. A split-belt treadmill has two belts, each that can be adjusted to different speeds. A person stands on the treadmill with one foot on each belt, and one belt is adjusted to run slower than the other. Researchers found that the leg on the slower belt had a longer stance duration (i.e., it stayed connected to the ground for longer). To compensate, the leg on the faster belt had a longer swing phase (i.e., it stayed in the air longer).

These experiments are fascinating because they prove how bizarre our bodies are. At first glance, it might seem obvious that if one leg is in the air, the other one would naturally stay on the ground: after all, we can't levitate. But it's only obvious because the body has been doing it for so long. Look at the split-belt experiment: the body will do anything to make our movement feel as natural and easy as possible—even if our legs are moving at two different speeds.

Most of us walk in an asymmetrical form, an asymmetry that is noticeable when we observe other runners, who often lean more to one side than the other when running. If we injure a leg, the body instinctively adjusts movements so that the healthy leg is doing more of the work and the injured leg is a passive pivot point. The symmetry in this scenario is an illusion—it feels symmetrical to us because our bodies work very hard to make it so.

Here's another bizarre example. When we run, we judge whether or not we're running in an upright posture based on where we're looking. We assume that if we're looking straight ahead, that means our head is angled correctly and thus so is our body. But research shows that even when the head is tilted forward, our eyes adjust to gaze at the same place that's straight ahead. So we could be running with the body out of alignment but our gaze levelled in a straight line, tricking us into believing we're upright. The consequences in the long run are terrible: in a forward head position, the neck muscles responsible for keeping our head lifted lengthen and weaken, making it harder for us to correct our head positioning. Worse, the sensory receptors in the neck are damaged, affecting feedback to the brain.

The feeling of smoothness, despite these dysfunctions, is simply a result of the body's ability to maximise its internal resources. It doesn't necessarily mean we are running smoothly, free of injuries. We can harness the strength within us, across the upper and lower body, to improve the fluidity of our form with our environment, as we will see later.

EARLY INTERVENTION

The three systems outlined earlier—neuromuscular, cardiovascular, psycho-emotional—are codependent. This means our physical movements are also heavily influenced by our emotions and state of mind. My shock at watching the video of myself running affected how I ran after that. Suddenly, I didn't feel smooth anymore or in control, and my movements became even more disjointed as a result.

In addition, when I tried to fix the problems I saw, in some ways I made things worse. Smoothness works at the brain level and cannot be consciously modified without an understanding of why the body is doing what it is doing. I reacted to what I saw in the video and tried to force out a larger and wider stride to compensate for my shuffling, crossover gait, but I lacked understanding of what was causing my gait in the first place and thus my interventions were incorrect.

But at least I was aware of the need to change. Seeing those pictures of me running was indeed a wake-up call. I realised I was fast because I was using brute force, not because I was working with my body to optimise movement. There was no built-in momentum; at every step of the way, I was battling with myself to move forward.

The truth is, there had been signs that I wasn't running smoothly long before I saw the Facebook pictures. I was getting injured repeatedly on one side of my body, especially if I ran on certain terrains. I couldn't run more than one hundred kilometres a week; each time I pushed beyond that, my body reacted negatively. Nor could I do high-intensity workouts more than once a week. If I did long races or difficult workouts back-to-back, my body broke down—as if I had inadvertently exceeded a load threshold that it couldn't handle—and I had to cut back immediately. I felt like a ticking bomb: I didn't know which run would lead to an injury or if it was preventable. I knew something was wrong, but I didn't know enough to connect the dots.

Don't wait for the next video to discover that you're not running as smoothly as you think you are. You can learn your body in-depth now, so you can investigate any patterns that seem problematic. Your body is a miracle machine; it can compensate for a million variables to smoothen your running experience. But that doesn't help you form an accurate picture of how you're running. You may have dysfunctional movement patterns, an awkward gait, and other biomechanical issues that go unaddressed because of how well your body calibrates. Intervene early. The next chapters will look at different aspects of our running experience at a biomechanical level to pinpoint what you can watch out for.

OFF THE ROAD

I ONCE HAD A FIFTEEN-YEAR-OLD CLIENT NAMED SAM, who was very active in sports: he'd been a competitive swimmer; was part of the National Police Cadet Corps, a cadet school club in Singapore; and was now transitioning to cross-country running.

He was frustrated with his progress with running, however. As a swimmer, he had been at the top level, but he wasn't able to reach those heights in cross-country. He was also experiencing neck pain every time he ran hard. It wasn't a crippling pain—about a 2 on a scale of 10—but it bothered him during and after each training session. He asked his teammates if they had experienced such pain, but none of them had. He asked his coach, who had also never encountered this kind of pain but thought it might be stress. Sam took a few days off, but when he returned to running, so did the pain. Frustrated now, he went to doctors and had X-rays, but no one could tell him why his neck hurt.

This is when Sam came to me. He told me the pain started in the middle of the neck and occasionally moved to the middle of his back, but it consistently happened in conjunction with intense interval training. It had come to a point where he dreaded running these intervals—not because the pain was unmanageable, but because he had no idea what was causing it.

Almost immediately, I noticed that Sam was holding his head incorrectly: his neck was excessively flat, without the normal curvature, and his chin tucked in, a pose learned from his time in the National Police Cadet Corps, where they had to stand for long periods of time in a rigid, upright posture. Since the rest of his cadet-mates were standing with arched backs and tucked-in chins, Sam didn't realise it was wrong.

Sam was also tall for a fifteen-year-old in Singapore: 1.75 metres (5 feet 9 inches). I watched the way he walked into a room and how he sat upright, and found his height affected his body posture. When he sat, for example, the chair seat was lower than appropriate for his height, which meant his knees were above the level of his hips and his hips were thus consistently curved. His friends were shorter than him, so Sam curved his lower back when talking to them. The same thing happened when he worked at a desk.

When we curve a part of the body, other parts extend to compensate and keep us upright. In Sam's case, there was an altered distribution of the bending motion across the neck and back, with the neck bending more than the upper back. He was standing in an upright posture, but without the appropriate curvatures in the right areas. He had a rounded lower back, a straight upper back, and a rounded neck. As a result, Sam experienced pain when running, because the muscles were forced to work against gravity to keep him upright. He didn't experience the same pain in swimming, where his body didn't have to support his weight in the same manner, or when he was sitting or lying down.

Over time, Sam developed poor postural muscles around the shoulder blades and down the lines of his upper back into his hips. For Sam to run well, and without pain, postural strength in the right areas has to be reintroduced.

Thanks to these developments, when Sam stood up straight to run, he couldn't engage the postural muscles around the shoulder blades because they were too weak. But he knew an upright position was correct, so he compensated by arching his mid-back and squeezing his shoulder blades together. Arching through the mid-back limits diaphragmatic breathing and lower chest expansions, which means he was using his upper chest to breathe, creating further tension in his front neck muscles, which worsened the issue created by his National Police Cadet Corps training.

When I took him to a mirror and showed him how to hold his neck in an ideal manner, Sam was shocked. He had a hard time understanding how his posture could be so off when he'd been so healthy and active all his life.

Likewise, most active people are surprised to learn that their bodies are not a blank slate—that, over the years, we accumulate small tissue adjustments that better facilitate our daily actions but deviate from the optimal movement patterns. Conscious running means not only being aware of our bodies—our form, the aches and pains we experience as we run—but also understanding the "off-the-road" routines, circumstances, and lifestyle choices that impact and even cause them. Only then can we learn how to make adjustments.

HOW TO THINK ABOUT YOUR BODY

Most people think that only intentional physical movements have an effect upon our bodies, but that is not the case. Our bodies are affected by how we sit, reach, stand, lean, and walk. All those daily, often sedentary activities can have a big impact on our muscles. Sitting slouched in front of the TV or leaning to the right atop the arm rest, for instance, changes our muscles as they adapt to that sustained posture. So does sitting with the neck turned, talking to a friend, while the body is facing forward. These moves are functional, and we don't do them with the intention of changing our bodies, but they have an impact nonetheless—as much as running, swimming, or Pilates.

We also don't think about how interconnected the body is, and how a change in one part affects another. Take slouching for example. Most people think that when we slouch, we curve the upper back, thus damaging it. This is true, but we also create other issues down the chain. Our head comes forward, our chin pokes out, and our neck arches. Because slouching brings our centre of mass forward, our lower body changes to compensate and prevent us from falling forward: we tilt at the pelvis and stand in a swayback manner, which means we drop the hips.

This interconnectedness exists at the muscular level as well. The body always chooses the path of least resistance to move forward, which often means engaging the stronger muscles over and over again, making the underlying joints excessively mobile. Simultaneously, the weaker, neglected muscles and their respective joints grow weaker and stiffen, because they aren't used as frequently. Running makes this imbalance worse: the excessive loading from gravitational forces further lengthens and weakens already weak muscles and shortens and tightens the muscles that are already overused, leading to repetitive-use injuries. Remember, the body chooses the most economical way to run, not the most sustainable.

Learn to think about your body as an interconnected system, where changes in one part have a knock-on effect, and recognize that every action and inaction—even the boring, daily ones—have an impact on how your muscles form.

HOW MOVEMENT PATTERNS ARE FORMED

If something isn't good for us, then we work on changing, right? If our posture isn't correct, won't we adjust it? If our neck is extended outwards, won't there be some kind of pain to tell us to straighten it out?

Not necessarily. Thanks to how well the body compensates for these issues, we rarely notice when something is out of alignment—at least not at first. Think back to the last chapter, where we talked about the forward head posture and how our gaze readjusts to give us the impression we're standing upright when we're not. It's the same with slouching: the body makes many tiny adjustments throughout to make sure we don't fall over.

We think of pain as the great indicator of what is not working with our bodies; if there is no pain, we assume everything is okay. But pain isn't always a good marker: you can have terrible posture or damaging movement habits and still not experience pain. Your body simply compensates.

When it comes to poor movement strategies, it's not so much what you do but how you do it. Repeated actions cause our muscles and tissues to develop differently, often freezing them into maladaptive positions. It's difficult for us to identify these positions as maladaptive because they feel familiar: they're comfortable because we usually learn them young. In some way, it's a vicious cycle: adopting these movements causes the tissues to develop in a certain way, which now means that any other movement—even if it's the correct one—feels unnatural.

Think about gait. Our legs can move forward using a variety of motions. For example, we can extend one hip back as we step forward with the other leg or we can lock the front knee in an effort to press forward. Some of us twist the front foot and others push with our back. Even for such a straightforward action as walking—arguably one of the most fundamental movements—we've developed many ways to do it.

We don't have benchmarks for what's a correct action; there is no internal system guiding us. A layperson observing one person walking by locking their knees and another person walking by using their back muscles won't be able to tell the difference: maybe the observer notices the first person moves a bit jerkily, but that's about it.

Poor movement patterns are hard to correct because we don't know they're poor. If they're getting the job done, if we don't experience pain, we see no reason to analyse and possibly change them. Thus, these patterns continue for years, until with age our muscles become less malleable, and the pain arrives.

HABITS AND DYSFUNCTIONAL MOVEMENT PATTERNS

Our lifestyles and habits have a deep impact on our bodies and can create tissue impairments that affect our running form and enjoyment. A right-handed woman who is breastfeeding, for example, will often use her right hand to hold her baby. Automatically, her body will rotate more to the right for the duration of the breastfeeding. Now multiply that position by seven days a week for about a year—it's bound to have a profound impact on her body. Her lower back and abdominal obliques will have shortened, tying her to the position and affecting the alignment of her ribcage and backbone.

The same goes for daily activities that are part of our career or our lifestyle choices. A stockbroker who has multiple screens in front of him may keep his head rotated to the left to look at one screen. Ideally, he should rotate his whole body while keeping his head in a neutral position, but that rarely happens. On days he's especially engaged with the charts, he may stay in that position, with his head turned, for a full half hour. When he turns back, he may not notice it, but the muscles in his neck have altered slightly: they've tightened at the left. Over time, he'll notice it's more uncomfortable to look towards the right or even keep his head in a neutral position, and he'll start tilting ever so slightly to the left.

This explanation is true for any position you hold for prolonged periods of time—like when you watch TV. If you are slumped on a couch, your head and neck are extended outwards and over time, they'll micro-adjust to this position. Or if you have an L-shaped couch and you sit at the corner seat, your head will likely rotate one way or another when you speak to others. Your shoulders will be more rounded in that slumped position because the tighter front muscles are constantly pulling you forward into a rounded posture, further lengthening and weakening your back postural muscles.

This applies to even the simplest of actions. Carrying your backpack on one side of the body was very cool when we were young, but it creates an acquired rotation in the upper back. Putting your wallet in your back pocket and sitting on it affects how your body tilts. Wearing heels throws your centre of mass forward, which means your back needs to arch or your knees lock to keep you standing upright.

All these lifestyle choices and habits can result in micro-trauma—slight shifts from the ideal posture or movement pattern. If we don't have the postural and core strength to reset, these habits can lead to the small aches, pains, and twinges we often feel if we continue these movements over weeks, months, or years. What often happens is that we feel a slight twinge, and we avoid using the pained body part in that particular way. If we feel pain in our wrist when we use the mouse in a certain way, we will probably adjust our hand position. If our left knee hurts when walking upstairs, we might lean more heavily on the handrail—or use the elevator when possible. We don't notice these decisions, but the body makes them. Over time, microtrauma and the body's compensatory mechanisms can result in macrotrauma—larger injuries that expand out of the smaller motions, thanks to progressive degeneration of the tissues.

Let's take one specific example: There are seven vertebrae in the neck, and not all of them move in the same way. Depending on how we hold the head and chin, some of these vertebrae will be hyperflexible. If our chins poke out—which can happen if we sit, slouched, on a couch to watch TV—then the bottom vertebrae will be flexed and the top vertebrae of the neck will be arched in. This microtrauma leads to the lengthening and tightening of certain muscles, which reinforces the poor movement pattern. Over time, that microtrauma will grow into a macrotrauma: we may get radiating pain down our neck, along with jaw pain and headaches.

The progress from microtrauma to macrotrauma is influenced by a variety of intrinsic factors (genetics, sex, and age) and extrinsic factors (fitness levels, type of work). But it's clear that the majority of injuries, both acute and chronic, result from cumulative microtrauma created by stress from repetitive motion in a specific direction or from sustained nonideal alignment. It may seem like your neck pain came out of nowhere, but it was likely seeded by your "off-the-road" lifestyle.

Even the way we walk on a day-to-day basis can affect our running form. For example, if you wear heels all day, your body makes micro-adjustments. If you then decide to go for a ten-kilometre run after work, your body will find it harder to maintain proper form because it has to reset: from holding your body one way in heels to holding it a different way in motion in running shoes.

Driving from the knees instead of the hips creates its own host of problems. When a person walks, ideally her butt muscles should work to push her forward, pivoting the body over a stable knee. But if someone has weak muscles or excessively stiff joint capsules that scramble her neuroreceptors, her knees slam back to create the necessary stability and momentum to move forward. The slamming of the knee into the locked position creates a lot of shear force on the knee, creating a lengthening of the posterior capsule of the knee joint over time. Thus, the meeting line of the joints is shifted even further back.

Walking in a locked-knee movement pattern is sometimes learned, and sometimes it results from genetic makeup. Either way, this pattern affects the gait: we will rely more heavily on our knee mechanics to drive ourselves forward while running, instead of hip mechanics, creating tightness in the hips (from underuse) and pain in the knee (from overuse).

Too much sitting is equally bad: when we sit for a long time, our hips are consistently bent, making it difficult to get up because our hip flexors have been stuck in a contracted position. Obviously, we have to sit to work, but if we haven't done the proper strengthening work for our core and postural muscles on a regular basis, our bodies won't be strong enough to reset properly for a run, thus impacting our gait.

Most poor movement patterns result in weak segmental dissociation. This means that we grow so used to a way of performing an action, we're unable to divide different parts of the body and use them individually. Consider the slouching example: Someone who slouches pushes his head and neck forward, shortens his abdominal muscles, and weakens his back postural muscles, which the body compensates for by standing in a sway-back position or leaning back at the hips. The person doesn't understand or feel this, however; the forward-head position is his normal. If someone asked him to stand up straighter, he wouldn't correct his head posture but would instead arch his back. In short, the person would be unable to isolate the head movement from his back movement—to him, they're one and the same.

Once we get stuck in a position, our concept of "normal" recalibrates, and our brain forgets the optimal internal reference point.

This kind of poor segmental dissociation in our postural muscles has a profound effect on running. Postural muscles are the muscles responsible for holding us upright against gravity, including muscles around the shoulder joints, shoulder blades, spine, lower back, neck, and tailbone. Running works closely with gravity—throughout the running motion, we aim to maintain a forward-leaning plank, using gravity to create momentum (without, of course, falling over). That is why postural strength plays such an important role. If we have weak movement patterns and maladaptation in our tissues, those issues will be aggravated with running.

OUR REORGANISING BODIES

Some of our muscles are postural muscles, intended to hold us upright against gravity for long periods of time. These muscles are located deeper, near the joints, and are closely integrated with the neurovestibular system. They are located at the base of our neck, around the shoulder blades as well as our pelvic and core region. When postural muscles are weak due to microtrauma or a previous injury, our bodies naturally reorganise so that we remain upright. The problem is that it uses non-postural muscles to do so—muscles that were not meant to bear that load—and we end up in pain as a result.

For example, if your head is always extended forward, you will have weak neck muscles, which means your jaw muscles are working harder to hold the head up. This can lead to jaw aches, grinding your teeth at night, and even headaches.

These issues get worse if you start running with a similar head-forward posture. Such a posture promotes the use of the head to drive a forward motion. Because you suffer from weak segmental dissociation—that is, you can't isolate your body parts and their functions—you remain slouched at the shoulders while arching your back instead. Worse, the more fatigued you get, the more you use your lower back to hold yourself upright, which creates additional issues.

It's not rare for a new runner to find themselves with prolonged jaw issues, headaches, and back problems. I've often treated a patient for back pain only for them to come back and say, "Hey, you cured my jaw pain as well!"

Often, I can predict how someone will run simply by looking at how they stand, how they rotate their head, or how they walk. These movements tell me a lot about what a person believes is the most effective way to move forward. You can't walk badly and run amazingly—it doesn't work like that.

Fixing these tissue maladjustments often requires a two-pronged approach. True dissociation requires strength. If we have tight abdominal muscles, we can't just work on loosening those muscles; we have to also work on strengthening our back. As we saw with the example of forward head movement, separate parts of the body are surprisingly connected, such as the lower back and jaw.

Nor is fixing these problems simple: it does require a customised approach. Two people can have the same problem, but for very different reasons. You need a professional to identify what the causes might be and what the best treatment is.

The goal of understanding how habits and daily activities might impact your tissue adjustments and create poor movement patterns is not to eliminate these actions. For most of us, that's impossible: you can't stop lifting heavy objects if you're a construction worker, nor can you refuse to look at a computer screen if you're a stockbroker. Even something as simple as not wearing heels might not be in our control if it's required by a professional dress code. But you can be aware of the connection so that you can begin correcting these habits, so that they don't adversely impact your running.

GENERAL EXERCISE AND DYSFUNCTIONAL MOVEMENT PATTERNS

Many runners use non-running workouts to keep fit for the track—cross-training, weight training, and so on. The initiative is great, but if done incorrectly, these exercises may end up doing more harm than good. They could become another habit that leads to dysfunctional movement patterns and impacts enjoyable running.

A good example is the lats pull-down machine. The point of this exercise is to strengthen the upper back muscles to hold the shoulders back. When pulling down, however, most people round their shoulders forward, and then arch their back when raising the bar to its starting position. This technique defeats the purpose and tightens muscles that are already tight.

In general, machines do not provide the best training for running because they offer isolated and single-plane strengthening exercises. As runners, we use multiple planes simultaneously, with multiple segments working together: we're trying to remain stable and stacked, with minimal rotation of the trunk and arms, and we're trying to maximise forward motion. For example, a knee extension machine isolates and exercises your quadriceps alone, but in running, you use more than your quadriceps to move forward. Together with the hip flexor muscles, hamstrings, and glutes, the quadriceps drive the hip upward during push-off and straighten the knee on landing. As such, building strong effective quadriceps goes beyond a simple knee straightening motion that you practise with a machine.

Using machines like the knee extension can create an imbalance. If you strengthen your quadriceps in isolation so that they become a lot stronger than your hamstrings and glutes, you'll run incorrectly. The body always chooses the path of least resistance: if one part of your body seems stronger and looks like it can carry the weight, your body will use it to move forward. It's the easiest way to save energy.

PAIN IS ONLY THE FIRST STEP

Like Sam, many clients come to me because tissue misalignments are finally causing them pain when they run, and they are surprised to learn that the root is found in everyday habits and activities. Without fail, however, those misalignments also show up in their running form.

To truly fix the issues causing pain, we have to look at the runner's gait, as well as standing posture and head position, for that will show imbalances and dysfunctions in action.

ON THE ROAD

I'LL NEVER FORGET SAM'S EXPRESSION WHEN I SHOWED him in the mirror where his posture was wrong. He believed he'd been standing straight, holding his neck in the proper position, and now he learned his postural muscles were badly developed.

As you know from the last chapter, Sam came to me when he couldn't figure out why he had pain in his neck during interval training. The first step was helping Sam understand what was happening in detail. In the mirror, I showed him which parts of his body were excessively arched and how his neck should be held. Then he got onto his hands and knees, and I taught him how to engage the different muscles in his neck and understand how to dissociate the parts of his body.

To better analyse how his posture was affecting his gait and how his form holds up when fatigue sets in, I had him run on the treadmill. I started the belt speed at three kilometres per hour, and I increased the speed every few minutes, progressing from a comfortable stroll to a running pace, slightly beyond comfort.

My first impression was how Sam sat back when he ran. Because his core muscles weren't strong enough to hold up his pelvis, he was limited in his ability to engage his hips in each stride and drive himself forward. As a result, Sam had to rely upon movement from the knees and feet, instead of his hips, causing him to tire out faster, which made his breathing heavier, which further tightened his neck muscles.

Think of a pendulum—if you swing a pendulum from the top string, it moves in a simple, free-flowing manner. If you try to move the pendulum from the ball, however, movement is restricted. It does not flow smoothly and freely. Instead, the ball only goes where your hand places it. Likewise, if we initiate our running stride from the top "string" (the hip), the "ball" (foot) follows along in smooth motion. If we initiate movement from the foot, it takes more effort to move the rest of the leg and there is more possibility of error.

The gait is a visual representation of the body's compensations, but it doesn't show us exactly where our weaknesses are. It simply reflects a culmination of our muscular strengths and weaknesses, flexibility, neuromuscular coordination, and echoes of past and present pains. And because our gait feels so natural, it almost seems like it can't and shouldn't be changed.

Before his gait analysis on the treadmill, Sam thought he was running well. He'd watched videos of elite runners who had a gorgeous back kick, heels lightly touching their butt. He tried to emulate a similar kick, or so he thought. The elite runners were driving their back kick from their hips, while Sam drove from his knees and ankles. Many amateurs do this. From afar, they look like they are running with a great back kick, but on closer examination, their strides remain closed up at the hips and only demonstrate an excessive butt kick.

Gait is a complex process that cannot always be understood

by watching others: you need to look at the underlying theory to grasp the hidden dysfunctions. Once you see what's really going on, the rewards are infinite.

Let's take a look in the mirror that is our gait and deep dive into how it works.

CHANGING BODY PATTERNS

As discussed in Mile 15, we don't begin our running journey with a blank slate. We start with the movement patterns we've picked up over the years, through lifestyle choices, cultural conditioning, and daily habits.

Thus, from our first stride, we already have some degree of misalignment in our body's musculoskeletal structure. And we carve this misalignment further into our form when we repeat the same movements to run further and faster. The more we run with these poor movement patterns, the harder it becomes to unlearn them. It's like a groove being etched deeper and deeper.

To the runner, these traits seem genetic. Excessive pronation at the ankle or stiffness in our foot resulting in over supination can feel inherited rather than learned. While there might be some degree of genetics involved, it's more likely that we have created or learned many of these poor movement patterns over the years.

We don't question our gait patterns because changing them feels unnatural and impossible. Yet, change can and should occur to develop a form that allows us to run more effectively.

THE IDEAL GAIT, AND WHERE WE GO WRONG

The ideal running gait maximises the forward motion of the entire body and minimises motion in other planes, such as side to side and rotation. In this ideal gait, the body is nicely stacked with the head squared between both feet and the torso held upright, which allows the body to move forward from the core. Successive foot placements land parallel with each other.

Unfortunately, without the learned ability to engage strength in the right places, the body does not naturally optimise for this stacked gait: instead, it opts for the path of least resistance and lowest energy costs, which often creates deviations from the ideal gait. Paradoxically, these deviations limit forward motion, but restricting them also impedes forward motion as these are the only ways the body knows how to move forward.

One deviation is a forward head posture. When the head is shifted forward, the body's centre of mass is also displaced forward. In this position, the body is unstable and almost crumbling to the ground. It has no effective leverage for the core to pull itself forward, which is why we instinctively use the head to move forward.

Here are some examples of other ways the body might compensate:

- *Excessive body lean:* An excessive sideways lean occurs when there is insufficient strength of the core and glutes. The body ends up leaning towards the weaker leg so that balance can be maintained on that side. When the core is weak, a backwards lean of the trunk can occur as well, which impedes the creation of a forward drive.
- *Excessive pelvis shifting:* Equally strong hips are required for a squared and stable pelvis. Insufficient strength in either hip can show up with the butt swaying from side to side.
- *Excessive body rotation:* Ideally, the legs extend straight back during push-off, but stiffness or weakness at the hip can

cause the body to rotate in an effort to achieve this long stride.

- *Excessive turning of the feet:* The foot position is a culmination of the motion, or lack thereof, going through the hip, knee, and shin. Restriction in the hip will result in a compensatory external rotation through the lower leg instead of the hip, resulting in the foot turning out. Sometimes, this external rotation simply doesn't occur and the entire lower leg, including the foot, remains turned in, resulting in an excessively shortened gait.
- *Excessive bounce:* Without sufficient hip mobility, the calves may take over the forward driving motion. As a result, the feet play a more active role, leading to vertical bounce.

Ultimately, achieving the ideal gait requires both strength and flexibility. You can have great flexibility, but if you don't have enough strength to back it up, ultimately it will lead to stiffness and compensations elsewhere. More specifically, a lack of balanced strength around the joint offsets its position, as the centre of the joint will be pulled towards the tighter and often stronger muscle group.

To the runner, however, the lack of strength and resulting stiffness feels like a flexibility issue that can be solved by "stretching it out," but stretching often proves ineffective. Take the hip, for example. The hip muscles are a glove-like structure around the hip joint. The pull of the muscles from all directions creates a suctioning effect that keeps the joint centred in its socket. Strength in those muscles, not stretching, is what gives the centring. The stronger the hip muscles, the more precisely the joint is positioned in the centre of its axis, and the greater the range of motion—in other words, the greater the flexibility.

AWARENESS AND ANALYSIS

Video is the best way to do an accurate gait analysis like the one I did with Sam. If possible, take video of your gait while running on the treadmill and ask a friend to record an outside run, so you can observe your gait in two different settings. If you have to pick one, get video of your stride on solid ground. In that setting, you're using the entirety of your mobilizer muscles to drive yourself forward, whereas on the treadmill the belt is doing that work for you.

That being said, you can still pick up fundamental weaknesses in your running gait by watching yourself in the mirror as you run on a treadmill. Take a look at your stride. Are you bending one knee more than the other? Is your body excessively rotating to either side? Are you striking the ground loudly? You'll still need the help of a professional to know how to fix what you notice, but noticing is a start.

In addition, pay attention to your body and your equipment, both during and after your run. You might be amazed at what you can learn about your gait from a little increased awareness. Here are a few examples:

- *Calluses:* If you have a lot of calluses on your feet, that's a sign you're not engaging your hips enough and instead using your feet and ankles to steady yourself, creating a lot of shear forces on your feet.
- *Stubbing of the toe:* Not lifting from your hip sufficiently at push-off can limit foot clearance and airtime. As a result, you can stub your toe on the ground when you land. If you're running on outdoor trails, you're more likely to trip over small obstacles.
- *Rolling of the ankle:* If you're pushing off from the ankle in

an unstable position, then you'll feel your ankle rolling—it's like you're always at the point of a sprain.

- *Heavy pounding or slapping of your feet:* This usually results from slouching such that your centre of mass has shifted backwards, which means you tend to land beyond your centre of mass, resulting in an overreaching in your stride. That overreaching means you are not landing squarely on your feet but slapping the ground instead.
- *Sweaty and sore feet:* The physical impact of the foot slapping can cause red blood cells in the capillaries of the soles to break down, causing a loss of iron. This phenomenon is called foot-strike hemolysis. Before the condition gets to this severity, you might feel the symptoms of sore feet and shoes drenched with sweat.
- *Chafing:* People feel chafing in different places—their inner thighs, armpits, arms, nipples (men feel this since they're not wearing a sports bra)—but in each case it usually indicates excessive rotation and cross-body motion when running, which creates excessive friction with their clothes.
- *Holes in socks:* If you don't use your core and glutes to control your run, you might end up gripping with your toes—you're basically using your toes to engineer stability.
- *Shoe wear and tear:* Take a look at the soles of your shoes. You will see more wear and tear in the places where you apply the most pressure during landing and takeoff. If you have a crossover gait, for example, you will find wear at the inner sides of the shoes where they hit or brush against one another (you can probably feel that as you run, too). Excessive pronation will often show up as wear on the inner sole, while excessive supination results in extra wear on the outer sole.

Awareness and observation of these signs are the best ways to understand how your body is moving, the first step towards doing work to achieve the ideal gait. Remember: you can't just implement a new arm swing or leg lift. Optimising your gait and fixing poor movement patterns involves proper and effective strength training. More on that in Part V.

OPTIMISING YOUR GAIT—IT CAN BE DONE

To fix Sam's posture and gait, I worked on correcting his postural muscles and undoing the bad habits he'd picked up throughout his life. I gave him exercises to do before and after a run, so that he can correct his posture and run with better body movements.

I also asked him to cut down his running training sessions by 10-20 percent—there is no point running if you're doing it incorrectly—and I replaced these sessions with rehab classes to increase his muscle strength. Rehab training is often more tiring than weight training; you're not just working out a muscle but waking up a muscle that's been dormant for a long time. That requires rest post-session, so the muscle can recover and readapt slowly.

The aim of the rehab session was to get his muscular system up to speed with his aerobic system. For a long time, Sam was using brute force to move forward—and it was working, to an extent. He was fast. But our goal was to optimise his movement by getting his muscles to catch up, so he can lean into momentum and work with his body to create speed.

By the end, Sam was running with a better posture and gait, the pain in his neck was gone, and he was able to see better results in his running.

The same is possible for you. It all starts with becoming aware of how you move.

THE UPPER BODY

BY THE END OF 2018, I WAS PRETTY BURNED OUT FROM running, and I thought a short detour in my distance running goals might refresh me. So I bought a road bike in January 2019, and challenged myself to try for the SEA Games Duathlon.

That was the beginning of my cycling journey. I spent 2019 doing a lot of cross-training, mixing a good amount of cycling in with my running. That new bike saw me qualify in the first round of the SEA Games Duathlon, took me to eighth position in the Powerman Malaysia Duathlon, and helped me secure first in the SEA Games Duathlon trials in Indonesia.

Despite my victories, the run after the bike always felt so difficult. It wasn't that I was more tired—that's to be expected after cycling forty kilometres—but I felt heavy and out of breath very quickly.

Running was what I was good at, so why was I suddenly finding it trickier? I analysed what had changed and realised that the sustained position of being bent over my handlebars had affected my running efficiency. In order for me to transit out into an upright running posture, I needed postural and core strength to adapt from a bent-over riding posture to upright running. The problem was that I didn't think the bike required upper body strength, so I didn't work on it and ended up negatively impacting my running form as well. My bent-over posture carried over, and this slouching affected my breathing as well as my ability to run light on my feet.

This was when I realised firsthand what a large impact the upper body has on our running economy. Many of us believe that running is all about the lower body. But the upper body—defined as the waist up—plays a vital role in how your lower body functions: ignoring one cripples the other. Let's take an in-depth look at how the upper body can impact running form, and the common mistakes runners make.

THE FASCIAL SYSTEM

As discussed, the ideal running gait is one that maximises forward motion, which requires muscular strength from head to toe. Most people who are unfamiliar with running assume the legs do all the work, but the upper body plays a vital role in the process of motion—largely because the upper and lower bodies are connected through the fascial system.

The fascial system consists of connective tissue that weaves together all the muscles, bones, and ligaments in the body. Think of it as the superglue that holds us together. Early theories on muscular movement believed that the muscles moved independently of each other, largely because each muscle had its own, unique insertion into the bone via a tendon. But further study proved that theory to be false: the muscles are in fact connected through this vast web of connective tissue we call the fascial system.

The fascial system works like a rubber band. When one body segment is stretched, it affects the connective tissues, which in turn create tension in a distal body part. That tension occurs throughout the body, not just with muscle groups that are close together. Poor head posture due to weak neck stabilisers can create extensive tension throughout the spine and even the calves and hamstrings. This shortens the stride during running, which impacts running economy: in the absence of an open stride, we compensate by shuffling and we tire faster.

The fascial system doesn't just connect the upper and lower body anatomically, but also physiologically. Tension created through the fascial system when we run regulates the blood pressure throughout the body, including the brain.

THE UPPER-LOWER CONNECTION

Viewing your body as an entwined web will help you understand how it moves and what might be impacting your gait. It may look like your legs and butt are doing all the work when you run, but that is not the case. You cannot ignore your upper body.

Consider your core, for example, one of the most important groups of stabiliser muscles. Your core is like a corset: its walls consist of the deepest layer of the abdominal muscles, and its base and lid are formed by the pelvic muscles and the diaphragm, respectively. The core is responsible for stabilising the upper body when the lower body moves, and thus plays a big role in the production, transfer, and control of force to the distal lower limbs. It also contains a high number of proprioceptors, which, as we saw in Mile 14, are necessary to help our bodies handle perturbations as we run and tell us where the body is positioned in space. When the core is weak, our stability is affected, as is the efficiency of our proprioceptors to correct any dysfunctions in posture.

The inability to hold the upper body upright impacts our ability to harness the strength and power of our lower body. Even if we develop strong glutes and calves, a floppy upper body will neutralise any power we can generate from these muscles. We need a well-stacked upper body to maximise strength in our legs.

Changes to that line of gravity also affect our centre of mass, which impacts our gait and running efficiency—that ideal forward leaning motion. Maintaining that forward plank is a battle between two forces: gravity and the ground forces acting on our joints (external forces) that are trying to pull us down versus the forces generated by our muscles and soft tissue structures around the joint (internal forces) that are trying to keep us up. It's a tug of war, and we need equal power between both—or better power internally—to generate forward motion.

With a poorly aligned centre of mass, greater internal forces are needed to offset the external forces on top of generating motion. In other words, our muscles need to work harder to counter the gravitational pull, which leads to a form that fatigues and falls apart faster.

Worse, the imbalance creates discomfort and pain. Because our muscles are forced to work harder to counteract the bad upper-body posture, we experience greater pressure on our joints. Thus, not only do we fatigue faster, but each run is painful, which further slows us down.

As we've seen in the past few chapters, our bodies are excellent at compensating enough for us to take that next stride—but that doesn't always mean those strategies are helpful for us in the long run. For example, if the head (upper body) is in a forward posture, it will not be neatly stacked above the pelvis, which means the centre of mass is shifted forward. To compensate, we may lift the knees (lower body) higher in an effort to propel the body forward. Or, ironically, the body may try to compensate by pushing the head even more forward, so as to pull itself ahead (for more details on how this occurs, see "Specific Upper Body Dysfunctions"). A strange vicious cycle is created: the foundational problem of a misaligned head is aggravated because the body simultaneously views it as the solution.

However your body compensates, it impacts your running gait and economy. This is why it is important to pay close attention to your upper body: if poorly stacked, it can throw off your whole form. It's like a tower of Jenga: if one block is off, it affects another block, and then another.

MUSCLES DON'T WORK IN ISOLATION

If you look at an anatomical diagram of a body, it's easy to think the muscles of the arm or leg or knee are responsible for movement in that area. In other words, to move your arm, you use your arm muscles, and to move your leg, you use your leg muscles.

To an extent, that's correct; the muscles associated with that part of the body do most of the work in moving it. But as we've said, muscles don't function in isolation. In order for one muscle to execute an action, it requires coordination and cooperation from muscles in distant parts of the body. For every main muscle executing an action, there are other muscles assisting or opposing the action.

Again, think of a rubber band: when you hold one end stable and pull the other end, you generate power. The same theory applies to the body as a whole. For your legs to move effectively, your upper body has to stabilise and function as a solid platform from which your lower body generates power.

At the same time, however, a rubber band can be stretched from both ends simultaneously, building potential energy on both ends. Likewise, the controlled rotation of the upper body above a stable core and extended hip creates a similar stretching at both ends, building energy to be transferred in the next stride. One researcher refers to this stretching as anatomy slings. This fundamental principle drives the forward motion of the body.[43]

SPECIFIC UPPER BODY DYSFUNCTIONS

There are a few common upper body dysfunctions that show up in runners, all related to misalignment that results from weak muscles and the body's efforts to compensate.

FORWARD HEAD POSTURE

The primary dysfunction runners experience is the forward head posture. The head is heavy and when it is extended forward, gravity acts on it to a greater extent, making it heavier. This weight puts a lot of pressure on the neck, spine, and even the jaw (as we saw in Mile 14). This is made worse when we run, because running creates strong vertical forces throughout the body that create compression pressures on the neck and the jaw, solidifying this extended neck and forward head position.

An extended neck makes it difficult to properly expand the chest when we breathe. Similarly, it's not easy to engage our core muscles to drive ourselves forward. This leads to the vicious cycle mentioned earlier, where we use the head to pull ourselves forward, further aggravating the problem of the forward head posture. We won't be able to engage our glutes either, which leads to an overreliance on our knees, feet, and ankles.

ROUNDED SHOULDERS

Ideally, the shoulder muscles should pin the shoulder blades back, against the upper back, which automatically pulls the entire arm closer to the body's centre of mass, which minimises the work the muscles have to do to keep the arms pulled in. In turn, this minimises the tension upon the neck, making it easier to hold our posture upright.

Proper shoulder posture also impacts breathing: the shoulder blades detach the arm from the chest so that the chest can expand with ease. Drooping shoulders constrict the chest and weigh it down, restricting respiration. Remember, the body is interconnected. The same muscles that keep our shoulder blades pinned to the upper back—thus preventing slouching—are also responsible for pushing the air out of our lungs when we breathe out. Thus, an ideal posture at the shoulder level not only improves your stability but also maximises our respiratory capacity and facilitates effective diaphragmatic breathing.

Good diaphragmatic breathing, in turn, strengthens our core muscles. There's an easy way to prove this right now: place your hands on either side of your chest. Take a deep breath and imagine using your chest to push out your hands. You should be able to feel your core engaging, as well as the simultaneous tightening of the fascia. Of course, the reverse is also true: a strong core means you are more likely to engage in good diaphragm breathing.

EXCESSIVELY ARCHED BACK

Connected to the core and diaphragm breathing is the excessively arched back many runners experience. An arched back makes it difficult to activate the diaphragm and thus engage in diaphragm breathing.

Weak core muscles are the most common reason for an arched back. Imagine your body as two parts of a stick, with a link in the middle. This link is your core. If the link is strong, then movement and power in one part of the stick will be able to transfer and affect the second part. But if the link is weak, the power will be lost and won't travel up the stick. It's the same with your body: a weak core negates the efforts of your lower body to move forward because it's not firm enough to transfer the effects along the whole body. Thus, one part of your body is moving forward, but the other isn't.

THE CHAIN REACTION

If we zoom out and take a look at the upper body as a whole, it becomes clear that a floppy upper body makes it difficult for the lower body to carry it forward with ease. The position of our head, shoulders, down to our back impacts our form and breathing, and thus our overall running efficiency and enjoyment. It's hard to enjoy our sport when we're not executing the way we'd like because we're tight and uncomfortable.

If you're trying to be a better, faster, and more conscious runner, you can't ignore your upper body. Make sure you include it in your training programs and are working to actively strengthen it. Always keep an eye on your posture and look out for compensation mechanics that may make it seem like your posture is fine when it's not.

THE LOWER BODY

IN 2016, I WAS BURNED OUT AND TIRED. I FELT DEVAS-
tated after messing up all my important races in 2015, so I
decided to spend the next year focusing on future-proofing
my running form. And that was when I discovered the significance of the big toe.

The big toe has always intrigued me. It's small, but it plays a
large role in locomotion. I understood the fundamental ideas
of its importance, in theory. But it was only when I experienced
it firsthand that I truly appreciated how it complements the
running motion.

When we run, we push off from the ground with the foot.
The ideal point of propulsion is technically fifteen degrees away
from the big toe, on the ball of the foot between the first and
second toes. In effect, our entire body is balanced on that point
during push-off, though it is equally important to have the
whole leg—foot, ankle, shin, knee, and up—aligned with the toe.
If everything is properly aligned, we create forward propulsion
by engaging the "windlass" mechanism. In this movement, the

plantar fascia stretches, like a rubber band, lifting the arch of the foot and creating a rigid structure, allowing the body to pivot forward in a more passive manner, creating a smooth motion from landing to push-off.

The big toe anchors the foot to the ground, engaging the windlass mechanism, which further contributes to the foot's stability. The stable foot allows for a synchronous engagement of both the inner and outer calves, perpetuating a continued balanced engagement of the entire posterior chain of muscles from landing to push-off. A floppy foot on push-off limits the effectiveness of our propulsion off the ground as well as our ability to absorb shock as we land, predisposing us to injuries at the foot and ankle region. In contrast, when the hip and knee are stacked in alignment with the big toe on propulsion, the foot is less likely to spin out because we are engaging the outer and inner leg muscles equally from the foot up to the hips and core.

The same year I discovered the big toe, I got the chance to participate in the Gyeongju Cherry Blossom Half Marathon in Korea. I hadn't planned on racing competitively in 2016, but I got an opportunity to work with a travel agency to promote this race through a slot at a half marathon, so I went with no expectations and little training. I'd been implementing what I'd learned about the big toe in my own running gait, making sure I was effective in my push-off; that was the extent of my preparation. I entered the race relaxed and curious to see how rolling off my big toe would affect my run.

That simple action changed my run. It helped me improve my foot mechanics and engage the right muscles, from the calves all the way to the core. I blazed through the course to a first-place finish, breaking the Singapore national record by two seconds. Inspired by my discovery of the big toe and its impact on my own gait, I co-founded a physiotherapy clinic two years later specialising in running gait analysis.

As runners, we're aware of how crucial the lower body is: we know our legs carry us forward, and that we simply need to drive them as hard as we can to move faster. But most of us don't understand the mechanics of the lower body and how seemingly insignificant parts—like the big toe—play such a crucial role.

Let's take a look at the biomechanics of the lower body and the elements you must keep in mind for the ideal gait.

SPECIFIC LOWER BODY DYSFUNCTIONS

Dysfunctions in the lower body affect more than our legs. Most involve our hips and pelvis, and are perpetuated through the upper body, making change difficult because of the built-up layers of compensation.

UNSTABLE PELVIS

The pelvis serves as a foundation on which the upper body sits, and works as a bridge between the upper and lower bodies. It consists of the pelvic bones (the two ilia) that connect with the sacrum along two sacroiliac joints and is held together by passive and active structures.

A stable pelvis facilitates load transfer between the upper and lower body, allowing the body to effectively move as a whole during the running motion. To achieve this stability, the pelvis (pelvic bones and sacrum) must lock into a firm unit throughout the running motion, with the pelvic bones rotating backwards while the sacrum tilts forward. The problem is that the pelvis and sacrum do not usually get held in a stable position because runners are unable to dissociate the different segments. When they try to tilt the pelvis back, they end up slouching backwards; when they try to tilt the sacrum forward, they end up rotating the pelvis forward instead. In either case, they end up with an unstable pelvis.

The most common posture among runners is the anteriorly tilted pelvis, where the pelvis tilts forward and the sacrum slouches backwards. In running, we naturally engage our lower back muscles to hold ourselves upright, but our frontal abdominals do not receive the same stimulus. The abdominal muscles weaken, and we end up relying excessively upon the hip flexors or the upper torso to drive ourselves forward. This running form perpetuates a muscular imbalance that holds the pelvis in a forward-tilted position. Without a strong core for bracing of impact, the vertical loading during the running motion creates a jamming effect through the spinal segments. Over time with repeated pounding, the weak muscles fail to support the back and the back moves into a greater arch, compounding discomfort and pain.

In addition, the sacrum is often slouched back due to inadequate strength from the butt to prop it up. During running, the impact of each stride along with the downward pull of gravity and weakness or tightness in the butt muscles can disrupt the pelvis alignment and stability. Butt muscles supporting the sacrum region lengthen and weaken, creating further strain on the ligaments supporting the sacrum. This creates excessive laxity in these ligaments over time, and affects their ability to hold the sacrum in place. The unstable sacral joint creates a sense of heaviness and ache at the tailbone, as if something is constantly pulling down from the back. To illustrate this sensation with my runner clients, I use my hands to manually support their sacrum as they walk, and immediately the heaviness goes away.

When the pelvis is stable, our centre of mass is aligned and we have more of a rolling motion through the feet and ankles. We lean into the forward momentum created by gravity to give us power, thus maximising our speed and minimising the pounding on the joints, thus decreasing the possibility of injury. When the pelvis is unstable, transference from force generation into forward motion is affected, resulting in jamming or jolting.

SHIFTY PELVIS

Think of the pelvis as a teacup, held in place by a balanced number of muscles around it. If one muscle is tighter or weaker, the teacup will be pulled out of alignment. Without an equal force from the opposing muscle to hold this teacup in place, the pelvis can shift side to side during running, which affects the path of force transference, causing the body to rewire a new path from distal feet to proximal core, which is ineffective and injurious. The body may also compensate by leaning to the side of the pelvic weakness, which can result in compression strains through the back.

For example, if your hip muscles are too weak to properly support the pelvis, the lateral back muscles will step in to provide support instead. The overworked and tight back muscles can hitch up the hip, forcing you to lean further towards the side, perpetuating an excessive side-to-side pelvis movement. Similarly, without adequate hip strength to support the weight of the body during landing, significant pelvic drop on the opposite side can occur because the shifty pelvis is unable to brace for impact.

It's quite common for runners to develop a muscular imbalance across the pelvis. In fact, we tend to develop a muscular imbalance over the stronger side of the body, mainly because we tend to depend on that side of the body more often. Right-sided dominant people, for example, may present with greater imbalances on their right side since they tend to push harder with their right, further strengthening their strong areas and neglecting their weaknesses, hammering in the imbalance.

RESTRICTION AT THE HIP

The pelvis position also affects the hips, specifically the articulation of the hip joint in its socket, where the femur (thigh bone) meets the pelvis. This means if the pelvis is not in an optimal position, the articulation and hence contact point of the hip joint won't be optimal either. This affects the hip joint's axis of rotation and subsequently the resulting mobility of the hip.

As mentioned in Mile 16, the hip joint is covered by a wide, glove-like patch of muscles called the glutes that extend from the front of the hip all the way to the back and into the tailbone region. The push and pull from these muscles in all directions centres the hip joint neatly in its socket. If any portion of the glutes is weak—whether the front or the side—then the joint won't be articulated in its socket, which will affect flexibility and mobility.

Strength in the glutes allows for effective hip motion independent of the pelvis. We have enough power in these muscles to articulate that joint to maximise its ability. We talked about this a little in Mile 15 when we spoke about the importance of muscle segment dissociation, that is, the ability to use each segment separately. In essence, muscular strength creates this dissociation. Remember, mobility is flexibility and strength.

Let's take a closer look at how this works. Ideally, when we're running, the hip should extend backwards. But if the hip is restricted, the extension has to go somewhere else such as the back. We may arch or rotate the back in trying to increase our stride length, compensating for the hip restriction.

From the way our foot strikes the ground, to the way our foot behaves when we push off, we are often obsessed about the foot itself, failing to realise that foot mechanics are often influenced by the biomechanics at the hips and pelvis. We are too quick to look at the foot, and footwear, as being the source of many running injuries. The new trend is to run barefoot, thinking it will solve all our problems. It doesn't, mainly because it doesn't solve an issue with hip mobility deficit (or any deficit elsewhere). The stride remains closed up at the hip with greater force engagement from the calves, potentially setting the body up for greater distal strain injuries.

It's a chicken-and-egg issue. Localised foot issues can indeed create issues at the hips, but more often, it's the hips that drive the foot issues. The foot is often compensating for the hip. For example, when one hip is restricted in motion, the body unconsciously tries to lengthen the stride to match the other limb by pushing off harder from the foot or by hyperextending the knee. Sometimes, to make up for the hip restriction, we overpronate, creating excessive tension in the plantar fascia, but pushing off on a pronated foot doesn't optimise the power drive from the hips. As such, while we might have a knee or ankle problem, it is often accompanied by a hip issue. Both must be addressed to disrupt the injury cycle.

Thus, optimal movement begins at the hip: hip mobility allows your entire lower leg to open up when you stride, subsequently allowing you to maximise motion and strength in the feet, ankles, and knees.

RESTRICTION AT THE KNEE

If we have poor hip, ankle, and foot mobility, then the position of the knee will be adversely affected. Think of the knee as a middleman: it can't disengage from what is happening above and below it. Thus, tightness above and below can restrict the mobility at the knee.

Ineffective gait patterns commonly result in an imbalanced activation of the knee muscles, restricting motion at the knee joint. For example, if you run with your leg turned out, it's likely because of an imbalance in muscular strength between your stronger outer and weaker inner chain of leg muscles. This imbalance creates a net pull of the kneecap outwards, restricting the normal motion of the kneecap as the knee bends and straightens during running. This creates excessive compression forces and irritation, resulting in the wear and tear of the articulating cartilage under the kneecap over time.

RESTRICTION AT THE FOOT

The hip also influences mobility at the foot. Tightness of the hip limits our ability to open the stride, which subsequently affects the loading at the foot. We can work on flexibility at the foot, but if our hips are tight or weak, we will never be able to put this flexibility into use. Weakness at the hip will limit our ability to extend the leg back, resulting in a premature lifting of the ankle during push-off, shortening our stride length. This also means that the ankle joint won't undergo the complete range of motion, and its surrounding muscles won't receive sufficient engagement as a result. Over time, the ankle adapts to a smaller range of motion and strength and loses its mobility.

Mobility at the foot is also maximised through the coupling mechanism of the ankle muscles supporting the arch and the toes. Any weakness can affect the ankle mobility, limiting a forward pivoting motion of the body. In response, the foot turns out, allowing for a forward translation of the body via a collapsed arch. Sometimes, the foot turns in excessively, the body pushing off over the outer aspect of the foot. Instead of translating into forward motion, the propulsive forces generated by the runner become absorbed at the ankles, knees, and hips and even into the back. This injury-inducing running form also limits the stride length and force efficiency.

As the runner pushes off the ground with his right foot, the right leg lifts at the hip together with the lifting of the big toe. Here, the big toe serves as a ladle, scooping the leg up with the hip leading the motion. The big toe remains lifted throughout flight, lifting up the arch and locking the foot into a stable unit to prepare for landing. As the foot strikes the ground, the body pivots over the foot and the big toe lowers itself to the ground, preparing again for the next stride.

In this series of rapid motion, what we don't appreciate behind the scenes is the coordinated coupling mechanism between the big toe, the ankle, and the hip. The muscles of the big toe, ankle, and hip work together to lift the arch. The engagement of the hip muscles provides further motion control down the leg to the foot. This coupling motion anchors the foot to the ground, allowing the body to pivot over the foot easily.

Press your foot flat on the ground and try lifting your big toe. You'll notice instantly that your arch is more pronounced. Now try lifting your big toe and bending it: your arch increases to its maximum height. This is because there is a coupled motion between the long and short flexors and extensors of the big toe, together with the muscles at the arch.

Next, dig your big toe into the ground and paw back into the ground. You should feel the butt muscles contracting. A stable foot allows for a more effective push-off, maximising the activation of the muscles up the chain. As such, any weaknesses in any of these muscles together with stiffness of either of the foot joints can impact the mobility of the entire foot and of the moving body.

A CYCLICAL MOTION

It should be clear by now that running is much more than placing one foot in front of the other. The combined coordinated functioning of both upper and lower body—with all segments of each side effectively performing their roles, carrying out their own motion in dissociation but just as much in coordination—is required to produce a smooth, efficient gait.

It should also be clear that this ideal gait starts from the hips. As stated earlier, we run in a cyclical manner: the left and right sides of our bodies communicate with each other throughout the different gait phases. If one side is unable to do its job properly, the other side is affected.

Most runners focus too much on the leg that is on the ground, because they believe they must push off hard from the ground to create force. They fail to see that the leg in the air generates an upwards lift by keeping the pelvis pushed up and preventing it from slouching backwards, all of which aids in force propulsion. Lifting from the hip, instead of the foot, builds momentum into the next stride, carrying the body from landing into propulsion step after step. This cyclical motion perpetuates a forward shift of the runner's centre of mass, allowing for a continued forward momentum upon landing.

If you were to go out right now and try to achieve this perfect gait, even knowing how you're compensating and which muscle groups are weak and which exercises might strengthen those muscles, chances are you would find it difficult to make changes to correct your dysfunction patterns.

Why? Why is it so hard for runners to change, even knowing what they're doing is wrong and potentially harmful? We'll explore that next.

WHY IS IT HARD FOR RUNNERS TO CHANGE?

WHEN NOVEMBER 2019 ROLLED AROUND, I WAS IN GREAT shape. I had won several duathlon events, and my running was on fire. I had just won the Sundown Half Marathon, and I was getting ready for the Great Eastern Singapore Half Marathon, the last race of the year. I was confident I'd win it.

One month before the race, on a rainy evening, I was running on the treadmill at my clinic. My colleague happened to be around, so I asked him to take a video. I felt fast: I was hitting my times, and my workout on the treadmill was going well. Honestly, I wasn't looking for running feedback as much as social media content: I thought a video of me in action would boost my presence.

But when I looked at the video, my heart sank. It had been ten years since I'd seen those pictures of me running on Facebook in 2009 and since then, I'd worked hard to correct my form. But here was proof of a whole host of problems, new and old. As in 2009, my knees were still caving in, but now it looked like the right knee was moving more than the left. I also wasn't driving my legs back enough, bouncing. And why was I always leaning so much to the right?

Part of me wished I hadn't taken a video. I was in the same place I had been all those years ago: with much to correct.

In retrospect, it's easy to understand why my form had changed. As we discussed in Mile 17, cycling had changed the muscular demands on my body. The long hours on the bike made me stronger aerobically, which translated into better running times, but I was also working out different muscle groups, and my form changed to accommodate those needs: instead of optimising 100 percent for running, my body needed to optimise 50 percent for running and 50 percent for cycling. Plus, I wasn't cycling the best either: my pedalling technique was unpolished, and my cleats were incorrectly attached, which was leading to an inverted foot while running.

Still, the video showed me a clear pattern. Over the years, as my lifestyle and activities changed, so did my gait. From student to working adult, I encountered a variety of stressors—both physical and emotional—that shifted my postural requirements and thus changed how I ran. Though I had been working on my form, it was naïve of me to believe change was a one-time thing. Progress is not a linear path; it is a complicated, winding route that shifts in real time. I had fixed the problems I saw in the Facebook video, but new activities and habits introduced over the intervening ten years had created new problems.

The truth is, change is hard. If we accept and embrace that truth up front, we are in a much better place to stay in tune with our bodies, consistently reflect, and act on what we know. Few people have a truly ideal gait, but we can keep working on getting closer to one that fits us.

CHANGE IS HARD

By "change," I'm not simply referring to our gait. Simply correcting our running form is not what we want; we want to be better runners, and that starts with focusing on and fixing our weaknesses. The moment we target our weaknesses, our gait naturally improves. The change I am referring to, therefore, is the willingness to reflect and improve: to learn to do this thing we are supposedly born to do.

Most runners just want to run. The more competitive runners want to run longer, faster, and more often. Change is the path to both outcomes. Change is the willingness to try something different outside of their habituated comfort zone. It is the willingness to examine our running form, unpack issues that show up in the form, and then to tackle these issues.

But change is not easy to adopt. There are several reasons why it is hard for runners, especially experienced ones, to recognise and work on their areas of weakness.

"MY GAIT PATTERN IS EFFICIENT"

Experienced runners have highly economical gait patterns. As they accumulate miles, their body finds ways to maximise efficiency and minimise energy expenditure. These movements are reinforced with repetition, and with corresponding changes in their nervous and muscular systems.

An efficient gait, however, does not mean a good gait pattern. Think of me at my peak: I was still winning races and clocking personal and national bests, but my gait was terrible. Most seasoned runners remain reluctant to change their established gait because they fear they will lose out on the well-practised and carefully honed speed.

This belief is backed up by the research: several studies have highlighted how incredibly inefficient it is to change the gait of experienced runners. They exhibit greater economical gait patterns and can transfer elastic energy in their bodies with less metabolic cost through self-optimisation. Any gait modification could increase the volume of oxygen consumed and hence the metabolic cost.[44] Thus, it's natural to assume a seasoned runner should just stick to their gait pattern.

But these studies focus on groups, not individuals. There is no data within the study that shows how many years each individual spent away from running while recuperating. In other words, the studies are quick to point out how economical the gait is, and very quiet on all the injuries it can cause.

Remember, an economical gait pattern doesn't mean a sustainable running form. A person who runs with her knee collapsing inward might do so because her body has self-organised to make this the most efficient gait pattern, given her presenting muscular and aerobic profile. Of course, you'll never notice the knee collapsing in for elite runners; their asymmetries are not as obvious. But their dysfunctions are present, and often present as fatigue during a race or during tough training sessions when their training stimulus exceeds that of their body's loading capacity.

"I DON'T NEED TO FIX WHAT ISN'T BROKEN"

It is true that experienced runners experience fewer injuries, though as you'll see, it's not necessarily because their gait is ideal. However, because they experience fewer injuries, they believe they don't need to fix what isn't broken.

The truth is, their form is often broken. They suffer from fewer injuries thanks to repetitive loading across their many years of running, which improves their musculoskeletal tissue tolerance. Moreover, their training programs are more sophisticated, with appropriate rest times and training that is designed to fit their metabolic and genetic profiles. The longer a person has been running, the more time he has to figure out what works for him and the more time his musculoskeletal system has to adapt to his style.

Thus, an experienced runner suffers fewer injuries not because he's running better, but because of factors outside of his form. According to one study, running experience does not significantly improve running mechanics. Experienced and inexperienced runners both demonstrate biomechanics that are associated with the prevalence of various injuries. It's clear that elite runners would therefore benefit from analysing their running form.[45]

"THERE'S NO TURNING BACK"

The more someone practises a certain style, the more comfortable he gets. Practise for long enough, and it can feel impossible to change. This is exactly what happens to elite and experienced runners: they've been running in a certain way for so many years, they cannot imagine doing it a different way. To them their gait is fixed. It's done, they say. There's no turning back.

It's true: gait can feel fixed. A runner who clocks eighty kilometres a week will have done more than four million foot strikes in a year. Altering any movement pattern that has been habituated and compounded over such extensive repetition will be very challenging. It requires an alteration of one's motor pattern, which is a complex integration of sensory and motor information performed at the level of the central nervous system.[46]

But it is possible, with enough motivation, time, and effort. Yes, there will be opportunity cost—time could be spent doing something else. Perhaps, we think, it's easier to get an "incorrect" run in rather than sacrifice run time with exercises and visits to the physiotherapist. Not true. In the long run, it's worth the time and effort spent on strengthening and mobility exercises customised to our gait. The whole process does require tremendous patience and perseverance, which leads us to the next objection.

"IT'S TOO MUCH WORK"

As mentioned, one of the reasons people are so drawn to running is that it seems effortless: you just put on your shoes and go. But running sustainably takes effort. It takes effort to get someone to record you on the treadmill. It takes even more effort to recognise that you have issues or injuries due to your running form. It takes vulnerability to recognise that a motion that is so natural to you may not be healthy and effective.

There is also the real emotional and physical difficulty of working on isolated areas of weakness when one is used to breaking age group records or completing tough and challenging hill repeats. Often, our areas of weaknesses are not as obvious as our strengths. We're used to seeing ourselves as fit and strong; it's not easy to accept otherwise. It's not easy to recognise that we can't engage our deep core muscles when we can hold a ten-minute front plank. Yet, it happens: I've had elite group runners—the fittest of the lot—unable to even support and lift up their lower abdomen on all fours, and I've had to personally provide assistance to guide them into activating these areas of weaknesses. It can be traumatic even to recognise muscular weaknesses so foreign to what you are used to achieving.

It's also hard to change because of how interlinked and complex our running form is. It's not only biomechanics that matter, but aerobics too. Hitting the optimal gait of 180 strides per minute and keeping that cadence going over long distances, especially with a good posture and form, requires remarkable aerobic fitness. Building up to that capacity takes effort, a lot more effort than most runners are willing to put in. That's why even an experienced runner's gait can often be dysfunctional: she makes adaptations to compensate for weaker aerobic fitness just to keep at the desired cadence.

EFFECTIVE, NOT PERFECT

The goal of making changes in running form is not to achieve the perfect, textbook form. Rather, we need to make changes that support our body structure and lifestyle, changes that will lead to the best gait for us, that will keep us from injury as much as possible. Once again, we bump up against the paradox of learning to do this thing we are supposedly born to do, and learning to do it so well that we are able to run sustainably for years to come.

That's the focus of our discussion in Part V.

Am I Running Sustainably?

RUNNING INJURIES

I ENTERED 2011 ON A HIGH NOTE. THE YEAR BEFORE, I'D landed my first sponsorship with Nike. I had won all my cross-country races. I was the junior champ in the 10K, having won the women's junior category of both the New Balance Real Run and the Nike 10K as well as the 10K in the women's open category at the Singapore Army Half Marathon. I was determined to keep my winning streak going. In my zealousness, I ramped up my training from several times a week to every day and doubled my weekly volume.

This was still early in my career, and I didn't know a lot about proper movement patterns. I wasn't a physiotherapist yet—I was a self-coached junior college student. Over the preceding four years, I had challenged myself across various elements of endurance, from swimming to recreational running to triathlons and then to running at a focused level. Within the running realm, I had attempted various plans recommended online and offline, from forums like LetsRun and magazines like *Runner's World*.

I was performing near the top of my level and found myself

acquainted with many passionate folks in the distance running arena. Yet not one person mentioned biomechanics, and though I knew of my awkward gait, I had no idea of its relevance upon my running efficiency. I just knew I was fast enough to beat most of my peers—to me, hard work was all I needed to achieve more.

As mentioned elsewhere, in early 2011, I had a chance to do what few student athletes had done: win the National Schools Cross-Country Championships for the second year in a row. Three weeks before the race, however, I found myself with a painful left shin in the middle of an interval workout.

Not again. I thought. *Another injury? Am I unlucky or what?*

I suspected it was another shin splint, which wasn't the end of the world; I'd worked through them before. I switched out some miles for some cross-training, while keeping the crucial workouts. In no time, I figured, the pain would disappear by itself. No biggie.

But the pain didn't go away.

I tried all the usual tricks for injuries—icing, heat rubs, stretching, massage, painkillers, acupuncture, herbal ointments—but every time I ran, the pain was still there. And it was different from the usual shin splint pain, which is diffused; this pain was more localised, which worried me. I was also beginning to feel the pain constantly, not just during runs.

Still, it wasn't so bad that I couldn't run, and the pain wasn't getting worse, so I was optimistic. Besides, the National Schools Cross-Country Championships was only 4.3 kilometres; I was certain I could get through it and win.

On race day, I popped a couple of Panadols an hour before taking my place at the starting line. As I watched the other competitors mill about in excitement, I felt nervous: everyone seemed to be in peak form, ready to give their best effort, but my shin wouldn't stop hurting. *Doesn't matter*, I reminded myself. *It's only 4.3 kilometres. It will be over soon.*

The race was held at Bedok Reservoir. It began with a short run across a grass patch, onto a gravel path to the turnaround, back across the gravel and grass, and then into the stadium, crossing the finish line on the track. Because of its unstable nature, the gravel terrain necessitates a greater degree of strength from the runner, which meant I had to cover more strides, with greater power, over the same distance. Because my stability was already compromised by pain, I really struggled to adapt to the shifting gravel. I willed myself to push harder upon my left leg, but the pain was limiting my conscious ability—my body wouldn't allow me to harm myself further.

Running on the painkiller high, I stayed in a position to win during the first half of the race. But in exponential fashion, the pain started screaming for my attention. It overshadowed my fatigue, and my form began to disintegrate. I dropped from first to third, and then all the way down to twentieth. As soon as I crossed the finish line, I collapsed, unable to put any more weight on my leg.

The next day, I went to the orthopaedic specialist for a bone scan and discovered I had one stress fracture on my left shin and four stress fractures spread out along the metatarsals and tarsals in my left foot. I was on crutches with an air boot for the next three months, and once I took that off, I had to stay away from running for an additional three months.

The diagnosis caught me by surprise. If I had addressed the issue when I first felt pain, rather than ignoring it for months, I wouldn't have been forced to spend months away from running. Plus, if I had understood that my awkward gait could lead to this serious injury, I would have started working on fixing the underlying issues.

Stress fractures and other injuries aren't a result of bad luck, as I used to believe. They stem from poor form and underlying issues that don't get addressed. In this chapter we'll look at some of the reasons runners get injured, while in Mile 23 we'll discuss prevention measures to keep you from being in that position in the first place.

WHY DO INJURIES SURPRISE US?

Injury is a tricky beast. In the process of achieving our goals, be it completing our first marathon or hitting that new personal best time for a 10K, we often find ourselves injured. When we do, we encounter the same thought: *Why didn't we see that injury coming?*

In other words, why didn't we see that breaking point *before* it was upon us? Then we could have taken steps to avoid being in an injured state.

The problem with identifying the breaking point is that it's not a point at all; it's a range, and that range varies from runner to runner. Some people can log two hundred kilometres a week, for several consecutive weeks, before they get injured, while others find that thirty kilometres a week is their breaking point. In either case, however, the key to staying on the injury-free side of the breaking point is being aware of the early signs, when you're still running without pain. And that awareness goes back to identifying the poor movement patterns in the upper and lower body that we've just discussed and then working on them through prehab exercises. Prehabilitation (Mile 23) increases this asymptomatic range in which the body can work, without the possibility of a surprise injury.

When we run with a dysfunctional gait, we don't carry the miles well. If the load still matches our capacity, we won't register this imbalance, so we'll keep running. The more we run, the faster we become, thanks to our improving aerobic and cardiovascular systems, so we don't see anything to correct.

But over time, the mismanaged load wears on the body. We develop small aches, but we usually ignore them because we can still run. The breaking point—the point at which we can no longer carry the mismanaged load asymptomatically—cannot be predicted because we can't see all the hidden damage going on when we are pain-free.

Running is a combination of stress and recovery, a unique balance of breakdown and adaptation. The stress of training breaks down the body; during recovery, we rest and adapt to stress to become stronger. Stress builds us up, but too little or too much can weaken and break us.

The key is finding a balance. If you want to maximise your performance as quickly as possible, and avoid injury, you need to figure out the minimum amount of recovery you require, and the maximum amount of stress you can handle.

To accurately gauge your needs, you have to develop a fine-tuned awareness of your body. This won't happen instantly. But slowly, through a process of trial and error, you'll learn to recognize which are the minor discomforts you can run through, and what pain needs your attention.

For the 2011 National Schools Cross-Country Championship, I should have recognized that my body wasn't reacting normally to the shin splint. My usual methods of fixing the problem weren't working—and that was a sign that the problem was bigger than I thought. I should have erred on the side of caution, but I insisted on irrational positivity. The result was months away from running.

A single race or workout or terrain is not to blame for any injury. These aspects simply expose underlying weaknesses that have likely been there for years, either in the form of poor movement patterns or insufficient recovery time. In my case, running in the cross-country championships wasn't to blame for my injury, though it was my breaking point. Had I not participated, I might have been dealing with one stress fracture, but running on the shifting gravel led to the acceleration of the injury, from a shin stress fracture to multiple stress fractures in my foot.

To keep yourself far away from the breaking point, you would want to increase the range in which your body can continue to run with no symptoms. It's important to minimise factors that could be closing the gap—that is, that could be reducing this asymptomatic range.

FACTORS THAT CLOSE THE GAP

Proper running form is really about knowing how to manage the body against gravity (knowledge) and our ability to do so (strength). According to Shirley Sahrmann, "The pattern of muscular recruitment is highly influenced by relationships to gravity, as well as the force required to move the extremity and react to external forces."[47] In other words, the human body is designed to adopt various strategies to create motion based on how we line up our centre of mass. Vice versa, the body also adopts strategies so that our centre of mass is sufficiently stacked up; if not, we will be falling to the ground. For example, when we run slouched, the body will naturally engage the knee extensors to propel itself forward. Activation of the core props the pelvis up and shifts the centre of mass forward. This allows the line of gravity to fall more anteriorly, facilitating the engagement of the hips instead of relying upon the knee extensors.

Strength allows us to take charge of our running experience, instead of succumbing to the mercy and detriments of a poor form. As stated, the goal isn't picture-perfect form. The goal is to run with a form that supports your body. In so doing, we broaden the range in which we can run asymptomatically and thus avoid injury.

The following factors in particular can disrupt a sustainable forward motion if we aren't aware of how they are impacting our gait.

ASYMMETRICAL FORM

Any time one part of your body is moving differently than its counterpart on the other side, you have an asymmetrical form—for example, if your right knee turns in on landing, but the left knee stays in line on landing. Asymmetry can present in any phase of the running motion.

In running, both sides of the body experience the same load, as we alternate between pushing off and landing on each leg. The body will run as hard as the stronger leg can handle, with the weaker leg playing catch-up. For example, weakness of the hip muscles on the right leg can result in greater inward motion at the hip and knee during weight bearing. This leads to increased demands of the weaker hip muscles and compensatory engagement of the stabilisers to perform more mechanical work with each stride in order to match up to the stronger left leg. The right leg will eventually arrive at a point of failure earlier than the left leg. Whatever the asymmetry, the side with greater instability and weakness will not handle the load as well as the stronger side, resulting in injury.

BODY LEAN

One particular type of asymmetrical form is a lean to the right or to the left. In earlier chapters, we mentioned that the body often leans towards the weaker side. It's the body's way of maintaining balance when the leg alone is unable to hold the body up. For example, a weaker right hip can result in compensatory body lean to the right to offload the hip muscles. But in doing so, this can create more impact forces over the right leg during landing and pushing off, resulting in the weakest links being injured first.

Most running injuries result from repetitive excessive weight bearing, often coupled with an aspect of movement and strength imbalance, such as leaning in either direction. At any phase of the running motion, the head has to be squared in the middle over both feet.

INSUFFICIENT STRENGTH

Distance running is a highly aerobic sport. As such, our cardiovascular system generally becomes stronger more quickly than our muscular system. Our bodies end up playing a tiring game of catch-up.

Sure, muscles get a heavy pounding, but because we rely on stronger muscles to drive us forward, we simultaneously leave the weaker muscles to grow weaker still. Because our stronger muscles get the work done, we're often surprised with an injury when we're at peak form. Just when we are able to run our farthest and fastest, an injury seemingly comes out of nowhere. Ironically, it is often at our peak that we are also at our most unbalanced. Building up our lungs and heart without strengthening our muscles is a recipe for disaster.

That said, there is a flipside to strength training: if not done correctly, it can actually do more harm than good. You risk reinforcing poor movement patterns instead of fixing them and making your running gait worse. Many runners simply follow videos and pictures on the internet about strength exercises and attempt to implement them without understanding the aims. Strength training should reinforce correct movement patterns utilised in the running motion so that your chances of getting injured are reduced.

INEFFECTIVE STRENGTH

In running, strength is only effective if it is helping with forward motion. To create the cyclical motion of the running gait, muscles work together, alternately stretching and shortening: contraction of one muscle group allows the other to stretch out, creating a constant cycle of storing and releasing energy with each stride.

To build effective strength that complements this coordinated movement, muscles need to be worked in combination. Building muscles in isolation can actually lead to ineffective strength in certain areas, which can lead to asymmetry and injury.

For example, many runners look to the seated knee extension machine to build their quadriceps, thinking this is what they need for more power in their stride. In reality, to achieve effective strength, they also need to work the opposing muscles—the hamstrings—as well as the stabilising glutes and core. Otherwise, the imbalance caused by overly strong quads could lead to injury.

One of my clients had very bulky right quads compared to his left, yet his right quad trembled whenever that leg was forced to bear weight, for example, during lunges and squats. We discovered that his right quads were hypertrophied to compensate for weaker hip muscles on the right-hand side. No matter how strong his quads were, they couldn't entirely compensate for weaknesses elsewhere. Without strength in the hip as well as the quads, he could not hold the knee stable. Had he continued without intervention, his right quads likely would have hit the breaking point, for there is only so much load they can take.

PAST INJURIES

For an injury to heal properly, the body needs sufficient rest so the injured tissue can fully reform. However, as discussed, injuries happen when issues with asymmetry, body lean, and insufficient or ineffective strength are present. If these underlying issues aren't addressed, the poor movement patterns will continue, and the chance of injury remains high. According to one stat, if someone sprains an ankle, she is twice as likely to reinjure it in the following year.[48] Chronic ankle sprains often result in lingering instability that creates long-term disability because disrupted proprioceptive ligaments affect the sensorimotor control and effective movement of the runner.[49]

In addition, a natural result of injury is the formation of scar tissue. If this tissue isn't broken down through massage therapy and strengthening, that tissue can restrict mobility and serve as a weak link in the kinetic chain. As such, with the combination of scarring together with the poor movement pattern still in place, the probability of the tissue being injured again becomes much higher.

Many of us succumb to the idea that our bodies are permanently compromised, and we will never be able to do the same miles as we used to. But so much of this comes down to poor rehab. If we are able to effectively rehabilitate our bodies postinjury, there is no reason why we can't reach the same heights we used to before we were injured (more on rehab in Mile 21).

BRAKING FORCES

Any motions that impede the forward motion of the body reduce the gap of asymptomatic running and put us closer to injury. These braking motions include vertical bouncing, side-to-side shifting, and excessive rotation in your arm swing or back.

These motions are amplified when we run on a treadmill. The backwards movement of the belt brings out movement inefficiencies. For example, stubbing the heel or slapping the foot may not be obvious in overground running, but on the treadmill, these motions will be louder against the belt and might create discomfort that may not be otherwise experienced running overground.

Research is clear that certain gaits have a higher injury risk, specifically those that involve braking forces that fight the forward motion the body is trying to achieve and thus place unnecessary demands upon the body, resulting in repetitive strain injuries of the smaller stabiliser muscles. Van der Worp et al. found that runners with a bouncy gait had higher vertical ground reaction forces, leading to a history of stress fractures.[50] Similarly, striking the heel against the ground when running puts more pressure on the anterior muscles of the leg, which then overdevelop and exceed the capacity of the fascial compartments, thus building pressure in the compartments and eventually becoming a source of pain.

EVEN ELITES GET INJURED

It's a common misconception that the longer you run, the more proficient you become, and the more injury-free you remain. But the truth is, for all their speed and brilliance, even elites get injured. In fact, many elites have had their careers suspended due to injuries. Many of these elites have to work hard behind the scenes to mitigate their injury risk, with a lot of time set aside for strengthening to optimise their efficiency, even if they were already talented.

For example, former British marathon runner Paula Radcliffe ran with a bobbing head. It was part of her classic running form, which saw her through countless marathon wins and a marathon world record that lasted sixteen years. It's easy to step back and say, "Well, Paula Radcliffe has won so many races. Surely the bobbing of her head while running is *good* for her?" To some extent, this is correct: her head bob might complement her running form and make it the most efficient gait pattern for her. It could be compensating for other irregularities in her gait, improving her running economy, rather than costing her energy.

In theory, a bobbing head is metabolically inefficient, as the movement expends energy that could be better directed elsewhere in the kinetic chain, but simply asking Radcliffe to stop bobbing her head would ruin the smoothness of her gait. In a 2008 interview with the *Guardian*, she revealed that "she has been wearing a mouthguard on her lower jaw to correct imbalances in her lower spine." And when asked if it will stop the famous nodding, she replied, "No, that's part of my running style."[51]

But her physiotherapist, Gerard Hartmann, recognised several areas of weaknesses and started Radcliffe strengthening her core and postural muscles. This greatly improved her running economy, reducing her injury risk and subsequently demonstrated a reduction in her head nodding. It was something that Radcliffe had to consistently work on behind the scenes. Without her consistent management, her head nodding motion might have worsened and aggravated her form.

So many elites have had their careers end over injuries, and many of these likely stem from ineffective gait patterns. Mary Keitany retired from running at thirty-nine due to a recurring back issue. European marathon record holder, Sondre Nordstad, has battled with a foot injury for four years, first picking up the injury after winning the U23 title.

Whether you're an elite or amateur, your injury risk is related to your choice of movement pathway. Running may be universal, but the strategies you use to run are not. These strategies are learned over time, and while some of them might make you fast, they don't necessarily make you less susceptible to harm.

But remember, you can't just force yourself to change; simply implementing a new gait pattern because you've read about it and believe it's better is counterproductive and unsustainable: it leads to more injuries, just in different areas of your body. Through exercises such as those presented in Mile 23, you must learn to organically change your running gait by strengthening the muscles and then working those new strengths into movement patterns, thus guiding your body towards a better running pathway.

What if you're already dealing with an injury? We'll discuss effective rehab next.

REHABILITATION

WHEN DANIEL WALKED INTO MY CLINIC, HE WAS PRETTY confident I couldn't help him. His injury was a "weird one," he told me. The shin pain happened in the same place every time he ran. He didn't feel it during the rest of his daily activities, but the moment he started running, it came back. This had been going on for the last three months.

Daniel was an experienced runner, and he knew his body well—better, he believed, than anyone else. He'd done all the usual rehab techniques: pain killers, icing, massaging, stretching, pool walking. Nothing had helped. So he was here, in my clinic, trying to find a solution but not really believing there was one.

On palpation, I found the pain was localised, close to the bone, with the probability of an inflamed tendon lining in the inner shin. I sent Daniel for a bone scan, which revealed a stress fracture. Clearly, the first step was to respect the structural failure and offload the fracture.

As you saw in my own stress fracture experience, that particular injury doesn't occur on its own; it is usually a sign of a dysfunction in how the body handles ground clearance or a problematic training plan. For Daniel, it was the former: his gait was asymmetrical. He ran with a lean towards the right, and instead of rolling off his big toe, his right foot spun out to the side. Because he wasn't lifting from the hips, his feet compensated for the lack of ground clearance through a circumducting motion.

Daniel's running form placed excessive load upon his foot and shin muscles. Over time, the work required to stabilise the foot was too much for the shin to handle, leading to the stress fracture.

I've seen many clients like Daniel: athletes who believe they know their body best, who believe they understand therapy and recovery but who don't really engage with their injury. Daniel only cared about fixing the pain because the pain was keeping him from running.

I don't blame him. As a runner myself, I'm aware most athletes have an unusual relationship to injury. They don't intentionally ignore their mechanism of injury or misreport symptoms, but they do so, either because they have a high tolerance to pain or have been running with the pain so long, they see it as normal.

In the end, most athletes try a combination of self-remedies to heal and get back onto the track as fast as possible. Sometimes, they *don't* wait. They try half-measures to ease the pain: they tape it up, they buy new shoes, they run on grass for a while. At each step, they test the injury over and over, hoping the pain will have disappeared and they can be their best running selves again.

But the removal of pain is not the only indicator of recovery. As you'll see, successful rehab involves several components.

Understanding the reasons for each part will allow you to work through each injury more thoroughly, taking away a greater understanding of your body in the process.

WHY REHAB DOESN'T WORK

Athletes often think of rehab as a generic process. You get injured, you rest the injured site, you do a few exercises to strengthen the injured site, and then you get back on the track.

But true healing needs more. Rehab is a complex and nuanced process that differs from runner to runner. Diagnosis and rest are only the first steps. In the case of Daniel, his first step was indeed to rest the injured shin and allow the muscles to recover. But if my analysis had ended there, Daniel would have been back in my office within months because we wouldn't have dealt with the mechanisms of injury, in order of priority. This goes beyond simply assessing the injured area. We can't let the injured site distract from the root cause. We need to look at how the body chooses to run, how it decides to compensate for its limitations. The answer to successful rehab is found in addressing the compensations that lead to injuries.

In Daniel's case, the root cause of the injury was his restricted hip mobility and his weaker foot muscles. For him to truly get rid of the shin pain, we needed to work on those areas to better redistribute the load and help his body move more sustainably.

Even healing something as basic as a sprained ankle isn't straightforward. A quick Google search will tell you to rest the ankle for six weeks, and then get back on the track. But that generic approach may not work for you: it depends on your body, your movement patterns, and your running goals. Good rehab is a dynamic and customised approach that follows several stages.

Why doesn't rehab work? Because people think healing happens in the rehab session itself. As you'll see, however, rehab involves much more than the exercises we do once a week. It involves a shift in our thinking about movement relative to the injured site, as well as the body as a whole.

STAGES OF RECOVERY

Let's walk through the stages of recovery so you have a better idea of what effective rehab might look like. Remember, this isn't a schema or guide for you to self-diagnose yourself. Self-diagnosis may only end up delaying your recovery. Rather, this information should empower you to seek help and take an active role in your recovery. If you're facing consistent injuries and you're at your wit's end, then this section will give you insights on how to think about rehab in a more sustainable manner.

STAGE 1: REST AND PROTECT

There's a spectrum to injury, from the moment you first feel pain to the point of not being able to run at all. Ideally, you want to address the injury as soon as possible to prevent it from getting worse. In hindsight, I should have intervened when I first felt the shin pain, rather than waiting until I could barely hobble across the finish line.

When you first feel pain and suspect you have an injury, the first step is to manage your symptoms. For the first twenty-four to forty-eight hours, make sure you rest the area, ice it, compress it, and elevate it (the acronym RICE can help you remember these steps). Your main focus should be to stop any movement that aggravates the injury and to control inflammation, which can get out of control.

Managing your symptoms is important because if you don't, the pain could inhibit effective communication between the brain and your muscles, preventing the muscles from fully activating. For example, pain and swelling, as well as joint laxity from damage to ligaments and tendons, can cause you to use the injured limb incorrectly. This drives poor movement patterns early on in the recovery phase, which often persist and are reenforced long after the pain is gone and structural healing completed.

Wherever there is pain, there is a movement issue. That's why it's important to head straight to a doctor and a physiotherapist. The doctor will rule out any medical red flags or structural issues that require further tests and scans, such as stress fractures, tumours, systemic inflammation, and cancer. A physiotherapist is trained to identify any movement impairments predisposing you to the injury, and to guide you in optimising your movements while managing your injury.

RECOVERY IS MORE THAN REST

Generic concepts of rehab sell you "rest" as an all-encompassing solution to your injury, but it's only the first step. Rest, braces, taping, painkillers, massage—these protecting measures are important and necessary, but they do nothing to rebuild tissue and fix dysfunctional movement patterns.

When you rest, both the injured tissue *and* the healthy tissue atrophy. The area isn't being worked out at all, so of course all the muscles lose some of their strength. Then when you move past the rest and protect stage and start running again, you're actually in a worse position than when you got injured: you're weaker overall. To regain your stability and control, you need active effort in addition to rest.

Balance here is key. You don't want to work out the injured area before it is ready. That is a recipe for disaster. You should be clinically guided to maintain mobility, especially in the healthy tissues, and provide healthier loading to the injured tissue when it is safe to do so early in the process.

In simple terms: Running develops healthy tissues. Excessive dysfunctional running breaks down tissues. Stopping running doesn't solve anything. That's why rest doesn't mean recovery—and the misconception that it does causes reinjury.

When your muscles atrophy due to excessive rest, they don't just weaken; they lose their passive stiffness, and "stiffness is the essential pre-cursor to stability and ... one of the keys to injury prevention."[52] Without sufficient passive tension in your core or back muscles, it takes greater conscious effort to stay upright when moving.

STAGE 2: RECOVER YOUR RANGE OF MOTION

The next stage is to recover your range of motion. This is achieved through a mixture of massage to work on soft tissue and scar tissue, joint mobilisation, and progressive strengthening through the full range of motion at the injured site.

As mentioned, traditional advice tells you to rest completely before beginning activity again. But it's better to train *around* the injury while you are rehabilitating it: this minimises the loss of healthy movement patterns while maximising optimal movement patterns. Think of it this way: your tissue got injured in the first place because it was compensating for weakness in the surrounding tissue. By allowing that surrounding tissue to further atrophy, you're making it difficult for your injured site to recover in an optimal environment. Improving the mobility of the surrounding tissue aids your recovery. For example, while recovering from the knee strain, you can work on mobility of the hip since restricted hip mobility can impose greater demands upon the knee and foot. When the tissue at the knee recovers, you will then be ready to focus your attention at the knee.

As part of recovering your mobility at the injured tissue, you will most likely need to deal with scar tissue. Not doing so is one of the main reasons people struggle to fully rehabilitate from an injury because scar tissue severely affects the mobility of a joint and increases chances of reinjury, as we have mentioned earlier.

STAGE 3: RECOVER YOUR LOADING CAPACITY

A full recovery requires your injured limb to have similar loading capacity as your non-injured limbs. Loading capacity is made up of three factors: strength, endurance, and power. All three components must be worked on equally. Often, the injured limb trails behind on one or more of these components long after "recovery," which of course affects the runner's overall health and their chance of reinjury.

Strength: By strength, we basically mean the ability of your muscles to shorten and lengthen safely under load. Running requires both types of strength: your muscles need to shorten to drive you forward and lengthen to absorb the shock during landing.

The key here is to build enough strength to handle various loads as well as fatigue. This is especially true when it comes to muscle lengthening. When you try to sprint without warming up or run hard when you're exhausted (for instance, at the end of the race) or when you have to transition between different sports in a triathlon, your muscles must be able to effectively shorten and lengthen in different postures or you risk getting injured.

Endurance: This is your ability to sustain your form over time—that is, over ten or twenty kilometres (or more), not just one. It refers to your capacity to *consistently* handle load in an effective manner.

Power: This refers to how well the muscles are able to lengthen or shorten in response to the load. There is an element of speed here: it's not just about the muscles' strength of response; it's also the rate of response that prevents injury. Plyometric exercises such as single leg hops and dynamic side jumps on the injured and non-injured sides can be used to assess and compare power in terms of height and distance.

Recovering your loading capacity requires continuous assessment of muscle strength throughout all ranges of motion. It's important that the injured area be able to move by itself throughout the full range of motion. Say you injured your right hip. You may be able to stretch your hip in all directions and even do the splits, but if you can't isolate the hip and move it without rotating the midsection or any other part of your body, then you still do not have complete mobility. As always, mobility is both flexibility and strength.

Because the body is so interconnected, the strength of the surrounding muscles will also impact the mobility of the injured area. For example, limited hip mobility will shift the loading towards the knee. This excessive loading can place unnecessary stress upon the knee, building up tightness over the structures at the knee and creating a set of dysfunctional movement patterns at the knee. Improving the hip mobility, together with optimising the upper body posture, can improve the loading upon the knee and thus provide a more optimal environment for the injured knee to recover in.

Begin rebuilding the loading capacity of your recovering tissues using non-body weighted exercises (i.e., using Therabands or manual resistance) and progressing towards using body weight, and then to using free weights. Weights teach the body to carry more than its own weight, increasing the loading capacity of the muscles to better cope with the shock absorption during running.

Next, the strengthening work should include compound exercises like squats, lunges, and bridges that work out multiple muscle groups together, including non-injured areas. Eventually, aim to progress to more running-specific strengthening exercises.

In all your exercises and progressions, strength rebuilding should be performed with optimal loading and movement patterns that reinforce the same demands in the running motion—upright stance, no leaning, minimised rotation, and so on. Again, we're not going for textbook-perfect form, but form that engages the muscles properly and allows you to move pain free. Think of it as building up good reserves, so that your body is ready to handle any situation without becoming injured.

STAGE 4: RECOVER YOUR FUNCTION

The last stage of the rehabilitation process is recovering your function. This is when you resume running with a good balance between rest and a progressive increase in loading, volume, and intensity across different terrains.

Often this fourth stage begins before the second and third stages are completed. Recovery in the real world is less black and white, less linear, and more dynamic. Healing scar tissue (Stage 2) and increasing your full range of motion (Stage 3) takes time, often months post recovery. You will probably be working on both stages when you rejoin competitions. It thus makes sense to begin working on your full function before Stages 2 and 3 are over.

That said, there is a risk here. The moment we rejoin training and competitions, many of us tend to forget we are still in recovery. We fail to monitor our rehab, and often forget to work on the rehab itself. This leads to reinjury.

It's difficult for runners to understand why rehab is important, especially once the pain is gone. Once we're back on the track, all the old narratives resurface: we no longer have time and are unwilling to choose between running and rehab work. Those who rush to Stage 4 and manage to stay pain free do so by cutting down how much they run. The moment they up their running intensity, the old pain recurs.

REHABILITATION IS MORE THAN BEING PAIN-FREE

Just as recovery is more than just resting, rehab is more than being pain-free. A lack of pain after prolonged rest does not necessarily mean a healthy body; it does not mean we've taught ourselves to move well. For rehab to be complete, we need to relearn our movement patterns to eliminate actions that led to the injury in the first place.

The body may heal enough to become pain-free, but that's only because the inflammatory mediators have been reabsorbed into the body. That doesn't mean our strength, range of motion, and loading capacity have returned—that takes active effort. Many athletes suffer from reinjury because they haven't fully recovered from their first injury.

Also remember that we begin running post-injury with limited strength. Because the human body is good at compensation, limited strength means the body relies on stronger muscles and neglects the weaker muscles—which means we often end up reinforcing dysfunctional movement patterns. Teaching our bodies the best and most sustainable way to move takes awareness and work, but it's worth the effort.

Finally, bear in mind that we are not working towards perfectly symmetrical motion. Our aim is to keep our imbalances in check as we run and increase the range of motion in which we can be injury-free. This range will reduce as we age, but we can future-proof our bodies by improving our strength and movement patterns.

So far, we've taken a good look at the practical steps you need to take to fully recover from an injury. But rehabilitation is not only a physical process: runners experience a variety of emotional states as they move through the various stages of rehab. In the next chapter, we'll explore what those states look like and how to handle them.

MENTAL AND EMOTIONAL ASPECTS OF REHAB AND RECOVERY

"LET'S TEST OUT YOUR CORE."

"What, like a plank?" Daniel said. "I can hold a plank for three minutes."

Daniel and I were in my clinic, beginning the rehab procedure for his shin fracture. He went into a plank position, and I could see immediately it was all wrong: his shoulders and neck were rounded, his upper back was curved, and his lower back was caving in. But he held the position with utmost confidence.

"Look in the mirror," I told him. "Your lower back is arched in. Now try to flatten your upper back and lift up the lower back."

To his bewilderment, Daniel couldn't engage his lower core to lift his midsection. He tried but ended up rounding his upper back and rocking his body forward and backwards instead. I tried to guide him with my hands, but his lower core muscles were not strong enough to follow through. So I got him into a modified position, on all fours, and did various dissociation exercises, having him move individual parts of his body one at a time, from his neck to hips. As we worked, a delicate air of frustration and despair developed and lingered. Daniel couldn't believe he was so weak.

I reassured him that he *was* strong. In fact, it was probably because he was very strong in some areas that his weak areas needed to do some catching up so that he could move in sync. I explained that because his core was wedged in between the upper and lower body, specifically between his shoulders and pelvis, he needed sufficient strength at both ends of the spectrum to support his core as it engaged. We simply needed to break down our goals into bite-sized pieces.

Slowly, Daniel transitioned from a place of frustration to hope. We worked through mobility exercises for his shoulders and hips, and he felt the change as he walked around between workouts: there was a strange sense of ease and lightness when he held his body. It instantly put less pressure on his injured shin and feet.

After some time, we revisited the core work. I got Daniel on all fours and he tried to flatten his upper back while lifting up his lower back. Thanks to the activation work we'd just done, he was able to guide his lower core up with my help.

By taking Daniel through manageable strength work, I gave him exercises that challenged him without defeating him so that he found hope in accomplishing tiny milestones. Without this kind of mental boost, many people quit before they're fully healed. The mind plays a big role in rehab: if you feel defeated, your journey to recovery will be so much harder. A good rehab strategy is to find positives in the smallest areas of growth, which helps more sustainable progression towards full recovery.

Athletes like Daniel are almost never prepared for injuries.

Most of them have invested a lot of time in building up their fitness, so seeing it disappear post-injury can be devastating. Physical loss is often accompanied with a perceived loss of identity, as the runner is forced to reorganise his lifestyle—especially the competitive runner, whose days before injury revolved around scheduling and preparing for runs. It's often not until confronted with the reality of being unable to run that these runners realise how deeply their self-worth is tied to their athletic performance.

Unfortunately, dialogue around the emotional states of rehab is often suppressed. People outside running view running injuries as self-inflicted. People within the running world often reduce the runner to their injury, with coaches and fellow runners inquiring about the knee or the shin rather than the person as a whole: their emotional and mental states are ignored.

This is made worse by runners themselves, who don't know how to deal with their emotions around an injury. They struggle with the feeling of being sidelined and their crumbling self-worth. So they don't talk about these internal, emotional aspects; instead they focus on the injury and the pain.

The result is a lose-lose situation: the injured runner fails to feel comforted, while her support team fails to provide comfort or effective help. The athlete feels isolated and may also experience shame and guilt: she may believe the injury was her fault, as is the inability to speak about her struggles. The runner feels lost: she doesn't know how to fix the situation.

Pain makes us acutely aware of our physical and emotional self by disrupting aspects such as the sequencing of our gait and how our body feels in motion, which usually escape our attention when we run. Pain brings the body to the foreground and disrupts the mind-body flow that we take for granted, thus putting enormous mental and emotional pressure on the runner.

A secondary set of emotional challenges arises during rehab, as we begin to appreciate the independent motion of the body's various segments (each with their own optimal patterns and roles to play) *and* their coordinated motion as a single unity. During rehab, we work through differentiating effective and ineffective body spatial positioning as we rebuild the injured site. It leads to a transformational shift in perception of their running, as we learn the relationship between the smoothness and accuracy of motion and its contribution to the development of our injury.

In short, rehab brings its own set of emotional and mental challenges, which mostly go unexplored. At the same time, it brings hope. We grow in mind and body as we successfully conquer these unfamiliar hurdles outside of running, unknowingly building upon the very same set of skills needed in distance running. The rehabilitation process is as much a challenging period as it is an empowering one, guiding us towards a more honest way of self-valuation, as well as serving as an opportunity to rediscover their physical and emotional self.

There is much courage and comfort to be found in this difficult period—far more than we realise.

PROCESSING THE EXPERIENCE

If you're in rehab, you already know what's going on with your body physically: you're in pain, you're stretching new muscles, you're trying new exercises. In this section, we want to explore the mental and emotional experience of rehab. There is much to learn from having an awareness of what's going on inside your heart and mind as you work through the physical reality of recovering from an injury.

The first step to coping with the emotional turmoil that injury and rehab bring is recognising the validity of your feelings.

The injured state can evoke strong feelings similar to being in a liminal space. The word "liminal" comes from the Latin word for "threshold"—*limen*. It describes a place of transition with an indeterminate time frame, uncertainty, and a state of being stuck in between. In other words, you've left behind a world of familiarity but you're not fully in another world. You're stuck in a transition zone, feeling alone and unsure. It's a directionless stage that feels chaotic and disconcerting. You want an immediate out, but there doesn't seem to be a clear exit. It can be unbearably tormenting.

This liminal space is made worse by the loss of the runner's identity. You feel like a runner, but you can't run. You miss the thrill: the dopamine high, the physical fatigue, the relief after a workout. You are also isolated from your community: no more chats during long runs or before and after workouts. Now you're just watching them from the sidelines. Running seems like a distant memory.

EXTERNAL PRESSURES

Elite athletes face an enormous amount of external pressure when injured. Their livelihoods are at stake: each day they don't train, there is a higher risk of them not being in competition form and losing their sponsorships.

Amateur runners also face external pressure, though not in the same way. When injured, runners have an acute sense of being left behind, which can lead to deep negative spirals when they log onto social media and watch their peers clock fantastic times or complete amazing training sessions. They begin to worry about whether their bodies will recover. They feel like each day they're not running, their body is getting older and older—they're running out of time to achieve their next peak. They begin to wonder how they're ever going to get to their next personal best if they can't even run, let alone train.

These may seem like internal pressures, but they are a consequence of living in the world that we do, training the way we do. No matter what level, none of us exist alone on an island; we're all constantly navigating what the world projects as the "ideal." These perceived external pressures feed into our anxiety. That battle is worse when we're injured and inching slowly towards recovery.

EMOTIONAL DRAIN

The rehab process itself is immensely emotionally draining. You're not just trying to teach your body how to heal or move better, but you are also coping with the realisation that you *can* get injured and that you weren't as strong as you believed. That realisation can add to feelings of defeat and loss, especially when coupled with factors of recovery that are outside our control.

No matter what body part is injured, runners of all levels typically go through several stages in the emotional journey of injury and rehab. Think back on the last time you were injured and see if the following sounds familiar.

- *Stage 1: Anxiety and fear.* When the injury first happens, you might feel unsure about the severity of the condition or what is causing the pain. As we saw in the last chapter, athletes have a complicated relationship with pain: they mostly believe they can just run through it. The realisation that you can't run through it and this injury is here to stay can create deep fear.

- *Stage 2: Alarm*. When you admit to yourself that you are injured, you might try your usual self-remedies, only to find that none of them work at reducing the pain. Your knowledge and experience—which you've gathered carefully over the years—are useless. You might experience great unease as you recognise that you don't understand your body as well as you thought.
- *Stage 3: Cautious optimism*. As you realise you need help and start looking for it, your spirits might lift. You might experience both doubt and quiet hope as you go through each new intervention, longing to get back on the track. This see-saw of doubt and hope is heightened by the trial-and-error embedded in this stage, most significantly in the search for the right practitioner.
- *Stage 4: Negativity*. At some point, you might find that a wave of emotions ranging from despair to despondency kicks in: it can begin as early as the search for the right practitioner, or a little later—after you've chosen a practitioner and rehab starts. You might struggle with the absence of running in your life. You might experience guilt and shame, blaming yourself for your injury and for not coping with the rehab process better. If progress doesn't happen quickly enough, you might also blame your practitioner. Your initial optimism can sour into disappointment. At this stage, you might either surrender to despair or regroup your emotions to stay on track.

You probably won't go through these stages in the clear-cut, chronological order I've presented here. You'll likely flip-flop back and forth in what will feel like a big mess. That's more than okay; it's completely normal.

Also, experiencing pain can be physically and psychologically draining, so don't be surprised if you're quite fatigued. Plus, you're suffering because you like running and being forced to take a break is hard. Be kind to yourself as you go through rehab. Don't punish yourself with negative self-talk. Prolonged negativity can delay your recovery as these negative emotions can keep you from a calmer state of mind, which can then lead to poor actions and poorer consequences.

Also remember that being injured and in rehab is only temporary. This too shall pass.

FACTORS OUTSIDE YOUR CONTROL

In every rehab process, there are factors outside of your control.

Even with the perfect rehab strengthening regime, you can't rush the biological timeframe needed for your torn fibres to heal. The strengthening process requires time: both to restimulate the torn fibres and for them to respond and adapt.

There is also a large element of chance and luck in the rehab process. Obtaining the right medical diagnosis is not within your control. Similarly, finding a therapist is often based on recommendations, which can lead you astray. It's also difficult to gauge the effectiveness of the treatment plan your therapist comes up with: you have to trust in it because you don't have the knowledge to assess it.

The side effects and ineffectiveness of many popular treatment modalities are often undisclosed to injured athletes, such as ultrasounds and steroid injections (especially when utilised on a standalone basis, without complementary treatment). In some cases, the severity of the injuries may be increased by these modalities. For example, steroid injections can create scarring through muscular tissues due to the physical disruption of the fibres from the injection itself.

OPPORTUNITIES FOR GROWTH

Difficult and scary as the rehab process may feel at times, it offers immense opportunity for growth. Learning to sit with and process the uncomfortable emotions that come with being injured is in itself an important skill set you can gain from rehab. Life throws all of us unexpected and often painful situations. Running, and specifically coping with injuries, can teach us mental and emotional resilience—the ability to bounce back rather than crumbling under the weight of despair and loss.

Sometimes, unhelpful emotions are borne out of fear or because we assume others will perceive us in a certain way. For example, we may believe fellow competitors are laughing at us for injuring ourselves yet again. As distance runners, we are used to spending a lot of time living in our own heads and being our own cheerleaders. If we are not careful, allowing others' perceptions of us to affect how we think about ourselves can make us very unhappy during recovery. Rehab can provide an opportunity to work on our self-talk and self-perception, even as we work on our bodies.

We can also be easily affected by what people say to us, or how much support we believe we are getting. If we feel people are uncaring or unsympathetic, our mental state may be affected. Non-runners who believe the injuries are self-inflicted and whose advice is basically "stop running and you'll be fine" don't help the cause. Here's another opportunity for growth: people may make these comments, but we are under no obligation to take them as truth. Our response is completely under our control. We can learn to find our own balance and calm by identifying our locus of control and filtering out the noises.

The truth is that running is not a purely physical experience; our mind and emotions are deeply intertwined. Likewise, running is not something that is separate from the rest of our lived experience. We are runners and daughters/sons and sisters/ brothers and wives/husbands and employees/employers—we're all these things at the same time, and what we learn in any one of these areas can be applied to the rest. Thus, what we learn as a runner, specifically during injury and rehab, can inform how we live the rest of our lives.

With that in mind, here are a few ways you can embrace your full rehab experience, ease your path to recovery, and practice life skills you can use in every area of life.

Be an effective patient. Don't focus on the helpless feeling of being injured, but instead concentrate on what you can do for yourself. Have a plan of action. Be aware of how you're responding to rehab, and make sure you're keeping an open mind to new rehab ideas.

Learn to communicate your progress with your therapist. Feedback helps the therapist recognise if things are not working and if you need a recommendation for a second opinion. Patience is a proactive process. Giving up would be entirely passive, causing you to dwell in negative emotions. Keep going. Recognise you are in another *part* of running. You're not outside of running. You're working on things required to run well.

Work on your emotional control. I don't mean repress your feelings, but reflect and process your emotions, as discussed earlier. Understand that this situation is not only unfamiliar to you, but also to the people around you. They may not know how to respond appropriately, how to comfort you effectively, how to give you the help you need, or even how to reach out to you.

Be open to change. An injury forces us to examine our sense of stability. In many ways, then, the injury can be seen as a stroke of luck; if we were healthy, we wouldn't take the time out of our running schedule to perform this same examination.

Somewhat paradoxically, perhaps, stability is a precursor

to change, but we sometimes need to embrace a change to see where we are unstable. We are often resistant to change until we experience for ourselves the need for it. Pain provides this need; it's an excuse to take a step back, reevaluate, and see where we are not as stable as we thought we were. In this way, our running form—and perhaps our life—finally gets the examination it deserves.

Clearly, we must have some stability and balance, or we wouldn't stay upright when we run. But because of the body's self-organising ability, this sense of balance often develops on its own, and thus can develop incorrectly. Proper development is often unappreciated and underestimated.

Developing more optimal stability and balance requires recalibrating our perception of equilibrium. This demands inner control and an understanding only achieved through relearning. Once that optimal stability is developed, though, it changes how we experience movement. A simple example would be walking straight versus crossing one foot in front of the other. So many of my clients cross their feet while walking but are confused when I tell them they aren't walking straight. Once I work on their sense of balance and proprioception, they understand what I mean: they can feel themselves moving to the left or to the right, and how to correct it.

A good sense of balance changes the relationship between the parts of the body in terms of intralimb symmetry, inter-limb symmetry, and the different body parts' relationship to the body's centre of mass. It also impacts your perception of the ground and the environment. When you are truly balanced and stable, you'll not only feel like you're running smoothly; you actually will be.

Yet developing this sense of balance is not easy: it takes conscious relearning and openness to change, which can be very physically and psychologically draining. Stick with it, because the rewards are vast.

Grow in awareness. Investing in a thorough recovery presents the opportunity to learn the intricacies of the body's movements. After miles and miles of running in a particular manner, we grow so used to certain strategies of moving forward that we forget there are other planes and types of motion out there that can help support the body when we run. There are movements close to the body and others that are distant from it. There are horizontal movements and rotational movements, both of which are present in forward motion and that work in coordination with it.

At the same time, our bodily awareness impacts our interaction with the environment. Before our injury, we may have thought we were running in the best form possible—pushing off the ground in the best way, moving our arms in the best way, and so on. Then we get injured and realise that's not the case. The same lesson can apply to any area of life: handling a conflict, solving a problem, and so on. Our current awareness of ourselves is the one which we are comfortable with but may not be the best.

Develop resilience. In a TEDx Talk about neuroplasticity, Dr. Lara Boyd says that our physical reactions and behaviours create new pathways in our brains. Whether we are pushing through a tough race and crossing the finish line or dealing with the physical pain associated with an injury, our response to these obstacles shapes the way our brain handles emotions, which in turn enables us to develop resilience in the face of future hardships. Our bodies, and our brains, remember that we got through it before, and we can do it again. This translates into greater perseverance the next time we encounter an obstacle, whether it's a tough workout or a personal tragedy.[53]

Remain conscious, in control. Most of us can run on autopilot very easily, but that doesn't mean we are in control of our bodies. Rather, it is often the body that is controlling us. We go along with movement patterns that our bodies have chosen for us without questioning them because we think these patterns are "genetic" or "inevitable"; we let our bodies take the lead. But rehab offers us a chance to take control back and rewire how we move to ensure a sustainable running career.

For example, we often run with our head pulling us forward. But if we were to be able to choose, we would be better off by driving the body forward from the core. It would be more efficient and more sustainable since it would lead to less neck and back pain.

This lesson can be expanded into life: how many of us bounce around between activities and jobs and relationships without conscious planning? Just as rehab can enable us to rewire the mind-body connection, it can also afford us the chance to take a more conscious, mindful approach to our choices.

EMBRACE THE SUCK

Trauma is not a requirement for growth. However, when injury does present itself, it is an opportunity for development and the reclamation of one's identity and authenticity. The very painful constraints of an injury can serve as liberating paths to freedom if we allow them.

Movement cannot be seen as purely mechanical or physical; movement is dependent on your thoughts, emotions, intention. Feelings are often expressed in the movement, especially when we allow the body to be in control. Have you noticed how you drag your feet on the days you're tired or depressed? Part of good rehab is learning how to take control of your body so that you are in charge and can shape a sustainable and satisfying running experience.

To truly get the most out of your rehab experience, you must recognise the emotional and mental growth you've made during this period. You haven't stopped running; you've acquired skills that can be used to help you run more effectively when you do get back on the track.

Above all, don't let negative thinking drag you down. Even when the process seems tough, remember that you are rewiring your body-mind connection to be as optimal and sustainable as possible. Of course that takes work! You have to disconnect before reconnecting at a more effective level. Embrace it. The challenges are difficult, but the rewards will last you for the rest of your running career.

And when it comes to mindset, work on developing a more sustainable approach. Difficult as it might be to see, the injury experience can be a positive transformation for your running identity—if you let it. Learn to be less vested emotionally in racing times and race positions; try not to base your self-worth on whether you achieved that personal best or won that race. Let go of the motto "no pain, no gain"—it can be inspiring, but it's not sustainable and can create severe long-term damage. Just learn to be more empathetic and forgiving towards yourself and the numbers on your watch.

This is not to say that recovery won't be hard. It's natural to feel upset, depressed, scared, and disheartened when you are injured. But the ability to grow through setbacks is itself a skill that must be learned. Once you do, it can be very empowering for the soul.

Without conscious management of our psychological and physical states, when injured, we can spiral further away from the empowered feeling that running offers us. We experience loss and pain. But we fail to see that our current state is also a consequence of running: injuries are a part and parcel of the running experience. With time and reflected learning, we can learn to minimise the damage or manage the hurdles to empower the next part of our running journey.

Everything you learn in rehab future-proofs your running experience. You learn to recognise the ineffective movement patterns that led to the injury and take steps to correct them. You develop proper training habits. You learn to see what is within your control and work within that sphere to achieve emotional and mental growth.

Growth happens *during* your recovery, not at the end. It's a pity we often underestimate the value of this transition into a stronger runner. Don't make that mistake. Injuries are difficult, but they are also opportunities. Make the most of them.

PREHABILITATION

ON SOCIAL MEDIA, I GENERALLY POST ABOUT MY DAILY work as a physiotherapist, how I help runners with their gait, and so on. A runner named James happened upon my posts and began following me silently. Finally, he was convinced enough to come in for his own gait analysis, though he was still suspicious about whether it would really help him.

When I analysed his gait, I spotted a few inefficiencies. I pointed out the priority issues and gave him a few exercises to try at home. We continued weekly review sessions for another eight weeks, reassessing his gait, reviewing the old exercises and introducing new ones, and progressing his strengths. We stopped meeting when I felt James had the sufficient skill sets to continue working on his form on his own.

A few months later, James contacted me and reported that he had noticed a difference in his form. He was running the same distance at about the same speed, but he found it easier to get lost in the music playing through his earbuds. He was actually looking forward to his runs because he didn't feel like he was working as hard. He didn't feel the same aches and pains in his knees and ankles.

As a result, James started running farther and faster without even meaning to. He went from running two or three kilometres every now and then, to training regularly for marathons. And he did so without getting injured. Because he was moving more effectively, he was able to enjoy his runs, improve his pace and distance, and avoid injuries all at the same time.

This is what prehabilitation can do for you, too. We can't think of injury prevention as being separate from performance. If we learn to maximise muscle recruitment and target strength training based on specific weaknesses and address the other fundamentals in this chapter, we will not only future-proof our bodies; we will also become better runners.

WHAT IS PREHAB?

Whereas rehabilitation helps you regain strength and function after an injury, prehab refers to work done to prevent injury from happening in the first place.

We usually think that prehab work is general strengthening exercises, so we do planks, or squats, or a whole range of generic movements and believe these protect us against injury. For any strengthening exercise to be effective, however, it must be tied into the running motion. Otherwise, we're just working out the muscle without strengthening how it's used in running, thus still leaving ourselves susceptible to harm.

Indeed, the whole concept of prehab work is misunderstood. Most of the strategies we use for injury prevention are actually useful in recovery from a hard workout or rehab, but not for keeping you safe from a muscle tear or bone injury. They help in lowering injuries, to an extent, but they don't do enough because they're not specific enough. Let's take a look at some of them:

- *Massage:* Massages are great both in rehab and for general recovery from a difficult workout because they help dissolve scar tissue. Its efficacy ends at some point, however, because it's not targeted enough: if we keep doing the wrong motion, scar tissue will keep building in the same place, and create the same forms of discomfort. Massages don't solve or prevent the problem; they only help alleviate the symptoms.
- *Cross-training:* There are many benefits to cross-training. It facilitates recovery from a difficult workout because we are building our aerobic capacity while minimising the vertical load on the body. It also pushes the body into a range of motion we don't usually get with running, thus future-proofing us to handle this range. But again, it's not specific: for example, if your gait is ineffective during the push off or in the way you land, cross-training won't help with that, and you'll still be exposed to injury.
- *Stretching:* This is a very general exercise that has limited usefulness. Usually, the tightness we feel requires specific intervention, but stretching lengthens the whole muscle. Strangely enough, we end up stretching out areas where we are already flexible; the areas that actually require lengthening often have a strength deficit and muscle imbalance that makes it hard to stretch them. Moreover, if we have too much flexibility, we may lose the passive tension in our muscles needed to generate force and help us go the distance.

The core of prehab is not stretching but mobility: we don't need the flexibility of a gymnast but must be able to move smoothly in the range of motion needed to run safely and effectively. Eliud Kipchoge, who set the marathon world record in 2018, can hardly touch his toes.

To make the most out of prehab, we must employ specific techniques that not only strengthen our muscles and move that strength into motion, but also work with our limitations to reduce our chances of injury.

FUNDAMENTALS OF PREHAB

Prehab is a combination of factors that works with our gait and body to future-proof our movement patterns and make us better, stronger runners. It helps us practise loading the body in the same way it will load when we are running so that the body isn't playing catch-up. Prehab aims to be one step ahead, preparing the body to handle the loading demands of each run, as well as the collective impact of many runs over time.

Here are six fundamentals of prehab.

LEARN TO DISSOCIATE

When we run, two types of movements occur: what we can see as the body moves through space and what is happening internally, at the joints. Not only are body parts working in coordination with each other—for example, the head works with the trunk, which works with the legs—but even within each part, there is coordination across its various segments.

For example, when we bend and straighten the knee, rotational motion happens at the joint that we don't see. This motion is made up of a rotation at both the shin and the hip joint. As a result, the hip and the shin must each have their own full mobility so that they can partake in the movement optimally.

Full mobility at each segment of the body is required before they can come together to allow for effective mobility as a whole. As such, we must learn to dissociate movement at each individual segment and ensure that each part is performing at full strength and mobility on its own. When this dissociation does not occur, body segments try to help each other in achieving the overall forward running motion. In so doing, they fail to perform their own roles effectively, whether that be providing stability or motion, the result being overworked muscles that are prone to injury.

REINFORCE EFFECTIVE MOVEMENT PATTERNS

Learning to dissociate the movement of individual body segments is essential to the next prehab fundamental: reinforcing effective movement patterns.

It should be clear by now that injuries happen because of repeated dysfunctional movement patterns; it stands to reason, then, that preventing injuries comes down to correcting those patterns.

We explored proper gait in Mile 15, and aspiring to that gait is crucial for good prehab. And the key theory you need to keep in mind for prehab is force transference. The aim of all good movement patterns is to effectively transfer force through the body so that we're not overloading a particular body segment and causing it to reach a breaking point.

For effective force transference, the body must be able to pivot on the stable foot that is anchored to the ground, and it must be able to do that with its own muscle movements. For this to happen, three basic principles need to be in place:

- The body must be upright and moving as a whole, not flailing or collapsing over itself. If it was, it couldn't pivot over the foot as a singular unit. This is why our postural and core muscles are so important: they keep the body together when in motion.

- The body must have a stable anchor on which to pivot: the foot. To effectively transfer force through the body, we need to have a foot that's stable and anchored to the ground.
- We need stable proximal force generators. This means our proximal stabilisers always have to be able to cope with the same load we're putting on the body. Running injuries are often a consequence of poor proximal stability—when our distal extremities are stronger than our proximal extremities, we face high injury risk.

Closed chain exercises can help us develop the strength needed to achieve effective force transference and thus effective movement patterns. These exercises work multiple joints at the same time, producing lower shear forces and higher compression forces, which mimics the coordination of multiple muscles and joints in the running motion. Open chain exercises, on the other hand, strengthen one muscle or joint at a time, which doesn't transfer into effective running patterns.

For example, the hamstrings muscles are important in running, but they don't work alone. They work in combination with the quadriceps, glutes, core, and trunk. Yet many people strengthen the hamstrings in isolation using the hamstring curl machine—in the seated version, the person rests their straight legs on the pad and curls by bending the knee down; in the prone version, the person lies face down and bends the knees up, curling towards the butt. In either case, the hamstrings alone are being worked, which does not reflect the actual running motion in which the hamstrings work in conjunction with the hip and knee: hamstrings lengthen to produce force when the hip is flexed and the knee extends to prepare for landing, and then they contract at foot strike, shortening at the knee while remaining lengthened at the hip. Because the hamstrings are attached to both the hip and the knee, they have to learn to contract and relax in different positions in relation to motion at the hip and knee. A machine cannot replicate this coordination. A better exercise would be a weighted squat, which engages not only the hamstrings, but also the surrounding muscle groups.

MAXIMISE SHOCK ABSORPTION

Most running injuries result from the body's inability to absorb the pounding that occurs during running. Muscles manage this shock by lengthening under tension during the swing and landing phases. For example, during the swing phase, as the knee and foot extend out to prepare for landing, the posterior kinetic chain has to lengthen simultaneously. During landing, muscles from the foot up to the hip lengthen as they absorb the shock going up the leg. In both cases, strength is required to move the leg properly to absorb the shock. When strength is lacking, muscular strains building into tears can occur at the weakest link.

Weight training, plyometrics, and resistance bands all teach the body to recruit larger amounts of muscle fibres under load, shortening and lengthening as needed to absorb shock. For example, I have runners work with a resistance band to mimic the landing, loading, and swing phases. I secure one end of a long looped elastic band and have them step down on the other end; this reproduces the landing phase. Then they "paw" the ground backwards (loading phase), and finally lift and swing the leg forward (swing phase)—all against the pull of the band. Performing the motion from landing to swing against resistance teaches them to control the lengthening of the posterior chain via the proximal hips and core. During a run, this control is demonstrated during the swing phase of the gait, when the leg swings forward after push-off. The posterior chain must continue to lengthen to create sufficient tension that translates into force generation upon landing.

MAXIMISE MUSCLE RECRUITMENT

As stated earlier, we can't talk about injury prevention as something separate from performance; they go hand in hand. This is especially true when we talk about maximising muscle recruitment. The more muscle fibres you recruit or involve in each stride, the easier it is to produce force against the ground, and the faster and further you will go—and it will require less strain to do so, thus reducing the chances of injury. A strong muscle—that is, one that maximises the number of fibres involved—is like a rubber band that can handle a great amount of lengthening without breaking.

As such, exercises that teach the body to recruit muscle fibres often build upon a lengthening motion. Here's a quick example: perform a squat with the knees moving forward and the pelvis slouching. Now perform another squat with the knees held stable. Sit back and stand up from the hips. Which squat felt more powerful? It should have been the latter. When you squat with the hips, there is a greater lengthening and tensioning of the posterior chain as you squat down, which then assists with the driving up motion.

The practice of translating stored energy—in the squat example, stored energy in the posterior chain during the downward motion—into movement teaches your muscles to recruit a greater number of fibres. It harnesses the elastic properties of muscles and tendons. Translated to running, the better the muscles are at producing force against the ground quickly, the less time you spend on the ground. And the less time you spend on the ground, the faster you cover the distance in the air.

MATCH LOADING CAPACITY TO RUNNING LOAD

Having good form is not enough: we need to be able to hold that form in context. This means the body should be able to sustain its form in the face of (1) a certain intensity of running and (2) a certain volume of running.

Simply put, maintaining form means the body is able to cope with the increased load being placed on it without deteriorating into flailing arms or dragging feet or hips shifting out or knees collapsing in. This involves strength translated into motion.

Our form must also be able to survive for a long duration. It's not enough to have a stable foot for the first kilometre or even the first five: as long-distance runners, we must sustain that stability across many, many kilometres. This is what prehab entails: building the body's loading capacity to handle the intensity and volume of our running (i.e., the running load) so that we're less susceptible to injury.

TARGET STRENGTH TRAINING TO SPECIFIC WEAKNESSES

As we've said before, the main value of strength training in prehab is translating strength into motion: that means using exercises to create force generation, absorption, and transference. General strengthening exercises make us fit, but they won't help us translate that fitness into force creation during running—and that's where we need it most if you're going to prevent injury.

To know what strength-based exercises you need, you must first analyse your weaknesses. This is what makes prehab work: specific interventions that fix your problems to guard against your vulnerable points of injury.

In the next section, we'll discuss assessments to find your weaknesses, followed by several prehab exercises to strengthen them.

ASSESSMENTS

When I see a client in person, I perform a range of assessments to pinpoint weaknesses. Based on the results, I then give the client exercises to strengthen those weaknesses.

As we've seen, every runner has different weaknesses and develops different compensations for those weaknesses. Thus, it isn't possible to provide every assessment to help you identify your particular weaknesses. Instead, I will provide the three that are easiest for you to do on your own and that tend to reveal the most common weaknesses I see among runners.

SINGLE-LEG STANCE

As you've read, running is a cyclical motion of synchronous propulsion—one leg pushing down while the other lifts up—that occurs at every phase of the gait. You can observe how efficiently your body performs this simultaneous engaging-lifting action by doing a one-leg single stance.

In front of a full-length mirror, stand on one leg, with the other knee lifted to waist height in front of you. Try to stand still for around five seconds. Look at your standing leg. Does that hip appear to shift out? Feel the way the load is distributed down your leg and in your lower back. Does it feel heavier at the ankle or in your arch? Look at the way you hold the leg in the air. Does the pelvis of the raised leg drop? Does the knee swing into the middle, instead of being held straight forward facing?

Now, switch legs and notice whether it is easier or harder to balance on this leg. Then look at your hip and pay attention to the weight distribution. Is it heavier in one place? Is it the same area that felt heavier on the other side?

This assessment reveals imbalances and weaknesses in your core and hips. The greater the difference between your right and left leg, the greater the chance that your running gait is also asymmetrical, and as discussed, asymmetry often leads to compensation techniques, which often leads to injury. If you notice a drastic difference, my advice is to see a professional.

WALK CHECK

Can you run without walking first? No, and as a result, your running gait can often be extrapolated from the way you walk since you use the same strategies to drive yourself forward. Analyse your gait by simply looking at yourself in the mirror as you walk on a treadmill.

Start with the speed at around four kilometres per hour, a speed you can walk with minimal effort. Is there a difference in your movement pattern when your right foot is in the air and on the ground, versus your left? For example, does your right foot drift towards the midline of the body as you bring it forward, while your left foot moves straight forward? When you push off, do you rotate your body instead of driving your hip back? Are you consistently leaning to one side?

Now increase the speed to six kilometres per hour. Do you

feel a jarring change in your walking posture? What was the largest change you felt? Do you feel yourself leaning back at the upper body? Does it feel more unstable on either leg?

Then analyse your gait at the minute level. Take this part overground, so you can slow or speed up at any time without feeling rushed by the moving belt of the treadmill. Don't walk the whole step: simply try and pick your heel up from the floor, with your toes still on the ground. When your heel lifts, do you feel contact with the ground under the outside of your foot or under your big toe? At the same time, are you able to keep the opposite hip stable or do you lean to the side?

If you aren't able to keep your hips square at any time of the walk, or if your head isn't squared in the middle of both feet, then you aren't loading correctly. This is probably because of weakness in the core or hip muscles that is preventing you from keeping your body aligned.

FOUR-POINT KNEELING

This is the modified plank assessment I performed on Daniel as described in Mile 22. You won't be able to watch yourself in the mirror during this exercise, so ask someone to observe and give you feedback based on the following guidelines.

Get into a four-point stance on your knees and hands, then go through the following steps:

1. Push yourself away from the ground using your hands. The tendency will be to round your back as you push. To avoid this, pull your shoulder blades together and down, and have your spotter give you feedback. If you are unable to flatten your back, then you most likely have weak upper body pos-

tural muscles—the muscles that help with bringing air in and out of your lungs.

2. While pushing your hands and pulling your shoulder blades together, lift your head from the base of your neck. Imagine that a string is pulling the back of your head straight up. Have someone watch to see if you jut out your chin as you lift. If so, you likely have weakness in the back of your neck at the base, which probably means you're slouching while you run.

3. Return your head and neck back to a neutral position. While pushing your hands and pulling your shoulder blades together, lift the lower core without slouching your pelvis or rounding your upper back. Imagine that you are pulling your navel towards your spine. If you slouch or round your back, you likely have weak deep abdominal muscles.

4. Now combine all four movements—push yourself away from the ground, pull your shoulder blades together, lift the back of your head, and pull your navel to your spine—and take a deep breath. In this optimised position, breathing should feel easier. This shows how keeping a tight, compact posture can help with breathing while you run.

This assessment is valuable for revealing weaknesses in the neck, core, and postural muscles. Weaknesses in these areas affect many parts of the running motion, including stability, breathing, and forward lean.

If you struggled with four-point kneeling, or any of these assessments, it's time to start addressing those weaknesses. Your ability to continue running sustainably and avoid injury depends on it.

PREHAB EXERCISES

As with assessments, I use many different prehab exercises to address the weaknesses that are revealed. The following three exercises address the most fundamental issues: inability to control sense of mass and keep oneself stable, because of weak core and postural muscles, and the inability to dissociate body segments, again because of muscular weakness.

The goal is to do three sets of ten for each of these exercises. However, if your form starts deteriorating before you hit ten, then start with three sets of five.

Following each description, I explain how the exercise translates to the running form.

PELVIS CONTROL

As mentioned earlier, upper body posture affects the lower body's ability to carry the upper and to efficiently move the body as a whole. This exercise teaches you to control your centre of mass, as well as the motion of your upper body over your lower.

Sit on the front edge of a chair with your feet on the ground in front of you. The seat of the chair should be high enough that your hips are above your knees. First, tuck your tailbone in. If you slouch and round your back when you tuck in, your tailbone will be tilted backwards, into the chair, and your sit bones will not be anchored to the chair. This is not what you want.

Instead, you want to find a neutral position. If you correctly tuck the tailbone in, you will feel a stretch in your buttocks and a deep engagement of the core.

Now, lean back from the waist, and notice how your tailbone wants to slouch back. Don't let it. Control that motion. Continue leaning back until you can no longer control that slouching action, then return to a sitting position by pulling the core forward as you drive the sit bones down into the chair. Here's how this exercise translates to your running form:

- When you do the seated exercise, you may find yourself unable to initiate and sustain control of the tailbone/sacrum throughout the back and forth leaning motion. As a result, you may initiate the forward lean of the trunk by rounding your shoulders or driving your body forward with the neck. Chances are that your body will move in the same ineffective way while running.
- The primary culprit in the slouch is the sacrum, more specifically, not being able to tilt your sacrum upright and slightly forward. To execute the proper movement, you need strong glutes and core to support the forward tilt, which lifts your body at the hips.
- When you run, picture yourself trying to maintain a slightly forward tilt of the sacrum. This is especially important later in your run, as you are more likely to start slouching as you fatigue. Maintaining a forward tilt leads to a continued forward weight shift of your centre of mass, which uses gravity to pull you forward. Though continuing this forward tilt may require concerted effort, it will help you run much lighter on your feet.

In running, acceleration begins from the pelvis, not from the head, shoulders, knees, or feet. This exercise mimics this proper sequencing. When you engage in a forward lift of the pelvis, you perpetuate a falling forward motion, allowing you to effectively speed up your strides and run faster. The knees, ankles, and feet simply complement pelvic mobility to generate an effective momentum.

SEATED KNEE STRETCH

Sit on the front edge of a chair with both feet on the floor in front of you. Straighten one knee so that your leg is parallel to the ground. Feel the tension of your hamstrings increasing as you straighten your knee. If your hamstrings are excessively tight, or if your core and glutes are weak, you will probably struggle to hold your leg up without slouching at the pelvis. If you can't resist slouching at first, then start with three sets of five knee stretches on each leg.

Here's how this exercise translates to the running form:

- The seated knee stretch mimics the running motion of extending your leg in preparation for landing. If you are unable to resist the slouching while seated, you will probably not be able to do so on foot strike while running.
- During the leg extension phase of the gait, any slouching of the pelvis will show up as a sitting back running form. You need to be able to keep your pelvis neutral and tailbone lifted while your knee stretches out before landing. To counter the increased tension of your hamstrings as the knee straightens, you need strength in your quadriceps, glutes, and core.
- Effective dissociation of your hips and feet allows you to maintain a forward acceleration at your pelvis and generate sufficient tension in the posterior chain of muscles for force absorption to take place on landing.

You can perform a standing version of this exercise as a dynamic pre-run stretch. Lift, bend, and straighten the knee of one leg, keeping the pelvis lifted and stable. Don't slouch back. Also, focus on keeping the raised leg directly in front of you through the whole motion. Your foot or knee should not drift across the body's midline. This exercise teaches your body to straighten the knee effectively, allowing for optimal foot placement upon landing.

BANDED DYNAMIC LUNGES

Step into a circular elastic exercise band and position it at thigh height. Stand with your legs hip-distance apart and then lunge forward by pushing your leg into the band with your toe pointed straight ahead. As you lunge, maintain a level pelvis—no rotating. Then step forward with the back leg, making sure you step in a straight line with your toe, knee, and hip facing forward.

To perform this exercise accurately, both glute muscles must be working at the same time throughout the lunging motion. When the front of the right leg pushes into the band on the way forward, the back of the left leg pushes into the band to establish a stable origin—and vice versa. The hip, knee, and foot should be in alignment with the pelvis and the rest of the body, all facing forward. The body should remain upright, not leaning to one side or towards the front or back.

Leaning back represents insufficient anterior core and hip flexors engagement. A forward lean often represents a compensation for insufficient glutes engagement, as a forward trunk lean reduces the need for the glutes to activate as much.

To make sure you are doing the exercise correctly, consider the following questions: Did you slam your foot on the ground when you stepped forward? Did your hips shift out in landing?

When you pushed up and forward from a crouched position during the exercise, were your knees in line with your body, with your hips moving over them? Or did your knees move backwards as you pushed forward? Your knees should serve as a stable point for your hips to pivot forward and over.

Here's how this exercise translates to the running form:

- If you have a hard time controlling body or pelvic rotation during this lunge, you will likely find a similar rotation motion in your running. To keep everything squared, you need a strong core—one of the primary results of doing this exercise.
- If your feet shift out during this exercise, chances are that you will use the same stabilising strategy in your running. This exercise will help you practise pushing the entire leg forward to engage the hip, rather than compensating for weakness by turning the foot or rotating the body.
- If you find your body leaning towards one side repetitively, chances are that you will do the same when you run. This body lean can create excessive weight bearing towards one side. Take smaller lunges and focus on keeping the head squared between the feet. If you still cannot achieve this, seek clinical guidance to nail down the root drivers to any underlying weaknesses perpetuating this.
- When you push off from the ground, the knees shouldn't be moving back and forth to drive the body forward. Rather, the knee should serve as the stable point over which the hip and upper body should pivot.

When you perform these dynamic lunges, don't rush the motion. Take slow, controlled steps and focus on driving from the hip while keeping the pelvis steady. Engage that core!

BE PICKY, NOT PERFECT

People often think of injury prevention as something separate from running performance, but I see them as inextricably linked. Prehab is all about learning and reinforcing correct movement patterns through assessments and exercises. When you learn to move in a more balanced and effective way, and then add load to these patterns, you not only prevent injuries but also run more effectively, which enables you to run more since you spend less time injured and off the road.

The key in prehab is to be picky and precise about reinforcing correct movement patterns. As we've said before, the goal is not perfection. If we can get to the place where our running form is consistently less wrong, we've done enough to prevent the next injury from occurring.

One more tool that can help you run sustainably and injury free is biomechanical data—but you have to know how to use it.

DATA FOR INJURY PREVENTION

IN MARCH 2021, THE ENTREPRENEURS OF A COMPANY approached me to be a cofounder for an app they were developing. The aim was to help runners understand their strides better. They showed me a minimum viable product: the runner would upload a short video clip of themselves running on a treadmill, from both the back view and the side view, and the app would judge their gait based on preset parameters of an ideal gait. The tech would look at angles of the hip, knee, ankle, and body swing across all gait phases, from initial contact to mid-stance to terminal stance. The runner's performance was marked in red and green, to indicate if it was excessive, suboptimal, or within the ideal range.

To me, the app was exciting because it automated what was currently a very manual process: the runner would come into a clinic, the clinician would measure their gait according to certain parameters, and then explain the results to the runner. Automation made this process easier, quicker, and more accessible.

Parameters for detecting one's injury risk could also be added. For example, if one's gait deteriorates very quickly when one's speed increases, then the risk of injury will be higher. Excessive body lean in one direction can create an unbalanced amount of weight bearing elevating injury risk on the side of the lean.

Secondly, the app stopped short of giving the user useful advice on what to do next. It told them where their gait was less than optimal, but it didn't tell them what to do with that information. As a physical therapist working with runners on a frequent basis, I could see how the app could be developed to help both runners and physicians. It could interpret the data in a way that enabled the early detection of physical impairments and injury predispositions. This information could then be passed on to physiotherapists for prehabilitation and rehabilitative treatments.

I also discussed a secondary use of the app with the founders: a machine learning component that would function as a human physiotherapist, guiding the app users on injurious gait patterns and how to correct them. We had a long way to go to develop this—the amount of data needed for this model to be accurate was large—but once it was fully developed, it would eliminate the need for costly and specialised sensor equipment, as well as the active supervision of a gait expert.

After I came onboard, we set about developing a product for the market. To make our visions reality, we needed extensive data to feed into the software. We recruited the first batch of fifty-five runners across a spectrum of running abilities and experience so we could study their gaits and develop advanced data analytics.

We collected information such as their height and weight, their current training and running levels, any past and present injuries, and any interventions they had done. We put these runners on a treadmill, and collected videos of them running at different speeds, from both a back and side view. I then analysed those videos to score different aspects of their gait on a 1-to-5 scale, with 1 indicating least severe and 5 indicating most severe.

For example, say a runner was leaning excessively to the left. Under the parameter "leaning to the left" his score would be 5, while under the parameter "leaning to the right" his score would be 1. I did the same process for aspects such as leaning back or forward, the degree of hip shift, body rotation, arm swing, and so on. I entered these scores into the software so that it had fifty-five models to choose from. The hope was that, with enough data, our app would be able to learn and compare any new user's running style with the models computed and then analyse their running gait as a human physiotherapist would.

Unfortunately, we didn't get enough funding to complete our development. But the research study and the data I collected for the project were deeply eye-opening. Because I had collected data on the recruits' past and present injuries and because several of them were my old patients—which meant I was already familiar with their running forms and biases—I was able to see how biomechanical data mapped onto injury risk at an in-depth level.

For example, runners who leaned more to the left developed more injuries on that side across the data sample. This is consistent with current research on the subject: the more weight and strain you put on one side, the more injuries you develop. This is why runners keep getting injured on the same side. Runners who had limited movement through the hips relied more on their knees and feet for force production and absorption, which increased the chances of repetitive injuries in these two areas.

If understood and used properly, biomechanical data can

clearly aid in gait analysis and identifying potential injury patterns. It objectifies our running form, serving as a mirror that reflects truth on the false fluidity we often feel. It's like Braille to the blind. When we run, we are blind to our form until someone gives us feedback or when we see a video of ourselves running. With data, we no longer need either.

As with video, however, these numbers can be useless and sometimes harmful without understanding how to use it for analysis and correction. In the absence of understanding, runners might try to force out the numbers to arrive within a more optimal range. Knowing optimal cadence is 180 steps per minute, for example, they might try to rush their steps or take other actions that will end up doing more harm than good.

Let's take a closer look at the types of biomechanical data that are out there and the ways to use it most effectively.

BIOMECHANICAL DATA AND ITS USEFULNESS

If we were to boil down the basic goal of running, it would be to run as quickly as possible over a given distance. At its core, running speed is the product of stride length (how much ground you cover with each step) and cadence (how fast your legs move). To run as quickly as possible, then, we must:

- Maximise distance covered overground
- Maximise leg speed
- Minimise vertical bounce
- Minimise foot-to-ground contact time

Many smartwatches provide information that can guide us towards achieving this goal, *if* we understand the numbers and know how to apply the information. More importantly, that data can provide greater insight into the loads running places on our bodies, which can be instrumental in preventing injuries.

DATA THAT'S USEFUL

Some smartwatches have become very advanced, providing information on everything from distance and pace to heart rate and VO2 max. However, without sufficient understanding of this information, the usefulness to application is limited. We're going to focus on five pieces of information that can be quite useful in injury prevention and running efficiency.

Cadence

In short, cadence refers to the total number of steps taken per minute. In other words, it's the frequency at which your feet land on the ground.

At the 1984 Olympics, running coach and Olympic medalist Jack Daniels sat in the stands and counted the steps of the runners whizzing by. After observing competitors in various distances, Daniels concluded that most had a cadence of approximately 180 steps per minute.

What would cause someone to have a lower cadence? Too much air time, excessive braking, or overstriding are three possibilities. Higher cadences are associated with lower vertical oscillation, or bounce, and shorter ground contact time, both of which reduce loading rates and thus injury risk.[54] A 2019 study found that ultramarathoners naturally increase their cadence and reduce their stride length to minimise ground contact time, so as to minimise fatigue and impact over their legs over the course of the race.[55]

Let's say your smartwatch shows your cadence averages 160,

instead of 180. If you're like many runners, you may think you can increase this number by quickening your stride, but it's not this simple. Cadence is the body's way of figuring out the best leg speed to achieve the fastest timing based on the target distance. As such, it may be unproductive and even injurious to force out an optimal cadence. The result could be increased back arching, knees turning in, or hips shifting out because you are trying to force a gait without sufficient hip strength and without effective muscle recruitment patterns at the hip, knee, and ankle.

How can you safely bring that number up without forcing an unnatural gait?

- Work on increasing your aerobic fitness. An unfit body cannot maintain a high cadence because it needs the endurance to sustain an opened-up stride at a certain rate.
- Incorporate running drills to improve leg stiffness, which increases the storage and release of energy in the muscles. Skipping, bounding, side hops—basically any drill that forces you to push off the ground quickly—can increase your cadence.
- Combine hip mobility and core/postural work into your routine to encourage landing closer to your centre of mass. Better hip mobility and core strength will naturally optimise your cadence and stride length.

The more you rely on your hips and core to drive you forward, as opposed to your calves and feet, the quicker your cadence will be. You will naturally open your stride and shift your step frequency into a more optimal range.

Stride Length

Stride length is the distance between successive points of initial contact between the foot and the ground. Unlike cadence, which takes into account both feet, stride length refers to successive points of contact on the same foot.

Short stride length might indicate weaknesses in the hip area that limit the stride from opening up and result in compensations that could eventually lead to injuries if not addressed. If short stride length results from lack of hip drive, push-off will be premature, which means the ankle unit will not be optimally engaged and musculotendinous units in the legs will not be fully stretched. As a result, you don't store enough energy in the push-off, which means you don't have as much force driving you forward on landing. When the ankle unit contracts and shortens without going through an adequate stretch, it can get tightened and overworked, resulting in repetitive strain injuries such as Achilles tendonitis.

On the other hand, long strides accompanied by low cadence can potentially lead to overstriding, which can lead to excessive braking forces and subsequent injuries through the knees and ankles, due to the excessive deceleration forces going through them. This also limits the perpetuation of a forward motion, translating to slower speeds.

Maximising stride length is not about pushing harder off the ground or consciously lengthening your stride. In fact, simply increasing stride length, without increasing cadence, can ultimately reduce the efficiency of the body's elastic recoil mechanism and slow you down. Likewise, solely speeding up your legs without increasing stride length can tire your legs prematurely and limit speed. It's the combination of optimal cadence and stride length that produces efficiency and speed.

To safely optimise your stride length, you need to maximise

the triple extension at push-off—initiated at the hip, extended to the knee, and completed at the foot/ankle unit. Stride length is then perpetuated with the leg swing as it drives an upward momentum from the hip and knee lift and facilitated by a forward body lean via a well-stacked upper and lower body. The banded lunges exercises introduced in Mile 23 can help you work on opening the stride from the hip.

Vertical Ratio

Vertical ratio is a cost-to-benefit ratio where the cost is the vertical oscillation (ground clearance or bounce) and the benefit is the distance travelled (stride length). The lower the vertical ratio the better, since spending more time in the air without covering much ground is inefficient.

Optimal VR, which is generally below 10 percent, is achieved by minimising vertical oscillation (VO), while maximising stride length. Most smartwatches will show VO as well as VR, and the ideal range for the former is five to ten centimetres. A number lower than five indicates lack of flight and length in stride, resulting in lack of power and slower pace. It usually means the runner is spending more time on the ground (higher ground contact time, discussed in the next section) and less time in the air.

VO higher than ten means the runner is probably expending too much energy in vertical movement, which doesn't translate to forward progress. High VO also means higher impact when landing, which can significantly increase injury risk.

What can you do if you learn that your high VO is causing a high VR?

- Check your gait: are you sitting back when you run or are

you maintaining a forward lean? Runners who forcefully push off from the ground without much forward lean tend to have a higher bounce. An effective forward lean requires strong core and postural muscles. The prehab exercises in Mile 23 can help you strengthen those muscles and maintain a forward lean that begins from the pelvis.

- Premature push-off often results from weakness in the hip, resulting from excessive knee and ankle motion, causing an upward vertical drive. Strengthen your hip muscles with hip mobility work such as the banded dynamic lunges (Mile 23).

In combination with the suggestions for maximising stride length, these tips can help you achieve an optimal VR, faster times, and less chance of injury.

Ground Contact Time

Ground contact time (GCT) refers to the turnover duration from landing to push-off. In general, the more ineffective the form, whether because you're overpronating or your hip shifts out, the more time you'll spend in contact with the ground and the greater the energetic cost of your form.

The optimal GCT range is generally below 300 milliseconds. If you find that your ground contact time is more than this, you can work on reducing that time in a few ways:

- Improve leg stiffness through running drills like skipping, bounding, and side hopping. As with cadence, exercises that force you to push off the ground quickly will decrease the amount of time each foot spends on the ground.
- Shoes with stiffer midsoles, specifically those with carbon-fibre plates such as the Nike Vaporfly, can facilitate usage

of the rebound energy you're creating with each foot strike. But don't even think of relying on these shoes! The better your form, the better you can harness the benefits of this technology.

- Incorporate speed workouts and a strength routine as these sharpen your ability to engage the fast-twitch fibres. The more fast-twitch muscles you recruit in your gait, the shorter your ground contact times will be.
- Practising running at faster speeds also helps to sharpen the body's neuromuscular system in its interaction with the ground. Try adding downhill running or stridings (short sprints) to your workout regimen.

A study comparing experienced and inexperienced runners revealed that inexperienced runners tend to have longer GCTs and demonstrate more ankle movement while the experienced tend to demonstrate more proximal movement at the hip.[56] An increase in ground contact time indicates a reduction in efficiency in force production. One can be running at the same speed, but an increase in ground contact time can indicate a fatigue in form, whereby force production is no longer as effective. When fatigued, novice runners in particular tend to lean forward more at the trunk and increase the width of their stride, both of which are inefficient and result in slower times.[57]

Research has also found that certain injuries are associated with increased GCT. "Runner's knee," for example, is connected with an underlying gait pattern that involves an increased turning out of the feet and increased pelvic drop, which results in increased time spent overground, delaying the speed from landing to propulsion.[58]

Ground Contact Time Balance

The final piece of data that can be most useful is Ground Contact Time Balance, which refers to the percentage of time one foot spends on the ground compared to the other.

GCT imbalance has the potential of increasing the body's metabolic costs. Research found that caloric unit costs were 0.0354 kcal·kg^{-1}·km^{-1} greater for every 1 percent increase in GCT imbalance. Let's say a male runner weighing sixty kilograms has a GCT percentage of 49 percent for the right foot and 51 percent for the left. That means he has a 2 percent GCT imbalance, which means that in a marathon, he's expending an additional 180 kilocalories. Such an increased rate of energy depletion and reduced running economy would presumably impair performance.[59]

In addition, this imbalance might have implications for muscle strength and activation patterns. This same study revealed significantly greater lean muscle mass imbalances in runners with higher GCT imbalances, compared with runners with lower GCT imbalances. Such muscle mass imbalances could perpetuate an asymmetrical gait, building up a greater injury risk.

So, how do you reduce such imbalances?

- Often, performing double-legged strength work such as squats or deadlifts may hide strength imbalances within the form. Performing these same exercises on one leg can help to identify and address strength asymmetries more effectively as you focus your attention on proper movement patterns across each leg.
- Strengthening your core and postural muscles can reduce sloppiness in form, which means the body spends less time stabilising itself on the ground. The best core-strengthening

exercise is the plank. Remember to keep your head and hips lifted and don't round your shoulders.

We cannot force out GCT balance based on numbers alone; trying to do so often leads to more dysfunctions. These exercises can strengthen our weaker areas and reduce imbalances, but because GCT numbers don't show the root cause of imbalance, the exercises can only go so far. To make best use of the GCT balance data, we need to look at it in combination with the other metrics to gain a more accurate picture of what's happening.

DATA THAT'S NOT USEFUL

Since 2014, running power measurement tools have started surfacing in the market, developed and exported from the usage of power metres in cycling. While the data provided by these tools is helpful to cyclists, it is not as useful for runners.

Cycling power metres measure the force that is applied during pedalling and convert that force to power, or the rate of energy use. For a cyclist, the power metre provides real-time feedback on how hard the body is working by measuring mechanical power. The greater the effort—that is, the actual pushing and pulling of the pedal—the greater the force production, and the greater the mechanical power.

This kind of measurement is possible for cycling because effort exerted more closely translates to the pedalling motion: the harder you pedal, the more power you generate, and the faster you move. The motion and effort are enclosed in the bike, and the power produced is driven through the bike into the ground.

In running, however, the "mechanical" work of pushing off and landing does not as neatly translate into power—pushing off harder from the ground does not necessarily translate into greater overground coverage as it does in cycling. This is because other factors are involved. For example, pushing off harder might simply feed into your compensatory motion, thereby limiting the very forward motion you are trying to create. The more you compensate, the more energy you put into stabilising the body instead of generating power. Some effort also goes into managing other planes of motion. In cycling, each pedal translates into force production; you're only working in one plane of motion. In running, however, you have to control body rotation, arm swing, pelvis tuck, and more to keep the body stable and to generate the most power. In addition, when you run you interact directly with the ground, which means you are absorbing forces with each step, in addition to producing them.

Thus, trying to measure and quantify mechanical power in running is nearly impossible. As a result, each smartwatch manufacturer comes up with their own method of computing power, so that the numbers generated are essentially useless. An article by Alex Hutchinson demonstrated that the power metre numbers indicated on the Stryde device represent more "the instantaneous metabolic demand rather than power."[60] In other words, the power metre number represents the energy consumed by your muscles, rather than force production by your muscles. In this case, a high number does not represent high power and forward motion. It could actually show that your body is coping with the energetic demands of a deteriorating form. Misunderstanding this number and thinking the higher the better could lead to disastrous results.

FUTURE OF DATA

Biomechanical data can be incredibly useful for understanding how your gait might be dysfunctional and what you need to correct for. However, most runners process and use the data ineffectively. There's a need for pairing technology with input from healthcare professionals and feedback about injury history and gait issues provided by the runner—as well as the guidelines provided in this chapter. Only then will currently accessible yet inaccessible data become useful.

There is simply no way of utilising biomechanical data from your running to improve your form in real-time. This data needs to be analysed post-run, the understanding then applied into focused strength work and training plans based on the particular weaknesses and compensations revealed in the numbers.

Part of what makes data useful also lies within the runner. Without the willingness to pay attention to his body and then to work upon his weaknesses, no matter how smart AI becomes, the usefulness of technology will always be limited. Until the day we have the body of a robot, strength will always come from within and to harness this strength, we will always have to tune into our body to learn its own unique ways of movement. Any translation of data to improve speed and prevent injuries comes from addressing the causes of our inefficiencies, and not merely the imitation of a more correct data set or via cues verbally or visually. There is a reason for the way the body runs, because of weakness, tightness, neuromuscular deficits, pain, or compensatory strategies.

It's disappointing that we never managed to push our app to the market because the potential is immense. Understanding how to analyse and apply this data is invaluable. An app that incorporates the learning of the data by a human therapist can

automate this understanding into application, which would
then allow for data to be made useful, for example, in the creation of individual training plans.

MORE FROM YOUR MILES

IN HIS BOOK *ENDURE: MIND, BODY, AND THE CURIOUSLY Elastic Limits of Human Performance*, Alex Hutchinson says, "A runner is a miser, spending the pennies of his energy with great stinginess, constantly wanting to know how much he has spent and how much longer he will be expected to pay. He wants to be broke at precisely the moment he no longer needs his coin."[61]

Have you ever run out of energy before finishing a race? If so, then you know what it feels like to be "broke" too soon. It's like hitting a wall, and your body simply cannot run a step further—not because you don't want to, but because you physically can't.

Training smart can help you avoid this situation. It builds miles in your bank, so that you have plenty available on race day. Training smart also teaches you how to spend those miles wisely and efficiently, so that your account reaches zero just as you cross the finish line.

Think of it this way: training helps you safely and quickly grow the bank of endurance, strength, and speed in your body. A mix of these "currencies" allows you to be a more versatile runner, manoeuvring through the elements in your competition with better control. It allows you to find your flow and finish the race strong, having maxed out your budget. If you have any percentage leftover, you will likely feel unsatisfied, which is almost as unpleasant as not having enough to finish.

The unfit runner has a smaller bank to begin with and is also unable to maximise expenditure of what he has, often feeling tired way before finishing the run even though he actually has plenty of untapped energy. Growing one's arsenal of resources and learning to use it efficiently is part of the training process.

Most people don't start running with a training plan. But at some point, when their love of running grows and they're wondering how to improve, a training schedule becomes relevant. How does one move from a 5K to a 10K or achieve that new personal best? The answer is a comprehensive training plan.

At this point, however, amateur runners usually pull up training plans from the internet—it's easy; there are a million out there. But what the internet won't tell you is how to interpret these plans. If a plan instructs you to run thirty minutes in Zone 1, do you know what that means? Do you understand the physiological goal of the numbers provided? After reading this chapter, you will.

MORE THAN MILES

The goal of any training plan is to minimise negative outcomes from running such as fatigue and injuries and maximise positive outcomes such as fitness and race day performance. The ideal training plan helps you to peak at a specific moment by getting the most out of the miles you put in. But you must be intentional about it. The first step to any plan is to set a clear goal. Be conscious of what you want—whether that's running your first marathon or getting a personal best in a 10K—and form a plan to get there.

The second step is to recognise that all miles are not the same.

It's easy for amateur distance runners to think that the more they're running, the better they're running. If you have ever hung around distance runners, you will have heard them compare weekly mileage, with high-mileage weeks being considered the yardstick of success.

There is some truth to this belief. The more we run, the more load we add to our neuromuscular, cardiovascular, and psycho-emotional systems, which makes us tougher and less susceptible to injury—assuming we're engaging in good movement patterns as discussed in previous chapters. So running more miles does, in fact, make us stronger and better runners, but only to a certain point.

However, while a good amount of load on our muscles causes them to grow stronger, too much too soon can actually cause them to break down, weakening them in the process.

Many of us equate miles with load, so more miles equals more load. Keep that equation below the breaking point, and we're good to go. But it's not that simple. Running five kilometres when we're fresh and sprightly will have a different load on the body compared to running five kilometres after a long day at work, when we're already tired. The *miles* have stayed the same, but the load differs. The body isn't able to differentiate stress from running and stress from other areas of life. It's all stress, and too much can create a breakdown.

Similarly, *how* we run those five kilometres makes a difference. Doing runs at a specific effort zone, in a specific amount of time, can elicit various physiological adaptations for our training benefit.

Equally, frequency and consistency matter. Say you plan to run twenty-five kilometres over the course of one week. How do you spread out those kilometres? Are you running an easy five kilometres daily or is there a variation in volume and effort across the week? On the days when you run twenty kilometres, are you running them all at once or are you doing half in the morning and half at night? All of this affects the cumulative load you're putting on your body.

Timing matters as well, especially if we're racing. How we run relative to the race day has a large impact on the race result. Research shows that it's more effective to train at race pace weeks ahead of the race, as compared to simply clocking more miles.

A good training plan maximises load effectiveness through yet another running paradox: to get stronger, we first have to get "weaker." When we train, our muscles suffer microdamage; this is why we feel sore after a hard run. Growth is in the recovery period, where our muscles heal and readapt to offer us a stronger level of support. It's in the tearing and healing that we progress. Load effectiveness is ensuring we have the right balance to keep this cycle going. Too little load, and our muscles won't be pushed to be better. Too much load, however, and our muscles won't have time to recover and grow stronger.

Thus, for effective growth, we need to load the body with miles that will build us, but not break us. It's not just about "high mileage" weeks; it's about including a carefully calculated sequence of both volume *and* intensity. That's what helps us go far and fast.

Don't beat yourself up if you don't know the perfect combination of volume and intensity as yet, though—the world's best running coaches have been trying to figure it out for ages. How many miles is enough? And how fast do we want to run those miles? In the 1700s, our training philosophy was high volume walking and some running. In the 1800s, that changed to high volume running. In the 1900s, we changed our minds every few decades, moving from high volume to high intensity, and then a mix of both high volume and intensity. To this day, we're still figuring it out.

MILES MATTER

Training aims to improve our efficiency at converting fuel into energy and energy into motion. The body does this via our aerobic and anaerobic energy systems.

When you run at a comfortable effort within your aerobic threshold, your body has sufficient oxygen to rely on for energy production. Aerobic respiration produces carbon dioxide and water, which are easily expelled via expiration. If you run faster and harder, going beyond this threshold, your body switches to your anaerobic energy system for energy production. Now, in addition to carbon dioxide and water, metabolites are produced, which requires a separate physiological process for removal. Moreover, the amount of energy produced through anaerobic respiration is much less than that during aerobic respiration, making it simultaneously more tiring and less efficient. As such, training helps us expand the limits of our anaerobic, as well as aerobic, capacities and allows us to run farther and faster. The greater the rate at which your body can utilise oxygen for energy and the better you get at clearing metabolites, the faster and longer you can run.

The longer the race, the greater the proportion of time spent in aerobic respiration. This would mean that for the average runner, the marathon is 99 percent aerobic and 1 percent anaerobic. Given that ratio, it might seem that running many easy miles would be the best way to prepare for a marathon, but in fact, there are many advantages to improving our anaerobic capacity as well. As stated earlier, aerobic capacity is represented as VO2 max, which is the maximum rate of oxygen the body can consume. Improving your anaerobic capacity will allow for a higher fractional utilisation of your VO2 max, which means you can run and endure a greater effort before your blood lactate levels rise.

The longer the race, the greater the amount of aerobic fitness needed and the less dependency on one's anaerobic fitness. However, regardless of the race length, there will always be a role for anaerobic training. A good combination of aerobic and anaerobic training allows you to stay longer in aerobic respiration before you enter into anaerobic respiration. You can run faster, harder, and longer because your muscles no longer need as much oxygen for the same effort, and at the same time are able to convert this oxygen into energy production more easily. In addition, the high intensity of anaerobic work teaches your body to be more fatigue resistant physically and mentally, as it learns to clear metabolites more efficiently, allowing for a faster recovery between training sessions. Anaerobic training also induces metabolic changes at the cellular level, increasing energy availability to muscles even at lower intensity of work. It comes in handy when you want to finish strong, outsprint against your opponent, or when you need to dig into your reserves to run that hill in the middle of the marathon.

Strength training also improves your running economy and should be part of your plan. Still all the strengthening work done in the gym doesn't translate to faster running unless you start running! The more comfortable you get running at different efforts, pacing, over varying duration and terrains, the more your body becomes efficient at force generation, absorption of force, and translation of force into motion.

In general, the right training plan provides a good ratio of aerobic and anaerobic stimulus. The primary physiological stimulus elicited is a result of a combination of effort and the duration of this effort.

THE RACE PEAK PYRAMID

Current schools of thought recommend training for no more than one major race per year, that is, one personal best or one race at a long distance. The idea is to dedicate your training towards one peak performance, as pursuing multiple peaks in a year often results in physiological or psychological fatigue or the risk of being undertrained in key fitness components for one or both races.

If you picture a pyramid, the bottom level is the foundation upon which you add different elements, all leading to the peak—the race. The components that make up this pyramid do build on each other, but the idea isn't that you complete one layer and then move on to the next, never to return to the preceding stage. Rather, you continue incorporating each component, prioritising important ones as you move closer to the race date. For example, the base of the pyramid is aerobic training, and this will be your exclusive focus at first. After a period of doing 100 percent easy runs (component 1), you might move on to 90 percent aerobic work and 10 percent of the second component, anaerobic training. Then you might shift to 80 percent component 1 and 10 percent combined components 2 and 3—and so on. The exact ratios and timing will depend on your fitness level, race distance, and training time frame.

The following components are involved in every race-focused training plan, whether you're running a 5K or a marathon, though the length of time spent focusing on each stage will differ. Someone running 3.1 miles will obviously not need as much base aerobic conditioning as someone running 26.2 miles.

Because every person's fitness level and goals are different, it's difficult to say how long someone should spend at each stage. For example, you might spend eight to ten weeks on component 1, six to eight on component 2, four to six weeks on component 3, and two to four weeks on each of the next two components. If you're a newbie, you may want to spend even more time building up your fitness on each component; if you're experienced, you may spend less time building up your base but more time on fitness components that you're lacking. For more specific time frames, consult reputable plans for your race distance.

HEART RATE ZONES

Throughout the race peak pyramid discussion, we'll be referencing heart rate (HR) zones and ratings of perceived exertion (RPE) in relation to the different components. In case you're not familiar with the zones, here's a quick cheat sheet:

- Zone 1: less than 70 percent max HR (less than 3 RPE)
- Zone 2: 70-80 percent max HR (3-4 RPE)
- Zone 3: 80-90 percent max HR (5-6 RPE)
- Zone 4: 90-100 percent max HR (7-10 RPE)

In general, Zones 1 and 2 are aerobic and done at an easy pace. You should be able to converse in short sentences. At Zone 3, you run at submaximal effort. You should feel like you are pushing and short of breath, but with some reserves left. At Zone 4, you're using maximal effort. Your lungs are screaming for air and your legs are burning, as if you are running for your life.

1. BUILD A BASE: GENERAL AEROBIC FITNESS

Goal: Build aerobic fitness

By focusing on easy runs of various lengths, you improve metabolic capabilities in your cardiac and skeletal muscles by increasing the size and number of mitochondria. Easy runs also provide a low-grade stimulus for improving joint and tendon strength and increase capillary density, which allows for more efficient delivery of oxygen and removal of carbon dioxide. Because it provides maintenance stimulus for continued connective tissue and cardiovascular development, aerobic conditioning will make up a big portion of the total training load throughout the training cycle.

How: Mix of long and short easy runs in Zones 1 and 2

At this stage, 100 percent of your runs will fall into Zones 1 and 2, where you are running below 80 percent of max HR. You'll start modifying the percentage to include hard runs when you move into the second tier of the pyramid.

As you develop greater aerobic fitness, you will be able to divide the easy runs more clearly into the two zones, with Zone 1 being used for warmups, cool downs, and recovery runs and Zone 2 being the place for the bulk of your training volume.

INCORPORATE A STRENGTHENING ROUTINE

In addition to easy runs in Zone 1 and Zone 2, the pyramid base is the best time to incorporate a focused strengthening routine. As you progress through the phases and move closer to race time, the amount of time spent in strength training will decrease. When you get to the Prepare to Peak phase, you can drop strength work altogether.

In Mile 23, we discussed the importance of running-specific strength training, that is, performing exercises that are tied to specific running motions. The same applies here. You can break down the running movement pattern into smaller focused areas to work on. For example, weighted squats or deadlifts teach you to leverage your body for force transference.

Strength training recruits large numbers of muscle fibres in a controlled setting that running cannot provide. When you run, you compensate for weaknesses by performing in movement patterns that engage the stronger muscles and neglect the weaker ones.

The same concepts we addressed in injury prevention also enable you to run faster.

In our bodies, we have a genetic ratio of fast- and slow-twitch fibres. We can't change this ratio, but we can change our ability to effectively recruit these fibres. Most distance runners are weak in recruiting fast-twitch fibres simply because their distance training does not prepare them to do so.

Plyometrics and resistance training teaches the body to recruit fast-twitch muscle fibres in a controlled environment—as opposed to sprint workouts where the body might use its learned compensations. In general, the easier it is for us to recruit muscle fibres, the less oxygen we need, and hence, the better we can maintain our running economy. Teaching your body to recruit both fast- and slow-twitch fibres under fatigue can reduce this decline in running economy. For example, at the start of the marathon, when you feel fresh, you recruit slow-twitch fibres, but if you continue to hold the same pace for the next three hours, you can dig into the fast-twitch fibres even as you fatigue to push through towards that last stretch towards the finish line.

2. BUILD STRENGTH: GENERAL ANAEROBIC FITNESS

Goal: Build strength in the form of anaerobic tolerance

After you've built an aerobic base, it's time to build your mental and physical tolerance for hard work and conditioning your body's efficiency at clearing the metabolites buildup that results from harder efforts of running.

How: Mix of short and medium runs completed between Zones 2 and 3

At this phase, you start moving from 100 percent easy runs, to 90 percent in Zone 1 and 2 and 10 percent in Zone 3, to 80 percent Zones 1 and 2 and 20 percent Zone 3.

There are a couple of ways to start building anaerobic tolerance. You can begin by incorporating one to two reps of twenty- to thirty-minute moderate to hard runs in the same session, completed at 75 to 85 percent of max HR, or you can do a higher number of shorter reps at a higher intensity, say, six hard runs of five minutes each, with equal time for recovery between reps. In terms of pace for these runs, you might use your target marathon pace.

You can also use hill running to increase intensity in a more free-flow manner. The key idea at this stage is to practise running at a harder intensity, and to balance the increased intensity by shortening the duration. You don't want to push too hard too fast. Your body needs to get used to harder runs, which takes time physically and mentally.

RUN EASY TO RUN HARD

In the past decade, several studies have compared the effectiveness of three different ratios of aerobic (Zones 1 and 2) to anaerobic (Zones 3 and 4) training: 50:50, 60:40, and 80:20. Of those three, doing 50 percent aerobic and 50 percent anaerobic is the least effective, primarily because it's hard to run 50 percent of your runs at high intensity. Many runners end up running slightly slower while minimally increasing intensity. They also don't recover sufficiently, which further impacts the results and puts them at increased risk of injury. In addition, studies suggest that runners fare better if they follow an 80:20 ratio early in the season and then shift to 60:40 about two to four weeks before race day. Any training over Zones 1 and 2 greatly stresses the autonomic nervous system, so intensity at Zones 3 and 4 should be closely monitored in the overall training load.

Among endurance runners, a debate remains regarding optimum time spent training in Zones 3 and 4. The conclusion is that the significance is highly dependent on the starting fitness of the athlete: high-intensity training is useful for improving performance in the highly trained, while moderate intensity is often sufficient for obtaining similar results in those with less training experience. Endurance events are usually raced in Zone 3, rather than Zone 4, so training in this zone more closely simulates competition scenarios.

After observing how elite runners trained, Stephen Seiler proposed that an 80:20 balance is most effective: large amounts of low intensity in Zones 1 and 2, small amounts of high intensity in Zone 4, and close to zero time spent in the middle. This theory follows the same "one hundred mile weeks" philosophy proposed by Arthur Lydiard in the 1960s. He preached that middle- and long-distance runners should regularly run one hundred miles a week during base training, believing that the cardiovascular system must be built up to its maximum before developing the muscular system to its maximum. Carrying the

80:20 idea started by Seiler, Matt Fitzgerald, author of *80/20 Running*, advises runners who put in less than thirty miles a week to run more miles rather than more time at a higher intensity.

The conclusion from all these studies? Run easy to run hard. Spend 80 percent of your training volume in easy running and 20 percent doing higher-intensity, faster miles. If you don't bolster your heart and lungs through easy runs, you won't have the capacity to truly benefit from the hard workouts. Your body might even break down from fatigue.

I recommend performing a self-assessment of your training level and racing performance to decide how to balance that 20 percent in terms of moderate and high intensity.

3. BUILD SPEED ENDURANCE: INCREASED AEROBIC CAPACITY

Goal: Improve VO2 max and increase aerobic capacity

As stated earlier, VO2 max looks at the maximum rate at which your heart, lungs, and muscles can utilise oxygen. The more efficiently your body can use this oxygen, the faster you can remove the metabolites that build up during hard running.

How: Repetition of runs in Zone 3 with adequate recovery

You increase aerobic capacity by increasing your tolerance of running at high intensity—but not so high that your body tips into purely anaerobic respiration (Zone 4). Including adequate recovery time between reps helps ensure that the training stimulus stays aerobic. Start by adding short bursts of fast running to your training plan, for example, four to six reps of 2,000 metres at 80-90 percent of max HR with adequate recovery—usually twice the duration of each rep. As a guideline, do your Zone 3 runs at mile race pace.

4. BUILD FATIGUE TOLERANCE: INCREASED ANAEROBIC CAPACITY

Goal: Improve anaerobic capacity

By now, you should have a good amount of anaerobic tolerance; it's time to sharpen it further. The effort at this stage can be very strenuous mentally and physically. As such remember to allow for recovery after each workout as well as at the end of this stage. The goal is to train yourself to easily recruit more skeletal muscle fibres even when fatigued so that you can change pace quickly and maintain that speed change.

How: Reps of one mile or less completed in Zone 4

Reps to build fatigue tolerance can be completed on hills or flats, but they should be done at 90 to 100 percent of max HR. You might do ten to twelve reps of 800 metres or eight to ten reps of 1,000 metres. Make sure you give yourself time for complete recovery, usually three times the duration of each rep.

5. PREPARE TO PEAK: RACE-PACE TRAINING AND SUPERCOMPENSATION

Goal: Practice race pace comfortably without overloading the body physically and/or mentally *and* allow the body to rest and adapt to a higher level of strength

The hard work has been done. During this period, you're not

going for extra growth or adaptation. You simply want to work on running your target race pace comfortably and sustainably so you can build confidence. If you're finding it difficult to sustain your target pace, it's time to modify your expectations and practise a more realistic race pace.

How: Reduce overall volume, perform short runs at race pace, and set aside time for rest

During the tapering period when you're preparing to peak, reduce your running volume and maintain or slightly reduce the intensity so that you're doing about 60 percent aerobic and 40 percent anaerobic. This ratio will keep the body rested but still prepared to run at race pace. For a marathon, you might include workouts of eight to ten 800-metre reps at race pace. For a 10K, you might do five to six 400-metre reps at race pace. You should be able to run these reps comfortably.

During this period, rest is as important as tapering because it allows for supercompensation to take place. The muscles recover from the microdamages induced in training and load bearing, allowing them to adapt to a higher level of strength.

Don't forget mental recovery! Go for a walk, or swim, or cycle. Go see a movie with friends. Your mind needs rest as much as your body.

As you work through these phases of the pyramid, it is crucial that you listen to your body. All along the way, you need to find the optimal balance of work and recovery and develop a plan that works for you.

A PLAN THAT WORKS FOR YOU

Like most amateur runners, I didn't begin running with a training plan—I didn't even know I might need one. As mentioned earlier, I started running around my neighbourhood, after which I began experimenting with distance running. "Training" at that point meant simply increasing the number of miles I ran—the more I ran, the more in control I felt, the more I felt like I was improving. While I did make progress this way, as you have seen, I ultimately hit a plateau. I began to dread my runs and I became increasingly fatigued, physically and mentally. I didn't know it then, but my balance between intensity and volume was off, and I needed to recalibrate.

I did know that something was wrong, so I started a diary to record my runs. I wrote down how tired I was, my mental state, and my training performance. I continued to run at the same volume, but I began to mix it up so that my body was getting more from my miles. I also took into account my personal preferences: I was bored with running five or ten kilometres a day, every day. I needed variety, challenge, and options.

PLYOMETRICS TO THE RESCUE

During the late 1990s, marathoner Paula Radcliffe was the "nearly girl of British sport." She would lead races from the front and then lose in a sprint at the finish. In 2000, Radcliffe finally realised that focusing on miles wasn't enough to give her an edge, and she started working on strength training with Gerald Hartmann.

At the beginning of their work together, Hartmann had Radcliffe do a simple test: hop on and off a forty-centimetre box twenty times. Her time was fifteen seconds slower than her teammate, Kelly Holmes, because Radcliffe's core and posture were weak. Hartmann introduced plyometrics and heavy weights, and after eighteen months, Radcliffe's body no longer tailed off at the end of races. She became nearly unbeatable. She bounced back from a fourth-place finish in 10K at the 2000 Sydney Olympics and set a new world record in the marathon in 2003. Over the next five years, she won seven big city marathons, the two world cross-country championships, and three world half-marathon championships.[62]

Throughout the season, I maintained a high volume of easy running each week, while modifying the two key interval workouts each week to suit my racing needs and to match my weaknesses. For example, when I expected to run a hilly course, I included more anaerobic endurance work to get myself comfortable at running at various pacing regardless of whether I'm fresh or tired. Further away from my key races, I worked on conditioning my aerobic and anaerobic system in an 80:20 ratio and as I became fitter, I changed up the intensity and quality of the training components. Instead of running at an easy pace for the entire long run, I added speed work, for example, doing a negative split where I run the second half faster than the first. Closer to race week, I reduced the volume of my training and focused on workouts at race pace.

I established some recovery rules for myself:

- A compulsory rest day each week
- An easy week every four weeks of hard training
- A twenty-minute strength routine after every alternate run session
- One to two weeks off—no running at all—after a major race

I found a template that worked for me and created a variable running plan that incorporated the various components:

- Monday: Low volume day. Short, easy run with stridings—short sprints to focus on form. For example, a forty-five minute run at conversational pace followed by five fifty-metre sprints. Prehab strengthening.
- Tuesday: High volume day split into two sessions. For example, fifteen kilometres in the morning and fifteen in the evening (back-to-back runs to build load endurance).
- Wednesday: Key interval 1: hardest workout of the week. For example, two four-kilometre tempo runs at 10K race pace with a ten-minute recovery jog in between. Personally, I like to get the harder workout done earlier in the week. Because, hump day!
- Thursday: Rest day.
- Friday: Key interval 2: a lower-load workout, either less intensity or less volume. For example, a thirty-minute fartlek workout: one minute sprint followed by one minute easy.
- Saturday: Low-volume day. Short, easy run with stridings. For example, a forty-five- to sixty-minute run at conversational pace, followed by five fifty-metre sprints with good form. Prehab strengthening.
- Sunday: High-volume day. For example, a thirty-kilometre run with friends.

At my peak, I averaged one hundred kilometres per week. During base training, I often reached higher weekly volumes, up to 120 kilometres per week. Moving into the season, I would reduce my weekly volume and replace miles with shorter, higher intensity runs. I also preferred two back-to-back hard training days. As I neared race day, I would taper off strength training, moving from weights to body weight, finally dropping strength training altogether in the days immediately prior. This practice helped me adapt to a higher volume of training stress, which translated to improved stress tolerance during the hard workouts.

This pattern of alternating between volume and intensity allowed me to maintain an overall consistent loading throughout the year. I was also able to stimulate various key physiological systems each training block, without feeling overwhelmed. However, it took consistent self-assessment to adjust my approach to training over the years to cope with my changing roles and work demands as I progressed from student to working adult. I kept a training diary in which I recorded my experience in each session. I wrote down my thoughts and feelings pre and post run, my rate of perceived exertion, resting heart rate, and heart rate during the session. In this way, I made sure I was minding my mental health, as well as my physical health, so that I kept my mind and body in sync and created the plan that was best for me.

MILES FOR THOUGHT

If you want to run farther and faster, rethink those miles. Training effectively is primarily about understanding how the miles you run impact your body. When you understand that, knowing why you do the miles you do and knowing how those miles bring you closer towards your goals allows you to run with greater intention and focus. Beyond the weekly volume, the way those miles are completed matters. You will still need to put in the hard work but at least you get the most out of it.

A training plan must be based on your goals and a clear understanding that not all miles are the same: there are various factors above and beyond distance that influence how much load is placed upon your body.

A good plan is adaptive to varying life demands. It accounts for a good balance of rest and recovery needed for adaptation, preventing overtraining, injuries, burnout, and plateaus, but with enough load and pressure to keep your talent growing.

Ultimately, the best training plans are the ones customised for the runner: their habits, preferences, lifestyle, and capacity.

THE LAST MILE

IN EVERY RUN, EACH MILE DIFFERS FROM THE OTHER. WE all have our emotional strategies to cope with the various miles—the first mile, the last, and everything in between.

For some, the first mile is the easiest. We're fresh, alive, excited. In a marathon, it's so easy to go hard for the first mile.

The last mile, though—the last mile is often the longest. It demands a thousand times more effort and willpower than the first mile. The end is so close, right there, but the physical and mental strain make it seem unattainable. You wonder, Am I really going to make it? You don't have the answer. That mile is an intense progression from doubt, exhaustion, disbelief, and anticipation to relief, pride, and happiness. While we physically push ourselves, our mental and emotional psyche are also training and adapting. Thus, the last mile becomes an opportunity for tremendous personal growth. It's almost as if the first twenty-five miles of the marathon are only important to get through so we can arrive at that final lesson.

In addition to the literal last mile of a race, we all experience last miles of a more figurative nature. For me, that happened in 2019.

Prior to competing in the SEA Games Duathlon that year, I had decided that this would be my last race. I was bringing the competitive running chapter of my life to a close. As a result, I really wanted to stand on a podium when it was over. I knew there were two strong contenders for first and second, but I had a good shot at third.

The SEA Games Duathlon in the Philippines, Subic Bay, consisted of a ten-kilometre run, a forty-kilometre bike ride, and a five-kilometre run. The first part of the race went well: I kept good time, and was feeling strong. I'd strategized such that I kept up with the chase pack during the run, so I would draft with the group when we transitioned to the cycling portion.

The first cycling lap went splendidly. I stayed with the group and put myself in a great position for a third position finish. On the second lap, however, my back tire got punctured.

There were two tire changing stations at the duathlon. I'd just passed the first one when I felt my ride becoming bumpier, but I kept going in the hope it wasn't what I thought it was: if you're stopping to change your tire, you're pretty much out of the podium race. Alas, it was a puncture; wishful thinking couldn't change that. I fell farther and farther behind the chase pack, until finally I was on my own.

Moving as slowly as I was, I had all the time in the world to reflect. I went through all the stages: denial, grief, frustration that it had to happen at this race of all races, and then acceptance. I felt at peace. I pulled into the second tire-changing station, replaced my tire, completed the final lap of the biking leg, and ran the last five kilometres. I ran my hardest, not for the podium, but for the fun of it and for the adrenaline and joy that this sport gives me.

I remember how upset people were when I crossed that finish line. They felt shattered for me, they imagined my disappointment to be crushing, and they felt so much love and sympathy. But I wasn't shattered. I had done so much growing over my running career—a journey that I've taken you on through the many chapters of this book—and I was at peace.

Interestingly, my loss was a vital reminder of the first victory in my running journey. It reminded me of how I was able to embrace discomfort, progress, and failures all together. It also reminded me that losing a race doesn't mean I've lost value as a person, just as winning doesn't make me a better person. Here, at the end of my racing journey, I truly understood that my value is self-created and is not determined by a race performance or the opinions of others. Racing that SEA Games was my last mile, for I had completed my lessons and achieved my goals. My running journey has given me answers in the form of experiences, to questions I had of myself and my life.

In every runner's career, there will be a point when they confront the last mile. It could be due to injury, lifestyle, physical decline, or, like me, personal choice. When that moment comes, remember that change is inevitable. No, not just inevitable—beautiful. It took me so long to leave racing because I couldn't think of anything else in my life that could give me the same rush. I was stuck in a pattern, and I couldn't imagine or act my way out of it. When I decided the SEA Games Duathlon would be my last race, it wasn't a spur-of-the-moment decision; a million small milestones had led me there, had made me ready to take the next step. I'm glad I did.

I still run. I still wear my shoes and hit the road and feel all the thrill that comes with flowing with your mind, body and environment. Many times we leave running when we're at our weakest physically, because of injury or age, but we fail to appreciate how we're, in fact, mentally and emotionally at our strongest. My last mile made space for new first miles—and I am leaning in.

Let's look more closely at the last mile, both the physical and emotional challenges of the last mile of each race you run, and the last mile of your running career.

OUR STRENGTH IS FOUND AT THE END

Our clearest memories of a race are always the stages that are significant and personal. These moments are important for reasons often we can't articulate because we haven't thought about them enough to understand what they mean to us.

The last mile in particular stands out. In the last mile, we persevere even though we're exhausted; we keep going, despite our desire to surrender. The moment we cross that line, we seek to capture this moment. We look for tokens or pictures that can capture the medley of feelings we went through. We collect racing bibs, medals, pictures of us crossing the finish line, but the truth is nothing can capture the sheer riot of emotions in us. We sleep really well that night, fatigue as our sleeping pill. And when we wake up the next day, and every other day, that specific race is forgotten physically and emotionally—yet we will never be the same again. That experience lives in our minds not only as a cherished memory, but also as a reminder of ourselves, of our perseverance and of our tenacity.

There are times when the last mile is over too soon, and we cross the finish line with energy reserves to spare. In moments like these, we feel almost cheated, as if finishing the race with anything less than absolute exhaustion makes the ordeal less satisfying. Disappointing, even. For if we're not exhausted, did we really push ourselves as hard as we could have? Could we have done more?

The last mile often elicits reflection from us because it's so gruelling. We confront our vulnerabilities and sense of self in that last mile: it holds a mirror to us, stripped of all pretence and illusions.

The thing is, it's almost impossible to prepare ourselves for the last mile. How can we? Nothing in everyday living comes close to the experience. What then is to be our dress rehearsal? No, we must take the last mile as it comes, encounter each challenge fresh and in the moment. It's a window through which our strength can shine—and we often don't even realise the strength we've developed until we're running down the last mile. The more last miles we run, the stronger we become.

I love the last mile because it pushes me—exhausts me completely—but it also makes it clear just how community-based running is. Our ability to take one step in front of the other when we believe we cannot move anymore is not only our doing; it's a strength given to us by every person and resource we've encountered along our running journey.

In many ways, the last mile is the most paradoxical. We feel excited that the pain is coming to an end, and yet when it ends, we feel sad that it is over. I felt this exact mix at the end of the SEA Games, both for that race and for the last mile of my running career. I was relieved that I would no longer have to train with the same intensity and put myself through that physical and mental fatigue, but I also felt tremendous sadness that this stage of my life's journey was over. And intermingled with the sadness I felt joy, knowing I had so much to look forward to, so many opportunities to apply the lessons I had learned over my ten-year career. That's the beauty of the end: you finally have time to reflect and celebrate and appreciate the journey for what it was.

The final mile teaches us we are bigger than we think, and

we have more to give than we imagine. Lean into the vulnerability and compassion of that time to see that you can overcome your preconceived notions of limits, and you can nurture the community around you.

JUST START LIVING

When we race, we all know there is going to be a last mile. To some extent, we even look forward to it—it's the last stretch, the moment before victory where all your hard work becomes apparent. But there's also a last mile in our running careers—and many of us don't look forward to that.

But we could.

The truth is, just as we can never know our peak fitness as a runner, we can never really predict when it becomes too late for us to continue running. Like any other sport, running requires muscular strength, which we naturally lose with age. As we get older, we lose muscle mass, and we don't respond as effectively to stressors because our tissues become more fibrotic and less elastic. Moreover, the body undergoes degenerative changes, and we start developing stiffness over areas of the spine due to poor posture across decades.

These changes are simply fact—they will happen, and we cannot avoid them. It's silly to think that in our fifties we can run the same as when we ran in our twenties: running will take a greater toll on the body when we're older.

But defining what that last mile of your career looks like is up to you. I defined it by stepping away from competitive running because I wanted to. I still run; I just don't race. Similarly, you get to define that last mile for yourself. C. Kunalan, one of Singapore's greatest sprinters, still runs three kilometres every day—and he's eighty-five. Three kilometres is obviously a lot less than he used to run, but it's the perfect amount for him now.

And that's what I want you to take away from this. Don't rail against the changes of your body; change is constant and inevitable. Instead, work with it. Find out what you truly want and why. Maybe as you grow older, it's no longer as important to set a new personal record as it is to simply run, whatever the distance might be. Then age doesn't prohibit you from hitting the track, because you just need enough power to complete the distance—any distance.

Look at your last mile as a change, not an end. Figure out how you want to shape that change. No one can say for sure whether you can run or not. That depends on whether you're willing to expand your definition and boundaries of what "running" means to you, adjust your expectations, and take the steps needed to run safely.

Running is a vehicle for self-discovery. On our first step in that first jog, we embraced this sport with open arms, taking in the unimaginable growth even though we didn't know what to expect. Remember to do the same wherever you are in your journey. They say that every athlete dies twice: once at an injury in one's peak, and the other when you retire. But what is forgotten in this statement is the opportunity awaiting us in the next stage of life, and the lessons we had undertaken from the miles we were lucky enough to run.

Above all, be compassionate to yourself. In doing so, you'll realise you're stronger than you thought and can do much more than you ever imagined.

BACK TO THE START

IN 490 BC, A GREEK SOLDIER NAMED PHEIDIPPIDES RAN from Marathon to Athens to announce the defeat of the Persians—a distance of approximately twenty-five miles. According to legend, he delivered the message "Niki!" (Victory!), and then promptly died from exhaustion.

To commemorate Pheidippides' historic run, the organisers of the 1896 Olympics in Athens included a race called the marathon. They mapped out a course from Marathon Bridge to the Olympic Stadium in Athens, a distance of 40,000 metres or 24.85 miles.

The race was part of the Summer Olympics going forward, though the distance changed slightly each time. The organisers figured the exact mileage didn't matter as long as everyone ran the same course.

For the 1908 London Olympics, for example, organisers laid out a twenty-six-mile course from Windsor Castle to White City Stadium, then they added 385 yards to locate the finish line in front of the royal family's viewing box. Thus began the tradition of yelling "God save the Queen" in the marathon's last mile.

Even still, it wasn't until 1921 that the International Amateur Athletic Federation adopted 26.2 miles as the official marathon length.

Distance was never the aim of Pheidippides' run, nor was it the aim of the marathons that followed in those early Olympic Games. It was all about the journey.

Similarly, if you want to revolutionise your running practice, you have to think beyond the miles. It's not a question of how far you run, but *how* you run.

AWARENESS AND EFFORT

As we have explored, we are born with a mind and body that allow us to run, but not necessarily effectively. This is the runner's paradox: having to learn on several levels—mental and emotional, as well as physical—to do this great, sucky thing we are supposedly born to do.

At every turn, this learning requires awareness: of how our body moves, of how we feel when we run, of our thoughts about ourselves and our sport, of the environments through which we pass, of our connections with those who share the journey. This learning also requires effort. There are no shortcuts. No magic pills. The lessons are in the miles themselves. We need to be willing to examine our running in full honesty, and then use tools such as this book to make changes, difficult though they may be.

I'm guessing you love running; you wouldn't have picked up this book if you didn't. We all know how precious the sport is to our lives, and we've sensed the strange dichotomies and depth that lie under the surface—depth that is just waiting to be explored. In this book, I've shown you how to unlock some of that depth. Now it's up to you to take that journey forward in your everyday practice.

TAKE THE FIRST STEP

The following five questions guided our 26-mile discussion, and they will take you through the .2 home:

- Why do I run?
- How do I feel when I run?
- Do I enjoy running?
- Do I know how to run?
- Am I running sustainably?

Which question stands out to you? Where do you need to gain awareness or alter your approach or up your effort?

Here are some follow-up questions to guide your contemplation. I found journaling to be a helpful tool in developing mindful running practice; you might do the same:

1. Do you know why you run? What drives you? Do you set goals? Which part of running satisfies you? What about running keeps you fulfilled?
2. Examine the quality of your running experience. Are you satisfied? Are you better able to enjoy the turmoil of running because you understand the benefits it offers? If you're unhappy, what areas are making you miserable: injuries, setbacks, losses, the inability to meet your goals? Then explore why you're unhappy—how is your relationship to running shaping this state?
3. How does running make you feel about yourself? What does not running make you feel about yourself?

4. Take a look at your running form. Begin with how you hold
    yourself, how you move, even with something as simple
    as walking, and then graduate to analysing your running
    motion. What do you see? What do you feel? Once you have
    a clear self-assessment, begin to correct it with a training
    plan that's aligned to your goals and physical state.
5. When you are chasing your goals, be it to win the next
    race or to set a new personal record, are you enjoying the
    journey? How do you grapple with both your victories and
    your losses? How do you see yourself when you lose? Do
    you beat yourself up over it and lose sleep for days? Or get
    mad at your loved ones and feel excessively frustrated? Do
    you experience an intense loss of self-value when you get
    injured? How do you pick yourself up when you plateau?
6. What constitutes progress in your running journey? How do
    you celebrate your growth? How do you gauge your prog-
    ress? Do you reflect beyond the outcome of your runs, into
    your feelings and emotions in the process?

Taking a more mindful approach to your running doesn't
just add new dimensions to your career—it also lengthens it.
Because you see your body as a tool of exploration, you're more
open to correcting dysfunctional patterns that may impact it.
Because you're always conscious, you're better able to catch
injuries before they happen and recognise the different pain
signals your body is giving you. Because you've tapped into
so many different aspects of running beyond just distance and
numbers, you're better prepared to shape your last mile into a
new beginning instead of an end.

The final .2 mile of a marathon is similar to the arbitrary
finish line we set for ourselves during each run. It's that random
white line we have to cross to know the workout is done.

Here's the thing: we create the lines we cross. We decide to enter that marathon or run fifteen kilometres before work or do five repeats up that horribly steep hill. We decide how early we get up, how often we run, how hard we train, what race we enter. We create our experience from beginning to end, in each workout and for the extent of our running journey.

We have the power to frame our mind, fix our form, and in so doing, find our high.

Here's to a journey well chosen.

ACKNOWLEDGMENTS

I WOULD FIRST LIKE TO THANK MY FAMILY FOR ALL THEIR love: My mom, for cooking all my favourite foods and insisting that I eat my fruits and vegetables, for keeping fresh slices of lemons available for my lemon water, for nagging me to get more rest and reminding me to avoid training too hard. My dad, for taking me to and from races and training to ensure I get enough rest, for bringing me food after my training sessions, for waiting at the airport for my return from my overseas competitions. My brother, for inspiring me to give my best in everything I do and for all the loving guidance throughout my formative running years. My late doggie, Rudy, for being the greatest Shih Tzu of all time, for greeting me with a wagging tail after a hard workout.

Thank you to my running friends: Sia, Desmond, Roberto, and many others who have been a huge part of my running journey. Thank you to my teammates back in my schooling days at Raffles Girls School, Raffles Junior College, and Nanyang Polytechnic. Thank you to my running group, The Coney Runners, for the weekly long runs at Bedok Reservoir, Macritchie, and East Coast Park, especially the key long runs in 2019, leading up to the SEA Games. Thank you to the Boulder Track Club for the short but very memorable and tough training stint in Colorado and for the countless brunches post-morning long runs.

Thank you to my patients for the unwavering support and for allowing me to assist you with your growth. I'm grateful for your dedication and perseverance in your rehabilitation. Without you, this book could not have come to fruition.

Thank you to Mr. C. Kunalan for his support and for believing in me. Thank you for sharing your stories, values, and motivation, which have inspired me in many ways in my running and writing journey.

Thank you to all my sponsors who have supported me one way or another in my running and physiotherapy journey: Nike, Rocktape, NZ Fulvic, Garmin, Oakley, and many others. Thank you to my teammates in Team Singapore and the supporting team at Singapore Athletics and Singapore Sports Institute for the assistance during my overseas races.

Thank you to everyone on my publishing team. Special thanks to my editor, Gail, for the keen insight, expert feedback, patient guidance, and dedicated support throughout the entire process. Thank you to Lindsey for putting my vision of my book into reality in a beautiful cover design. I would not have been able to pull through this arduous journey from the creation of the book's road map to its final publication otherwise.

Thank you to all my friends for listening to my rants and grumbles during the tough periods in my writing journey. Thank you to Alex for lending me a pair of sharp eyes in the proofreading process. A big thank you especially to my wonderful friend, Jess, for showing me around Enschede and for waiting for me to finish my three-hour run with an amazing breakfast. I truly appreciate the friendship we have.

And finally, thank you, my reader. This book represents everything that has been and is important to me—my family, my sport, my passion, and my values. Thank you for being a witness to my journey.

ABOUT THE AUTHOR

MOK YING RONG is a physiotherapist specialising in movement analysis and prehabilitation. A passionate entrepreneur, Ying has built and developed groups dedicated to rehabilitation for patients across a spectrum of movement disorders, from neurological conditions to sporting injuries. Her deep interest in running stems from her decade-long dedication to the sport. For twelve years, Ying represented Singapore in distance running and held the half marathon record from 2016 to 2019. Ying has partnered with schools and national teams to help athletes maximise their performance and minimise their injury risk. Ying is also a frequent speaker on all aspects of the running gait.

NOTES

MILE 1

1   Dennis M. Bramble and Daniel E. Lieberman, "Endurance Running and the Evolution of *Homo*," *Nature* 432, no. 7015 (2004):345–52, https://sci-hub.wf/10.1038/nature03052.

2   Travis Rayne Pickering and Henry T. Bunn, "The Endurance Running Hypothesis and Hunting and Scavenging in Savanna-Woodlands," *Journal of Human Evolution* 53, no. 4 (2007): 1156-1159; Martin Hora et al., "Comparing Walking and Running in Persistence Hunting," *Journal of Human Evolution* 172 (2022)

3   Mikko Ijäs, "Fragments of the Hunt: Persistence Hunting, Tracking and Prehistoric Art" (PhD diss., Aalto University, 2017).

MILE 2

4   Jeffrey J. Summers et al., "Middle-Aged, Non-Elite Marathon Runners: A Profile," *Perceptual and Motor Skills* 54, no. 3 (1982): 963–69.

5   S. K. Stoll, "Loyalty: Why Is It So Problematic in Athletics?" *Journal of College and Character* 13, no. 2 (2012), https://doi.org/10.1515/jcc-2012-1891.

6   Alister McCormick et al., "Self-Regulation in Endurance Sports: Theory, Research, and Practice," *International Review of Sport and Exercise Psychology* 12, no. 1 (2019).

7   Linda Linton and Stephanie Valentin, "Running with Injury: A Study of UK Novice and Recreational Runners and Factors Associated with Running Related Injury," *Journal of Science and Medicine in Sport* 21, no. 12 (December 2018), 1221–25.

8   Lieke Schiphof-Godart and Florentina J. Hettinga, "Passion and Pacing in Endurance Performance," *Frontiers in Physiology* 8, no. 83 (2017), https://www.frontiersin.org/articles/10.3389/fphys.2017.00083/full.

9   Daniel Pink, *Drive: The Surprising Truth about What Motivates Us* (New York: Riverhead Books, 2009), 54.

MILE 3

10   Anil Ananthaswamy, "The Exercise Paradox," *New Scientist* 218, no. 2919 (2013): 28–29, https://sci-hub.ee/10.1016/S0262-4079(13)61368-8.

11   Lieke Schiphof-Godart and Florentina J. Hettinga, "Passion and Pacing in Endurance Performance," *Frontiers in Physiology* 8, no. 83 (2017), https://www.frontiersin.org/articles/10.3389/fphys.2017.00083/full.

12   Ananthaswamy, "The Exercise Paradox," 28–29.

13   "Trending Topic: Physical Activity Guidelines," American College of Sports Medicine, https://www.acsm.org/education-resources/trending-topics-resources/physical-activity-guidelines.

14   Benjamin M. Ogles, Kevin S. Masters, and Scott A. Richardson, "Obligatory Running and Gender: An Analysis of Participative Motives and Training Habits," *International Journal of Sport Psychology* 26 (1995): 233–48.

15   Erin Beresini, "Distance Runners Are a Paradox for Insurers," *New York Times*, October 15, 2010, https://www.nytimes.com/2010/10/25/sports/25coverage.html.

MILE 4

16   K. S Masters, B. M. Ogles, and J. A. Joton, "The Development of an Instrument to Measure Motivation for Marathon Running: The Motivations of Marathoners Scales (MOMS)," *Research Quarterly for Exercise and Sport* 64, no. 2 (1993): 134–43.

17   T. J. Csordas, "Somatic Modes of Attention," *Cultural Anthropology* 8 (1993): 135–56.

18 Jenneke van Geest, Rosemarie Samaritter, and Susan van Hooren, "Move and Be Moved: The Effect of Moving Specific Movement Elements on the Experience of Happiness, *Frontiers in Psychology* 11 (2020), https://www.frontiersin.org/articles/10.3389/fpsyg.2020.579518/full.

MILE 5

19 Jacquelyn Allen-Collinson and Helen Owton, "Take a Deep Breath: Asthma, Sporting Embodiment, the Senses and 'Auditory Work,'" *International Review for the Sociology of Sport* 49, no. 5 (2014): 592–608.

MILE 9

20 Débora Godoy-Izquierdo et al., "Exercise Addiction in the Sports Context: What Is Known and What Is Yet to Be Known," *International Journal of Mental Health and Addiction* (September 2021), https://link.springer.com/article/10.1007/s11469-021-00641-9.

21 Anna Lembroke, *Dopamine Nation: Finding Balance in an Age of Indulgence* (New York: Dutton, 2021).

22 Flora Colledge et al., "Individuals at Risk of Exercise Addiction Have Higher Scores for Depression, ADHD, and Childhood Trauma," *Frontiers in Sports and Active Living* 3 (2021), https://www.ncbi.nlm.nih.gov/pmc/articles/PMC8825800/.

23 Emmanuelle Larocque and Nicolas Moreau, "When Sport Is Taken to Extremes: A Sociohistorical Analysis of Sport Addiction," *International Review for the Sociology of Sport* (June 2022), https://journals.sagepub.com/doi/full/10.1177/10126902221104956.

24 Volker Scheer et al., "Potential Long-Term Health Problems Associated with Ultra-Endurance Running: A Narrative Review," *Sports Medicine* 52 (2022): 725–40, https://link.springer.com/article/10.1007/s40279-021-01561-3.

25 Zoe Hrom, "When Running Becomes an Addiction," *Trail Runner*, May 14, 2020, https://www.trailrunnermag.com/people/culture-people/when-running-becomes-an-addiction/.

MILE 10

26 Lauri Nummenaa et al., "Maps of Subjective Feelings," *PNAS* 115, no. 37 (2018): 9198–203.

MILE 11

27 Nir Eynon et al., "Genes for Elite Power and Sprint Performance: ACTN3 Leads the Way," *Sports Medicine* 43, no. 9 (2013): 803–17; Ysabel Jacob et al., "Genetic Variants within NOGGIN, COL1A1, COL5A1, and IGF2 Are Associated with Musculoskeletal Injuries in Elite Male Australian Football League Players: A Preliminary Study," *Sports Medicine* 8, no. 1 (2022): 1–14.

MILE 12

28 Alex Hutchinson, *Endure: Mind, Body, and the Curiously Elastic Limits of Human Performance* (Boston: Mariner Books, 2018), 26.

29 Jim Blascovich, "Challenge and Threat," in *Handbook of Approach and Avoidance Motivation*, ed. Andrew J. Elliot (New York: Psychology Press, 2008), 431–45.

30 Lauren A. Gardner, Stewart A. Vella, and Christopher A. Magee, "The Role of Implicit Beliefs and Achievement Goals as Protective Factors in Youth Sport," *Journal of Applied Sport Psychology* 30, no. 1 (2018): 83–95, doi:10.1080/1041320 0.2017.1334160.

31 Andrew J. Carnes and Sara E. Mahoney, "Cohesion Is Associated with Perceived Exertion and Enjoyment during Group Running," *Journal of Exercise Physiology Online* 19, no. 6 (2016).

32 Arran J. Davis, Pádraig MacCarron, and Emma Cohen, "Social Reward and Support Effects on Exercise Experiences and Performance: Evidence from Parkrun," *PLoS One* 16, no. 9 (2021): e0256546.

33 Noel E. Brick et al., "Altering Pace Control and Pace Regulation: Attentional Focus Effects during Running," *Medicine and Science in Sports and Exercise* 48, no. 5 (2016): 879.

34 K. Martin et al., "Superior Inhibitory Control and Resistance to Mental Fatigue in Professional Road Cyclists," *PLoS One* 11, no. 7 (2016), https://doi.org/10.1371/journal.pone.0159907.

35 H. K. N Lam, H. Middleton, and S. H. Phillips, "The Effect of Self-Selected Music on Endurance Running Capacity and Performance in a Mentally Fatigued State," *Journal of Human Sport and Exercise* 17, no. 4 (2022), https://doi.org/10.14198/jhse.2022.174.16.

MILE 13

36 Shirley Sahrmann, *Diagnosis and Treatment of Movement Impairment Syndromes* (St. Louis, MO: Mosby, 2002).

MILE 14

37 N. Hogan, "An Organizing Principle for a Class of Voluntary Movements," *Journal of Neuroscience* 4, no. 11 (1984): 2745–54.

38 Nidhi Seethapahi and Manoj Srinivasan, "Step-to-Step Variations in Human Running Reveal How Humans Run Without Falling," *eLife*, March 19, 2019, https://elifesciences.org/articles/38371.

39 A. S. Voloshina and D. P. Ferris, "Biomechanics and Energetics of Running on Uneven Terrain," *Journal of Experimental Biology* 218, no. 5 (2015): 711–19.

40 S. F. Donker et al., "Adaptations in Arm Movements for Added Mass to Wrist or Ankle during Walking," *Experimental Brain Research* 146, no. 1 (2002): 26–31.

41 Hyung Suk Yang et al., "Effects of Arm Weight on Gait Performance in Healthy Subjects," *Human Movement Science* 60 (2018): 40–47.

42 E. P. Zehr et al., "Neuromechanical Interactions Between the Limbs During Human Locomotion," *Experimental Brain Research* 234 (2016): 3059–81.

MILE 17

43 A. Vleeming, et al., "The Sacroiliac Joint: An Overview of Its Anatomy, Function and Potential Clinical Implications." *Journal of anatomy* 221, no. 6 (2012): 537-567, https://onlinelibrary.wiley.com/doi/full/10.1111/j.1469-7580.2012.01564.x

MILE 19

44 Ben T. van Oeveren et al., "The Biomechanics of Running and Running Styles: A Synthesis," *Sports Biomechanics* (March 4, 2021), 1–39, doi:10.1080/14763141.2021.1873411.

45 Christine E. Agresta et al., "Experience Does Not Influence Injury-Related Joint Kinematics and Kinetics in Distance Runners," *Gait and Posture* 61 (2018): 13–18, doi:10.1016/j.gaitpost.2017.12.020).

46 C. J. Winstein, "Knowledge of Results and Motor Learning—Implications for
Physical Therapy," *Physical Therapy* 71, no. 2 (1991):140–49.

MILE 20

47 Shirley Sahrmann, *Movement System Impairment Syndromes of the Extremities,
Cervical and Thoracic Spines* (Maryland Heights, MO: Elsevier/Mosby, 2011), 6.

48 Phillip A. Gribble, "Evidence Review for the 2016 International Ankle
Consortium Consensus Statement on the Prevalence, Impact, and Long-Term
Consequences of Lateral Ankle Sprains," *British Journal of Sports Medicine* 50,
no. 24 (2016): 1496–1505.

49 Tricia Hubbard-Turner, Adam Lavis, and Michael J. Turner, "Fitness and Body
Composition as Consequences of Chronic Ankle Instability," *Athletic Training
and Sports Health Care* 13, no. 6 (2021): e419–e424.

50 Henk van der Worp, Jelte W. Vrielink, and Steef W. Bredeweg, "Do Runners
Who Suffer Injuries Hae Higher Vertical Ground Reaction Forces Than Those
Who Remain Injury-Free? A Systematic Review and Meta-Analysis," *British
Journal of Sports Medicine* 50, no. 8 (2016): 450–57.

51 Patrick Barkham, "Picking Up the Pace," *Guardian*, December 15, 2008, https://
www.theguardian.com/sport/2008/dec/16/paula-radcliffe.

MILE 21

52 Juan Santana, Stuart McGill, and Lee Brown, "Anterior and Posterior Serape,"
Strength and Conditioning Journal 37 (2015): 8–13.

MILE 22

53 Lara Boyd, "After Watching This, Your Brain Will Not Be the Same," TEDx
Talk, November 14, 2015, https://www.youtube.com/watch?v=LNHBMFCzznE.

MILE 24

54 Douglas Adams et al., "Altering Cadence or Vertical Oscillation during
Running: Effects on Running Related Injury Factors," *International Journal of
Sports Physical Therapy* 13, no. 4 (2018): 633–42, https://www.ncbi.nlm.nih.gov/
pmc/articles/PMC6088121/.

55 Gianluca Vernillo et al., "Energetically Optimal Stride Frequency Is Maintained with Fatigue in Trained Ultramarathon Runners," *Journal of Science and Medicine in Sport* 22, no. 9 (2019): 1054–58.

56 Wenjing Quan et al., "Competitive and Recreational Running Kinematics Examined Using Principal Components Analysis," *Healthcare* 9, no. 10 (2021): 1321, https://www.ncbi.nlm.nih.gov/pmc/articles/PMC8544359/.

57 E. Maas et al., "Novice Runners Show Greater Changes in Kinematics with Fatigue Compared to Competitive Runners," *Sports Biomechanics* 17 (2018): 350–60.

58 S. Willwacher et al., "Running-Related Biomechanical Risk Factors for Overuse Injuries in Distance Runners: A Systematic Review Considering Injury Specificity and the Potentials for Future Research," *Sports Medicine* 52 (2022): 1863–77.

59 Dustin P. Jourbert et al., "Ground Contact Time Imbalances Strongly Related to Impaired Running Economy," *International Journal of Exercise Science* 13, no. 4 (2020): 427–37, https://www.ncbi.nlm.nih.gov/pmc/articles/PMC7241633/.

60 Alex Hutchinson, "Rethinking What Power Meters Mean for Runners," *Outside*, December 19, 2020, https://www.outsideonline.com/health/training-performance/running-power-stryd-research-2020/.

MILE 25

61 Alex Hutchinson, *Endure: Mind, Body, and the Curiously Elastic Limits of Human Performance* (New York: HarperCollins, 2019), 26.

62 Sean Ingle, "Paula Radcliffe: Behind the Smile, and Tears, a Desire to Be Better Than Great," *Guardian*, April 25, 2015, https://www.theguardian.com/sport/2015/apr/25/paula-radcliffe-behind-the-smile-and-tears-a-desire-to-be-better-than-great.